Satanism, Magic and Mysticism in Fin-de-siècle France

Palgrave Historical Studies in Witchcraft and Magic

Series Editors: **Jonathan Barry, Willem de Blécourt and Owen Davies**

Titles include:

Edward Bever
THE REALITIES OF WITCHCRAFT AND POPULAR MAGIC
IN EARLY MODERN EUROPE
Culture, Cognition and Everyday Life

Alison Butler
VICTORIAN OCCULTISM AND THE MAKING OF MODERN MAGIC
Invoking Tradition

Julian Goodare, Lauren Martin and Joyce Miller
WITCHCRAFT AND BELIEF IN EARLY MODERN SCOTLAND

Jonathan Roper (*editor*)
CHARMS, CHARMERS AND CHARMING

Alison Rowlands (*editor*)
WITCHCRAFT AND MASCULINITIES IN EARLY MODERN EUROPE

Rolf Schulte
MAN AS WITCH
Male Witches in Central Europe

Laura Stokes
DEMONS OF URBAN REFORM
Early European Witch Trials and Criminal Justice, 1430–1530

Forthcoming:

Johannes Dillinger
MAGICAL TREASURE HUNTING IN EUROPE AND NORTH AMERICA
A History

Soili-Maria Olli
TALKING TO DEVILS AND ANGELS IN SCANDINAVIA, 1500–1800

Robert Ziegler
SATANISM, MAGIC AND MYSTICISM IN FIN-DE-SIÈCLE FRANCE

**Palgrave Historical Studies in Witchcraft and Magic
Series Standing Order ISBN 978–1403–99566–7 Hardback
978–1403–99567–4 Paperback**
(*outside North America only*)

You can receive future titles in this series as they are published by placing a standing order. Please contact your bookseller or, in case of difficulty, write to us at the address below with your name and address, the title of the series and the ISBN quoted above.

Customer Services Department, Macmillan Distribution Ltd, Houndmills, Basingstoke, Hampshire RG21 6XS, England

---

Satanism, Magic and Mysticism in Fin-de-siècle France

by

Robert Ziegler
University of Montana, USA

First published 2012 by
PALGRAVE MACMILLAN

Palgrave Macmillan in the UK is an imprint of Macmillan Publishers Limited, registered in England, company number 785998, of Houndmills, Basingstoke, Hampshire RG21 6XS.

Palgrave Macmillan in the US is a division of St Martin's Press LLC, 175 Fifth Avenue, New York, NY 10010.

Palgrave Macmillan is the global academic imprint of the above companies and has companies and representatives throughout the world.

Palgrave® and Macmillan® are registered trademarks in the United States, the United Kingdom, Europe and other countries.

ISBN 978–0–230–29308–3

This book is printed on paper suitable for recycling and made from fully managed and sustained forest sources. Logging, pulping and manufacturing processes are expected to conform to the environmental regulations of the country of origin.

A catalogue record for this book is available from the British Library.

A catalog record for this book is available from the Library of Congress.

10 9 8 7 6 5 4 3 2 1
21 20 19 18 17 16 15 14 13 12

Transferred to Digital Printing in 2013

Contents

Acknowledgments

To begin with, I wish to express my deep thanks to Willem de Blécourt for coming to me with a proposal to undertake the current project. It has proven to be an enriching and profoundly instructive experience.

To my cherished daughter, Mary, I give thanks for her untiring editorial assistance, her patience with my refractoriness, and her unstinting support throughout. She is a keen and perceptive reader, an artful advisor, and a precious source of comfort.

To my wife, Louise, who knows my mind better than I, I give thanks for her review of the entire manuscript. Where there was confusion, Louise helped to create order. Louise is my partner in my scholarly work and in my life.

I have received invaluable insights from colleagues steeped in arcane matters and conversant with great mysteries. To Professor Jack Crowley, possessor of a marvelous library of esoteric texts, to colleagues and friends, Professors Allan Pasco, Marc Smeets, Jennifer Forrest, and Elizabeth Emery, I express my warm gratitude.

I wish to thank the staff of the Montana Tech library for dependably obtaining the most difficult-to-find works. To Evelyn Merkle, whom I can count on to assemble my scattered papers into a coherent and professional document, I give my thanks yet again.

A portion of this work appeared in article form. For his permission to use this material in revised and expanded form in the present volume, I wish to thank the editor of *French Forum*.

Introduction

In a letter to a friend, J.-K. Huysmans once explained that what sparked his interest in the occult and supernatural was a wish to find "some compensation for the horror of daily life, the squalor of existence, the excremental filthiness of the loathsome age we live in."[1] Horrified by the trend toward secularism and money worship, he had seen the crooked streets of Paris made straight, robbed of their charm, the city's beauty destroyed by Baron Haussmann's geometric urban grids. Human interaction, with its complexity and richness, had given way to business dealings with their emphasis on profit. Even the sacraments had been profaned by tradespeople and merchants, who diluted Communion wine by adding alcohol and alum and who substituted oat flour and potato starch for Eucharistic wheat. It was Huysmans's ambition to use his art to mask the vulgarity of life that explains in part his fascination with the aesthetics of Satanism. It is also what motivated him to uncover the clandestine practice of devil worship in turn-of-the-century Paris, what fueled his research into the monstrous crimes of medieval Satanist Gilles de Rais.

Born in Paris in 1848, Huysmans was baptized in the Latin Quarter at Saint-Séverin, a church that would figure prominently in his later religious writings. Huysmans's early work gave little foreshadowing of his eventual turn toward supernaturalism. Instead, books like *Sac au dos* (*Knapsack* 1878), which fictionalized his service in the Mobile Guard during the Franco-Prussian War, his rollicking account of working-class life and romance in *Les Soeurs Vatard* (*The Vatard Sisters* 1879), situated the fledgling novelist squarely in the emergent naturalist camp. However, Huysmans's association with Emile Zola and his inclusion in the Médan group proved short-lived as he soon judged naturalism as presenting an incomplete picture of human life. Huysmans's metaphysical

1

ruminations, his plumbing of the unconscious are already evident in his gaudy masterpiece, *A rebours* (*Against the Grain* 1884), and in the labyrinthine dream narratives woven into the country novel *En Rade* (*Becalmed* 1887). Huysmans's growing interest in religion and the occult was in part motivated by a need to explain the mystery of suffering. In the years following the publication of *En Rade*, the health of his long-time mistress, Anna Meunier, worsened dramatically. Literary colleagues and close friends like Barbey d'Aurevilly and Villiers de l'Isle-Adam died in quick succession, the latter after a painful, protracted illness. Suffering to Huysmans could not be a matter of accident or circumstance, and instead presupposed a supernatural causality that gave it purpose and meaning.

At the same time, Huysmans's impatience with the aridity of naturalist aesthetics moved him to investigate the domains of the diabolical and sublime. However, his immersion in esotericism was inspired by more than disillusionment with the triumph of materialism in fin-de-siècle France. Unable to find in Catholic teaching an explanation for the apparent cruelty of God, impervious to human suffering and slow in returning to save the downtrodden, Huysmans evolved a personal belief system grounded in mystical eschatology, whose adherents formed an aristocracy of self-sacrifice and genius. The problematic deity found by Huysmans and his fictional heroes in Catholic orthodoxy was the heartless, detached, impassive figure mentioned in *A rebours*. Like des Esseintes, Huysmans had been scandalized by the doctrine of original sin, revolted by the apotheosis of the scoundrel and the oppression of the innocent. He thus agreed with Schopenhauer, who had famously observed: "If a God did make this world, I should not like to be this God, for the misery of the world would break my heart."[2]

By following Huysmans's evolution as an esotericist and man of faith, one finds that – more than any other public figure – his career followed the trajectory of fin-de-siècle occultism. He stands out as the author of the most notorious Satanic novel of the era, *The Damned* (*Là-bas* 1891); he interacted with virtually all of the leading hermeticists of the day; he engaged in necromantic warfare with his diabolical adversaries, warding off their spells with magic apotropaion and exotic, mystic rituals. Huysmans later became conversant with the apocalyptic doctrine of Eugène Vintras, adopting from the heretical cultist a belief in the coming Third Age of the Paraclete. Following his conversion and apparent return to traditional church dogma, Huysmans evolved a personal view of Catholicism as a religion of martyrdom and miracles, in which supernatural wonders fought eternally with monstrous evil, striving for dominion in the daily lives of ordinary people.

A denizen of the French capital, Huysmans spent much of his life as a functionary at the Ministry of the Interior. This unremarkable career as a government employee contrasts with his colorful and turbulent role in the world of fin-de-siècle mysticism and art. First a full-throated partisan of Emile Zola and the naturalist cause, Huysmans proclaimed that the artist's place was in the raucous confusion of the world, among real people whose coarseness was grist for naturalist depictions. Naturalism, in Zola's view, was a democratizing force, a scientific instrument used to diagnose social evils and prescribe remedies. While Huysmans dismissed the theory in Zola's *Le Roman experimental* (*The Experimental Novel* 1880), he had welcomed naturalism's interest in the lives of common people, had embraced the goal of examining the plight of the poor and dispossessed. Defending Zola, whose *L'Assommoir* had been characterized as pornographic, Huysmans argues that a writer should escape the prison of Romantic subjectivity: "we go into the street that teems with life; we try to plant on their feet beings of flesh and bone, beings that speak the language that was taught them, beings that throb with life."[3]

From 1879 to 1880, Huysmans, increasingly involved in art criticism, had taken to championing the innovative works of the Impressionists, writing laudatory essays on Gustave Moreau and Odilon Redon, publishing a collection of his reviews in *L'Art moderne* (*Modern Art*) in 1883. Huysmans's own subjectivist aesthetic placed him at odds with Zola, his erstwhile mentor. Yet his disaffection with naturalism had more to do with its scientific apparatus, its diagnostic methods, and utopian pretentions.

In *Là-bas* (*The Damned* 1891) Huysmans's protagonist, the novelist Durtal, denounces naturalism's emphasis on appetites and instincts, on insanity and sex. It had degenerated, as Durtal argues, into a "sentimental surgical support, a spiritual truss."[4] While naturalism had taken Huysmans outside, into the streets, his Decadent masterpiece, *A rebours*, barricades him in a cloistered world of artificiality. For the hero, Jean Floressas des Esseintes, art's realm is an aestheticizing consciousness. Visitors are forbidden in his retreat at Fontenay. Soundless servants wearing slippers are consigned to the mansion's upper floor. Surviving on a diet of rare perfumes, flowers, and poetry, des Esseintes admits no mistresses, etherealizing women into memories.

But with elimination of the outside world came a craving for unreality, as des Esseintes furnishes his bedroom with the austerity of an anchorite, collecting religious bibelots, consecrated custodials, and chasubles – and intuiting that beyond literature lies the domain of the transcendental. Sharing the author's skepticism, des Esseintes had scoffed at the "psychology of mysticism," yet had toyed with the idea of worshipping a divinity *a rebours*, summoning God by invoking Satan, following a liturgy of sacrilege. Fantasies had come to him of "shameful and impure abuses of the holy water and the holy oil." He had imagined God's antagonist, "a rival full of vigor, the Devil, [...] cabbalistic excesses, black masses, witches' Sabbaths, thoughts of exorcism, all these came into play."[5]

Foreshadowed by des Esseintes's dilettantish interest in diabolism, Huysmans's own path toward conversion had led him to an investigation of the Satanic, both in medieval history and in the reality of contemporary Paris. In Huysmans's blockbuster novel on the mysteries of devil worship, he presents a picture of the occult world in fin-de-siècle France. There, as Richard D. E. Burton claims, Huysmans's "reader gains access to a curious and disturbing (anti)religious underworld, part real, part inverted, in which spiritualism, sexual perversion, and madness intersect, populated by men and women who, thirsting for some kind of absolute gratification but despairing of or hostile to orthodox Christianity, turn to Satanism as a way out of the 'materialist prison house' of late nineteenth-century France."[6]

Biographer Robert Baldick questions whether Huysmans ever witnessed a Black Mass of the kind he describes in a memorable chapter of his novel. However, Baldick's commentary underscores the ambiguous status of Huysmans's book, as well as the complex reaction it elicited from the public. Part novel, part documentary on contemporary Parisian mores, part archeological reconstruction of medieval Satanic practices, Huysmans's text became popular by appealing to audiences' love of sensationalist invention as well as to serious readers' concerns with the religious problem of good and evil.

In his book, pederast choirboys with powdered cheeks and carmined lips attend a priest presiding over a ritual enveloped in the smoke of toxic incense. In a later scene, Huysmans's hero is taken to a squalid chophouse, to an upstairs bedroom whose filthy mattress is strewn with desecrated Hosts. Huysmans's hero had been sickened by the ignomininy of contemporary devil worship, and while Satanism as it was practiced in the distant Middle Ages had been haloed with the sulfurous mystery of conjecture, the Black Mass Durtal witnesses enacts only the banality of evil.

By 1887, Huysmans's research into the occult had put him into contact with the foremost magicians of the day. Stanislas de Guaïta, with his vast knowledge and personal wealth, had established himself as the Eminence Grise of the esoteric movement and would publish in 1890 *Au Seuil du mystère* (*On the Threshold of Mystery*), an encyclopedic overview of Occidental occultism. Gérard Encausse, whose pseudonym, Papus, was taken from the works of Apollonius of Tyana, had authored popularized analyses of the Kabbalah and the Tarot, and, in 1888, together with Guaïta, he had founded L'Ordre de la Rose-Croix, intending to reawaken the traditions of Rosicrucianism and alchemy in turn-of-the-century France. Most important was the acquaintance Huysmans made with the visionary Jules Bois, author of *Le Satanisme et la magie* (*Satanism and Magic* 1895), for which Huysmans contributed an important introduction. There Huysmans chronicles the spread of nineteenth-century Luciferianism, warns of the malignancy of Palladism, a Satanic cult linked to the Freemasons and which was later exposed as an imposture perpetrated by master hoaxer Léo Taxil.

However, it was not until Huysmans made contact with the notorious Joseph-Antoine Boullan, whose expertise in Satanism Huysmans viewed as essential in documenting his novel, that the author finally penetrated into the dark heart of fin-de-siècle necromancy. One of the fin de siècle's most colorful figures, Boullan had been the target of criminal prosecution and the object of church sanction on numerous occasions before Huysmans began corresponding with him in 1890. Co-founder in 1859 of the Society for the Reparation of Souls, Boullan had become infamous for his sorties into supernaturalism and sacrilege. Accused of ceremonial child-murder, of authorizing orgiastic rituals, Boullan was allegedly an accomplished exorcist conversant with an array of occult practices. Aware of Boullan's spotted reputation, yet wishing to be accurate in his writing, Huysmans had set aside his reservations and had written directly to the controversial cleric. Huysmans's hope had been to disprove materialism's impoverishing principles, to demonstrate that the devil did exist, to "show Zola, Charcot, the spiritualists, and the rest that nothing of the mysteries which surround us has been explained."[7]

After an extended exchange of correspondence between the cleric and the writer, Boullan, in 1890, sent his housekeeper, the eccentric oracle Julie Thibault, to inquire about Huysmans's intentions in an interview conducted face to face. Not long after Julie had delivered a positive report to her employer, Huysmans had been inundated with information about the secrets of black magic: incubism, succubism, bewitchments, and counter-spells, ceremonies for warding off attack by deadly larval beings.

Huysmans's indebtedness to Boullan as his initiator into occult matters had led him to take sides in the ensuing conflict between initiates. Years before, Guaïta's ally, fellow occultist Oswald Wirth, had infiltrated Boullan's sect with the goal of exposing its sacrilegious practices, rituals devolving into adultery and incest. Having found Boullan guilty and passed a death sentence against him, Guaïta dispatched against the priest a host of invisible assailants. Warned by ornithomantic messages and astrological charts, Boullan had protected himself by conducting the Sacrifice to the Glory of Melchidedek. Huysmans had been challenged to a duel, Guaïta and Bois had exchanged pistol shots, and Boullan had died mysteriously in 1893, "done to death by magic," as Huysmans would steadfastly maintain.[8]

When *Là-bas* first appeared in February 1891, it became an instantaneous bestseller catapulting the author into fame. While some readers of *L'Echo de Paris*, in which the book appeared in serial form, were sufficiently scandalized to cancel their subscription to the paper, the novel's reception was generally favorable, and the controversy surrounding Huysmans's work resulted in impressive sales. Several prominent occultists disputed the authenticity of Huysmans's research, as Péladan dismissed the book as fraudulent invention, and Papus claimed that Huysmans's sources had largely been encyclopedias on Satanism. Yet even these acrimonious denunciations had generated publicity, and Huysmans's star continued rising as his novel flew off the shelves. "And when, on its publication in book form in April, the Bibliothèque des Chemins de Fer banned the novel from its railway stalls, its success was assured," as Baldick adds by way of summary.[9]

Yet Huysmans's association with Boullan and his visionary handmaiden, Julie Thibault, continued to direct the author's spiritual evolution long after his anatomy of Satanism was published. Huysmans's disgust for reality and its enshrinement in naturalist art had prompted him to seek escape into the otherworldly and supernatural, "anywhere out of the world," as Baudelaire described it. And while Huysmans's misanthropic temperament had made the truth of Satanism seem more plausible, once the writer had explored the netherworld, he had turned his eyes heavenward, *là-haut* (up there).

Little by little, Boullan had instructed Huysmans in the doctrine of the notorious heretic and prophet Eugène Vintras, whose controversial teachings on sexuality and suffering had continued to affect disciples long after Vintras's death. The so-called "Prophet of Tilly," relentlessly persecuted by the church, Vintras had advanced a powerful message on the imminence of the apocalypse, attracting important members to his messianic cult. Boullan shared Vintras's unorthodox views on adultery and redemption and professed the same mystical expectation of the forthcoming world's end, and, following Vintras's death in 1875, Boullan had successfully positioned himself as his successor.

It was from Vintras that Boullan drew his views on expiatory suffering on behalf of others. And so, when Huysmans's mistress, Anna Meunier, had declined into insanity and had been interned in the asylum of Saint-Anne in 1893, he likely recalled Boullan's explanation of the doctrine of Mystic Substitution. Boullan's theory was that Anna's ordeal had been divinely ordained, and that those whom Christ loves best are those he allows to suffer most. As Baldick remarks, it was from Boullan and from his coreligionist Léon Bloy – "those two apostles of pain"[10] – that Huysmans was initiated into the mysteries of Dolorism, the belief that suffering was a privilege, a mark of election – that the torments of a few purchased the redemption of the many.

Huysmans's meditation on the expiatory plight of Anna Meunier – his admiration for the pilgrim/prophetess Julie Thibaut – had softened the antipathy for women he had exhibited for so long. Initially, Huysmans had been infected by Schopenhauerian misogyny, believing that the female animal was what imprisoned man in a world of instinctual automatism. Like many of his Decadent contemporaries, Huysmans had despised woman "in her pure carnal existence." He had come to believe that sexual passion could be experienced only "on the level of culpability," that it could be understood only as "a privileged expression of Satanism, a fundamental impulse toward self-debasement that constitutes true perversity."[11] However, in the teachings of Vintras, Huysmans had found an image of women as avatars of the Mater Dolorosa, intercessors whose bodily suffering secured a deliverance of the spirit.

When, in 1891, Huysmans's spiritual quest first put him in contact with Abbé Arthur Mugnier, the priest who would guide him toward his eventual conversion, the novelist was still torn by his warring images of women: as the Beast of Revelation, the Maenad or the Harlot, a Schopenhauerian instrument of man's utter degradation, or as the embodiment of compassion who mourned her son beneath the Cross. During his visits to Mugnier's residence, Huysmans confessed to his sexual obsession with a prostitute, Fernande, transposed in his unpublished novel, *Là-haut*, as the boyish sex worker, Florence, "who with her tomboy's open face goes about with her nose up in the air."[12]

The drama that played out in much of fin-de-siècle fiction – in the works of Léon Bloy as well as in the pre-conversion books by

Huysmans – describes male authors as helpless pawns of Satanic Lust Goddesses or as grateful beneficiaries of the expiatory trials of female martyrs. In Bloy, these roles are often played by an identical female figure: the prostitute rescued from the street who undergoes a spectacular awakening, becoming a saint whose tears wash the author's sins away. Transformation of man's pruritus into a glorious salvation – effected by a woman who suffers unspeakable torments on his behalf – suggests that Dolorism is supported by an unconscious sadism, as women are made to suffer to redeem the men whose perdition they had caused. Huysmans's ambivalence toward woman takes the form of a Manichean drama: "Lust and the Church, however implausible it seemed, worked together to share him equally. Wishing to possess him, they raised themselves up and resolutely joined in the struggle."[13]

Vintras's alleged institution of the ritual of the *ladder of life*, where women use their sexuality as the instrument of the Fall, in order to raise the sinner up and ensure his spiritual redemption, illustrates what, for Huysmans and other fin-de-siècle mystic writers, would define Eve's relationship to Mary.

Huysmans's conversion and retreat at the Trappist monastery of Notre-Dame d'Igny (begun on July 12, 1892), a sojourn recounted in detail in his autobiographical novel *En Route* (1895), marks a disappearance of the she-devils who formerly had tortured him and whose evil majesty he had heralded in his essay on Félicien Rops (*Certains* 1889). These give way to gentle soul-guides like Durtal's housekeeper, Madame Bavoil, or to Warriors of the Lord, the mystic Sin-eaters, the *gluttons for pain*, who were propitiatory victims transmuting guilt into forgiveness.

Already in *Là-haut*, Huysmans had contemplated undertaking *a white book*, a counterweight to the biography of the medieval child-murderer, Gilles de Rais: "he jumped at once from one extreme to another, and after digging into medieval Satanism in his study of the Maréchal de Rais, he had found nothing interesting left to probe than the life of a saint. It was then that a few discoveries made in Gorrès's *Mystique Divine* had launched him on the trail of the Blessed Lydwine, in search of new documents."[14]

From the brothel to the church, from Fernande to the Virgin, Huysmans moves from the black book of the devil to a hagiography of suffering immaculacy. Published in 1902, *Sainte Lydwine de Schiedam* describes not only the end of Huysmans's journey from misogyny to hyperdulia. It also marks the humbling of the foremost Decadent supernaturalist, whose name and narrative presence are eclipsed by the glory of his subject.

Huysmans's remarkable reconstruction of the life of the fifteenth-century Dutch visionary is both a clinical record of religion as psychopathology and a study of the operation of a soteriological economy – of suffering as it redresses the balance of good and evil in the universe. It also illustrates a dialectic at work in fin-de-siècle supernaturalism, between elitism and fraternalism, isolation and the gift of self. A generation of artists who had started with a sense of solidarity, resolved to go into the streets and tell the stories of those they saw there, had become an aristocratic coterie of occultists and Magi, inaccessible in their fortresses of esoteric wisdom. Huysmans' character, Durtal, had climbed into the bell-tower of Saint-Sulpice where, with his initiate-acquaintances, he had discussed the odiousness of life, the oafishness of common people, and the dawning of the Third Age of the Paraclete.

Huysmans's apparent confusion, manifested during the writing of *Là-bas*, between exorcists and necromancers, Satanists and their adversaries, might be expressive of an underlying ambivalence toward the devil – not as the champion of the rich, not as the vassal of the banker, but as the spokesman for the ostracized, as Huysmans's friend Jules Bois describes him. In certain centuries, as Bois says, humanity sometimes falls so low, humanity dishonors itself so much that it calls on Satan, not on God. Herein lies the devil's power: "he suffers" as Bois concludes.[15]

Indeed, suffering is the leitmotif in the mystical writings of the fin de siècle. Although it is endured alone and thus defines an aristocracy of chosen victims, it is welcomed and undergone on behalf of an anonymous collectivity of sinners. From Vintras and Boullan, Huysmans had received the message of apocalypticism, and in the opening of *Sainte Lydwine*, he describes the harrowing of fifteenth-century Europe, the ascendancy of despots, perverts, and blasphemers whose transgressions must be counterbalanced by the agonies of saints. The turn of the nineteenth century, like the conclusion of Lydwine's era, saw the weight of evil grow so great that God would soon unleash his vengeance.

Included in *Là-haut*, with the account of Huysmans's 1891 pilgrimage to La Salette, is the text of *Mélanie's secret*, the message delivered by the Virgin to the unlettered cowherd Mélanie Calvat at the time of the Apparition on September 19, 1846. Warning of dire events to come – famine, pestilence, church turmoil – if the clergy did not reform itself and the faithful failed to observe the Sabbath, the Virgin's message reinforced the millenarianism of numerous fin-de-siècle Catholics. Among these were Huysmans and his nemesis, Léon Bloy, both of whom seemed to long for a detergent Armageddon.

The era of the Holy Spirit, as envisaged by Vintras, is explained in a discussion among intellectuals and occultists in *Là-bas*. With the conclusion of the Second Age of the crucified Redeemer, the need for expiatory suffering would similarly end. No longer would man be the slave of his sexual desires and, in accordance with a mystical eugenics, only the elect would reproduce. Having served as redemptive martyrs or as instruments of Satan, women would usher in the Paraclete at the same time that their roles became obsolete. Yet in professing Vintrasian doctrine, Huysmans had not moved beyond his original misanthropy, his loathing for the insolent triumphalism of the "fetid bourgeoisie," "the apotheosis of crooked politicians and financiers."[16]

It was only in the aftermath of his conversion that Huysmans left his novels' center stage, that the voice of the aesthete grew less clamorous and shrill. Huysmans had resembled his occult brethren for whom magic was an insignia of distinction, for whom *Gnosis* or privileged wisdom permitted membership in a new elite. Yet in the writings of his contemporaries, there had been a willingness to go down among the people. Guaïta had referred to the need to descend the ladder of secret knowledge. Papus had assumed the role of popularizer of arcane doctrine. And Joséphin Peladan, the most overweening of the hermeticists, had seen the need to mentor neophytes in writing *Comment on devient mage* (*How One becomes a Magus* 1892).

When Huysmans next had heard the devil speak, it was after his taking of Communion, when a disputatious voice had denied the authenticity of the sacrament. Whereas, in *A rebours*, des Esseintes is locked in his soliloquizing consciousness, pleased to pursue a dialogue exclusively with himself, Durtal in *En Route* hears his own voice as the devil's, and so prays for inner silence so that he can hear the word of God.

The decentering of Huysmans's character is traced by his positional relocation. In his historical analysis of the architectural symbolism of Chartres (*The Cathedral* 1898), the narrator does not expand to fill a sumptuous Thebaïd but is dwarfed by the magnificence of an edifice built by a mystic collectivity. In 1889, Huysmans became an oblate at the Benedictine Abbey of Saint-Martin in Ligugé, living outside the cloister, adjacent to, but not belonging to, the Order – moving toward it (*ob*), as is etymologically suggested by his title, remaining marginalized by choice in the practice of his faith. And finally, in *Les Foules de Lourdes* (*The Crowds of Lourdes* 1906), the last novel of Huysmans's life, his narrative alter-ego, the self-analyzing Durtal, finally disappears so that the writer's subjectivity ceases to be his sole material.

The naturalist who, in the street, had mingled with the people "throbbing with life," becomes a naturalist observer of the crowds of pilgrims who throng to Lourdes. Wishing to emulate Claude Bernard in using fiction as diagnostic medicine, Zola had proposed that his methodology treat the sick and the insane, curing poverty and alcoholism with science-based enlightenment.

In the writings of other fin-de-siècle Satanists, occultists, and mystics, the suffering of the poor emerged as a prominent concern: in the compassionate revolt of Jules Bois's empathetic Lucifer, in Vintras's image of the downtrodden as the crucified members of Christ's body, in Léon Bloy, for whom the flesh and blood of the poor were Eucharistic substances. On the one hand, monsters and pariahs sought compassion from the devil; on the other, martyrs' pain was the alchemy that turned self-pity into altruism.

In Huysmans's last book, he returns to naturalism that had been the point of his departure. He goes out in the street, studying those deformed by lupus, ravaged by cancer, twisted by paralysis. In writing *Lydwine*, Huysmans had learned that suffering only prepared the way for rapture and that, in being crucified with Christ, the martyr was blessed with mystic ecstasy. For the saint, the only sickness she is impatient that Christ relieve is the affliction of corporeity, the martyrdom of life.

Already in the spring of 1900, Huysmans had begun to exhibit symptoms of the cancer of the jaw that would take his life seven years later. By 1905, when he undertook his work on *Les Foules de Lourdes*, his physical condition was little better than the invalids who made their way to the pilgrimage city.

In Lourdes, Huysmans describes repairing to the clinic of Doctor Boissarie, seeing a physician trace the interface between medicine and miracle. Charged with scientifically ascertaining the authenticity of divine cures, the doctor applies his medical knowledge to determine the point at which it fails. Fin-de-siècle occultism is positioned on this threshold – between science and supernaturalism, chemistry and alchemy, mathematics and Kabbalism, empiricism and magic. However, the most important boundary that the Magus learns to cross is between a self immured in pride and others needing comfort. More than the Virgin's miraculous healing of diseased organs and shattered limbs are the acts of solicitude and kindness done by people for their brothers.

Huysmans had never felt God's presence more strongly than when he witnessed wealthy women leaving home and coming to Lourdes to serve as caregivers and nurses. The aesthete once enshrined in the opulent refuge of his solipsism becomes a magician whose clairvoyance allows him insight into others. The benighted female animal, controlled by ignorance and instinct, becomes an intercessor whose suffering allows her empathy and compassion. This is the occult miracle Huysmans sees done every day in Lourdes: selfishness fired away in the crucible of pain, then ennobled and transmuted into generosity and service. The occultist journey, guided by the mystery of suffering, moves from the self into the street, from introversion to fraternalism. Sharing in the Passion of the Savior or in the bereavement of his Mother, the decadent occultist becomes an adept in the divine alchemy of pain. "After the necessary period of incubation," as Huysmans writes in *Lydwine*, after self-love turns to service, "the Great Work is completed." From the retort of the soul comes the purity of gold, which Huysmans equates with Love that cures "despondency and tears." This is the true Philosopher's stone," he writes in a coda to the era:[17] suffering that ends suffering and inaugurates the Holy Spirit's Reign. "Neither shall there be mourning nor crying anymore," after an elite joins their stricken brothers to complete God's work on earth.

Following J.-K. Huysmans in his migration through the rarefied, sometimes infernal precincts of fin-de-siècle supernaturalism, this volume begins by touring the devil's lair, then visits the austere chamber of the Magus, and finally climbs to the celestial plane of miracles and mysticism.

In turn-of-the-century France, an encounter with the devil often inspired the seeker to begin a quest for the divine. Chapter 1 explores Decadent Satanism both as an aesthetic and a belief system. Serious occultists like Stanislas de Guaïta and Gérard Encausse (Papus) initially dismissed the devil as nothing but a bugbear that appealed to deviants and fools. Jules Bois, in his masterly study of both traditional and modern Satanism, evokes a colorful image of the country Sabbath as an anarchic, rollicking event, yet depicts clandestine Black Masses celebrated in nineteenth-century churches as despairing, cold, and evil ceremonies inspiring only respectful dread and horror. At the same time, the devil who captivated artists of the era as an urbane sophisticate emerged as a charmingly wicked reflection of the author himself.

In an age in which both faith and art had been robbed of majesty by science, the aesthetics of diabolism were held up as a source of expressive innovation. Thus, the mysterious allure of Satanism set in the remoteness of the Middle Ages, the sacrilegious banality of fin-de-siècle devil worship, and the rehabilitation of the Evil One as a glamorous avatar of the writer are themes explored in an analysis of Huysmans's bestselling exposé on Satanism.

While Satanism provided material for serious literature, it was also perceived as a genuine threat by the church, re-energizing an institution recently demoralized by the ascendancy of reason and materialism. Perpetrated over a number of years, Léo Taxil's elaborate and masterly hoax – his invention of the Luciferian cult of Palladism – is the object of study in Chapter 2. Reconstituting Taxil's imposture as a source of popular entertainment, this examination also describes it as a response to the prevailing culture of xenophobia and anti-Semitism, and as fuel for the propaganda campaign waged by Pope Leo XIII, who warns of the evils of Freemasonry in his 1884 encyclical, *Humanum Genus*. "Emerging from the shadows of an occult conspiracy," the Freemasons, as Leo warns, had enlisted Satan's aid in order to separate the interests of the church and the state, and to promote "the monstrous systems of the Socialists and Communists."[18]

As is argued in Chapter 3, the leading esotericists of the day often sought to distinguish magic, as an initiatic discipline, from necromancy, deemed a refuge for criminals and pariahs. As the aesthetics of Satanism had promoted an ideal of urbane transgressivity, occultism also pictured the Magus as a narcissistic character, a superior, if lonely, being. However, in the works of Stanislas de Guaïta, Gérard Encausse, Edouard Schuré, and Joséphin Péladan, the Magus is shown as learning the virtue of self-sacrifice, mingling with the people whom he edifies.

Chapter 3 traces the evolution of the fin-de-siècle thaumaturge as an adept conversant with the numerological secrets of the Kabbalah, the hidden symbolism of the Tarot, the esoteric traditions of Rosicrucianism. However, the Magus is also depicted as a pedagogue and mentor, obedient to the church, respectful of its doctrine, willing to bestow his privileged knowledge on the people whom he serves.

Chapter 4 explores the process by which this ideal of self-abnegation was carried to the extremes of penitential martyrdom. Explaining the practice of mystic substitution, whereby the suffering of innocents redeems the guilt of unrepentant sinners, this chapter reviews the controversial and little-known teachings of heretical cultist Eugène Vintras. While Vintras began by denouncing the Vatican, excoriating a Pontiff regarded as immoderate and self-glorifying, the way in which Vintras's teachings influenced the generation of fin-de-siècle mystics was by elevating the poor, stressing the sanctity of human suffering, and according a special status to women as the Lord's sacrificial vessels. Touched by Vintras's precepts, writers like Ernest Hello (*Prières et méditations* [*Prayers and Meditations*]), J.-K. Huysmans (*Sainte Lydwine de Schiedam*), and Léon Bloy (*La Femme pauvre*) [*The Woman Who was Poor*]) adopted an unusual brand of mysticism predicated on anti-intellectualism, rigorous self-mortification, and an embrace of suffering allowing the visionary to re-enact the Passion of Christ.

The end of the era of Decadence – with its celebration of an aristocracy of aesthetes, its apotheosis of an elite of artists and intellectuals – was also accompanied by a renunciation of literature as a forum for private and exclusive expression. During the flowering of fin-de-siècle occultism, what had been the proud solipsism of the Decadent aesthete was translated first into the hauteur of the Magus with his esoteric wisdom, and then into the raptures of a saint whose religious visions were indescribable in the profane idiom of the people. However, as Chapter 5 establishes by way of concluding, the fin-de-siècle emergence from the fortress of the self, the mingling of a privileged subject in the throngs of fellow-sufferers signaled the end of occult practices as exclusive and incommunicable. When Huysmans departed from his sanctuary of scholarly monasticism and recorded his sojourn at the pilgrimage site of Lourdes, his chronicle marked a redefinition of turn-of-the-century supernaturalism. *Non sibi*: extraordinary blessings were shared with the unfortunate, secret wisdom was imparted to earnest seekers, miracles, experienced collectively, were performed as good works done on behalf of one's fellow man. Occultism, ceasing, as is etymologically suggested, to mean knowledge that is hidden, became a gift the initiate henceforth consented to shower on his brothers.

1
The Satanist

Perhaps the most spectacular manifestation of fin-de-siècle supernaturalism was the country-wide explosion of reports of the meetings of secret cults and the bloody rituals of Satanic societies. So deep was concern over the spread of devil worship that the Catholic Church published *La Revue du Diable*, whose mission was the exposure of clandestine Satanic practices. Among its targets, a prominent socialite, Lucie Claraz, was excommunicated in 1895 for engaging in Satanic activities. Another object of religious and legal sanction, a farmer, Bernard, from the Département of Allier, was convicted as "a sorcerer in scientific relations with the Devil," and sentenced accordingly to six months' imprisonment.[1]

Counterbalancing anxieties over Satanism as a metaphysical threat was a perception that the devil was an instrument used by impostors skilled at profiting from popular fascination with supernatural evil. Dismissed by detractors as scandal-mongering or hysteria, the fad of devil worship was also widely regarded as being sustained by an interest in the commercial exploitation of the public.

In Britain, renowned occultist Alfred Waite characterized France as fertile ground for the spread of black magic since it was, as Waite believed, a place where gullibility and superstition flourished. While crediting the authenticity of J.-K. Huysmans's *succès de scandale Là-bas*, an 1894 exposé of devil worship in contemporary Paris, Waite devotes attention primarily to recording instances of imposture, chronicling growing concerns over the malignant influence of Freemasonry. Waite focuses in particular on the origins and history of the Luciferian sect of Palladism, describing at length the paranoid extravagances of Dr. Bataille's *Le Diable au XIXe siècle* (*The Devil in the Nineteenth Century*), a compilation of spurious memoirs about Satanism and its rituals, practices occurring from Charleston to Ceylon.

Serialized in the press, beginning in 1892, and devoured by a public that made it one of the decade's bestsellers, Bataille's work purports to be the diary of a ship's physician recording manifestations of Satanic activity in France and around the world. A sprawling 2,000-page excursus denigrated by Waite as "a perfervid narrative issued in penny numbers with illustrations of a highly sensational type,"[2] Bataille's book is replete with colorful anecdotes of the kind that Waite reports: a witch doctor's cottage tenanted by a Tamil-speaking ape, the summoning of Beelzebub that culminates with the emergence of zombie fakirs, "eaten to the bone by worms," dragged out among skeletons "while serpents, giant spiders and toads swarmed from all parts."[3] Waite's dismay is clearly offset by a measure of amusement so that, ultimately, his panning of Bataille has the effect of popularizing an already successful popularization.

The often-contradictory reactions to Bataille's treatise on Satanism show how the issue of devil worship was viewed at the turn of the century from a surprising variety of perspectives. For serious practitioners of the occult sciences like Waite, the question of the devil's existence was primarily a matter of truth or deception. Refusing to judge Bataille's narrative as entertainment or diversion, Waite argues that the book contained no believable miraculous material. It is absurd, Waite asserts, that apes should talk, in familiar or exotic languages. It is impossible, Waite remarks about another tale Bataille tells, that a "female pythoness, aged 152 years, should allow herself to be consumed in a leisurely manner by fire."[4] Failing to evaluate Bataille's work on the basis of the pleasure afforded readers, Waite asserts the obvious in dismissing its contents as "transparently fabulous." "To attribute a historical veracity to the adventures of Baron Munchausen might scarcely seem," Waite summarizes, "more unserious that to accept this *récit de témoin* [eye-witness account] as evidence for transcendental phenomena."[5]

Lively and protean in popular narrative, the fin-de-siècle Satan became repellent and cold in first-hand accounts – like those documented in Huysmans's *Là-bas*. Unlike the devil who presided over contemporary ceremonies – banalized by witnesses' experiences – the uncertain Satan of folklore was the product of the imagination of the people invoking him. From an overview of literature on the fin-de-siècle devil, one sees the being first threatened by science, then assaulted by skepticism, and finally revitalized in art works whose creator worshiped the devil inhabiting his mind.

Those who disputed the reality of the devil's existence were motivated by different concerns. There were the dabblers in the dark arts who wished to avoid criminal prosecution or the threat of excommunication. And there were serious occultists condemned as Satanists or frauds who therefore sought to uphold the legitimacy of their own study. Thus, a broad confederacy of rationalists, intellectuals, occultists, doctors, and scientists often spoke in similar terms when denying the devil's existence as a physical being. A psychiatric disorder, a crude appeal to a foolish and credulous public, a symbolic embodiment of the human propensity toward cupidity, violence, and lust, the devil was widely described as the product of a primitive and disordered brain.

However, the Decadents also intuited that Satanism was not just an issue of fact, and that – more than an entity whose existence was demonstrable – the devil was the product of fear and nostalgia. The Satan who receded into the remoteness of history, who withdrew into the implausibility and vagueness of folklore, could be summoned forth by those whose creativity cast him in the shape of their desire. As Satan migrated from the domain of ontology into the realm of fiction and fantasy, he grew in stature, his avatars multiplied, and his majesty was enhanced by style and artistry.

The multifaceted richness of the devil who presided over the fin de siècle is most thoroughly represented in Huysmans's *Là-bas*, a work whose own genre complexity emerges as one of the story's underlying themes. Part autobiography, part history, part fiction, the novel resembles the devil it pictures, showing that what empiricism makes poor is what conjecture enlivens. Huysmans's lessons are echoed by contemporaries like his nemesis Stanislas de Guaïta, who also realized the connection between fantasy and evil. Guaïta may dispute the factuality of Huysmans's account of a Black Mass seen in Paris, showing himself "anxious to bring a corrective to Huysmans's affirmations,"[6] yet in his historic overview of sorcery, Guaïta's anatomy of Satan shows him to be a rich and complex figure. Guest of honor at midnight Sabbaths, the devil known as *Maître Léonard* mutates from a creature the size of a squirrel into a monstrous goat with twisted horns. With his body emitting "a vague fluorescence" that radiates in spirals, pestilential effluvia enveloping him in "a pale atmosphere,"[7] the devil baptizes the Sabbath bride with urine on a plain lit up by torch-fire. This is a different devil from the being who, to modern intellectuals, is only a symbolic embodiment of human ignorance and vice.

Following Huysmans, Guaïta traces the evolution of the devil who, from the fearsome Sabbath sovereign, dwindles into a ridiculous anachronism, the Decadent devil characterized as a petty charlatan and pervert. Despite their antipathy for one another, Huysmans and Guaïta were in agreement that only art could save an Evil One imperiled by sophisticated cynicism. A study of Huysmans's novel and Guaïta's history of Satanism discloses the future of the Decadent devil, who, having vanished from the text of ancient grimoires, emerges on the page of an imaginative artist.

The devil denied

For purportedly serious occultists like Papus (Gérard Encausse) and Guaïta, the issue of the devil's existence first had to be framed in a way that credited the morality and authenticity of their own practice. Seeking to counter the slanderous, if comical, characterizations given by Bataille of Protestants, Buddhists, thaumaturges, and metaphysicians held in thrall by malevolent powers, these writers confronted the dilemma of arguing that occult study involved neither diabolism nor imposture.

Typical of the strategic campaigns of the devil-deniers is Papus's 1896 polemical tract *Le Diable et l'Occultisme* (*The Devil and Occultism*). A prolific writer, Papus had established his credentials as an occultist with links to the French branch of Madame Blavatsky's Theosophical Society and the Golden Dawn. Together with Guaïta and Péladan, Papus had founded in Paris the Kabbalist Order of the Rose-Croix, emerging as one of the leading voices in the occult movement of the turn of the century. While characterizing him as leading spokesman for the occultist movement, Jean Pierrot deprecates Papus's esoteric knowledge, describing him as a vulgarizer whose learning was broad but often superficial: "Largely devoid of original ideas and endowed with only a limited knowledge of philosophy and literature,"[8] Papus, in Pierrot's view, was nonetheless an influential figure. Author of a study of the Tarot and an interpretive analysis of the Kabbalah (1892), Papus stood in the forefront of the disseminators of esoteric teachings who were sensitive to accusations that occultism and Satanism were synonymous.

While Papus begins his book by refuting the most preposterous of Bataille's allegations, he further issues a challenge to Positivists for denying the authenticity of the supernatural, and to Catholics for stigmatizing occultists for their heterodox beliefs. A regrettable by-product of the triumph of empiricism, for Papus, was the enthronement of irreligion and materialism. Conversely, Papus argues, in cultivating anti-intellectualism, the church had rejected the good offices of its natural allies. Whereas "[o]ccultists sought to bring back France's intellectual elite to a belief in the Beyond and in the existence of an immanent justice,"[9] the Catholic hierarchy had attacked hermeticists for linking religion to the practice of diabolism. Blamed by both sides, occultists like Papus had been forced to counter claims made by scientists that magic evidenced no more than megalomania and delusion, while disproving allegations made by sensationalists like Bataille that any unorthodox practice entailed paying obeisance to Lucifer. "People accuse magicians in vain of these preposterous designs; Satanism and Magic stand at opposite poles, and only several generations of scientists will be able to restore them to their rightful place in the field of human knowledge."[10]

Used as a forum for self-exonerating clarification, Papus's book devotes little attention to Satanic ritual and belief. Fearing to be associated with Bataille's commercial ambitions, Papus retreats to the more intellectually defensible position of characterizing diabolism as the absence of God. As Papus reasons, the devil is no more than an abstention from virtuous action, blindness to the divinity at work in Creation. Scientists, church leaders, occultists like Papus all illustrate the apothegm that the devil's greatest triumph is to convince the faithful he does not exist. Like the psychiatrist who diagnoses Satanism as hysteria, the occultist equates the devil with the inoperativeness of God's will. "There is no personal Devil in the ordinary sense of the word. The being mystically referred to as the Devil is the negation or the opposite of God. God is Light, Truth, Order, and Harmony. Consequently, the Devil is darkness, deceit, discord, and ignorance."[11]

In Papus' sensible assertion, one sees foreshadowed the impending fate of the Decadent devil – put to death by the enlightened pronouncements of medicine, marginalized by occultists stressing the delusional selfishness of devil worship. Similarly, in his apprentice manual, *Comment on devient mage* (*How One Becomes a Magus*), Joséphin Péladan denies the reality of spell-casting and necromancy. He deprecates the efficacy of sorcerers' violence, impugns the credibility of the vision ary prophet Eugène Vintras, and mocks Huysmans for engaging in an exchange of spells with his enemies. Huysmans's occultist/mentor, Abbé Boullan, referred to as Doctor Johannes in *Là-bas*, stands in relation to Huysmans, his acolyte/protégé, Péladan says, as would "a prophetic Tartuffe in face of a mystical Orgon."[12]

With his apocryphal Chaldean ancestry, his vatic bombast, flowing toga, and prodigious beard, Sâr Péladan emerged as the most controversial and flamboyant of the Decadent occultists. A self-styled aesthete, founder of the Salon de la Rose+Croix, Péladan was also a prolific writer, author of *L'Amphithéatre des Sciences mortes* (*The Amphitheater of Dead Sciences*) as well as various treatises on astrology and eroticism, one of which he describes as an "ascetic practice of transcendental sexuality." Péladan's multi-volume *Ethopée, La Décadence latine*, links the workings of the devil to the pervasive corruption of Occidental culture by intellectualized vice and moral laxity. For Péladan, evil is manifested as an unquestioning acquiescence to the values of militarism, nationalism, and materialism. In Péladan's view, the devil is not witnessed at Black Masses. Instead, Satan's temple is the *café-concert*, the newspaper office, the gambling den, the brothel, or the racetrack.

Péladan also dismisses the authenticity of black magic, which he characterizes as social or mental pathology. "Keep this in mind, my disciple," he admonishes a follower, "that sorcery comes from an exaltation of nervous energies among people who are at once believers and criminals."[13] Rather than learning secret techniques for the manipulation of objects, the Adept achieves mastery through the exercise of self-control. While, in his fiction, Péladan ascribes to his Magus-hero a host of impressive occult abilities – chiromancy, magnetism, anesthetic insufflations, divination, astral travel – to his student, Péladan insists that such powers are fake. Adopting the reductionist idiom of science, Péladan claims that supernatural evil is only criminal imposture: "Those claiming to be sorcerers are simply thieves and murderers, magnetizers of people unaware of their own guilt, spiritualists, all of whom suffer from a form of mental alienation."[14]

As Decadence augurs the extinction of Occidental culture, the fin-de-siècle devil is similarly an endangered entity, threatened with annihilation by doctors and skeptics, reduced to the burlesque antics of swindlers and imbeciles. But, as Decadence reassigned value from knowledge to beauty, engaging less in truth-seeking and more in aesthetics, the Decadent devil migrated from the realm of religion and sensational literature to art. Rejecting the capering caricature of tabloid accounts, the Decadents relocated the devil to the iconography of history.

The people's devil

In Decadent fiction – in fin-de-siècle treatises on occult tradition – the devil is most animated, most implausible and entertaining when he appears in folktales, legendary accounts, and popular stories of indeterminate provenance. For the Decadents, the devil featured in these colorful tales is the object of nostalgia, the devil they wish still existed.

In his rollicking anatomy of turn-of-the-century diabolism, *Le Satanisme et la magie* (*Satanism and Magic* 1895), Jules Bois distinguishes between the traditional devil – presiding over ceremonies held at night in the countryside – and the cold, urban Satan invoked in sacrilegious ceremonies in churches. Bois's floridly exuberant image of the traditional devil gives way to the descriptive poverty of the contemporary Satan: "As soon as the Black Mass moves from the open air into a church, it becomes hypocritical and refined, losing the grandeur which came from its essentially human element."[15] Like the readers of Dr. Bataille's fanciful narrative, Bois yearns for the devil who justifies descriptive excess, a Satan as picturesque as the language that celebrates him.

Bois's own writing alternates between naturalism's detached neutrality, clinical analyses of scenes like those Huysmans witnessed, and revelry that abandons all pretense of objectivity, as when he pictures a Sabbath at a forest crossroads or in a moonlit cemetery. On an early winter evening, hordes of malcontents and pariahs aspirated up chimneys climb on goats or straddle broomsticks and set off across the land. No embittered aristocrats or intellectual cynics flood the livid back roads of the country at night, but a ragtag gang of freaks and grotesqueries: "gypsies, peasants, vagrants, jugglers, false clerics,"[16] specimens not offered hospitality in respectable literature. The rural Sabbath Bois pictures is part Miracle Fair, part circus, and features mountebanks and exhibitors of dancing bears: showmen skilled in amusing an audience like Bataille's: "everything needed to delight the people's foolishness."[17]

Uncircumscribable because unseen, the devil is a collective projection of his worshippers, misshapen like hunchbacks, ridiculous like idiots. Bois's devil also animates the gamut of the medieval bestiary, assuming the theriomorphic richness of anathema and fancy. Wolves, toads, and roosters, basilisks, and serpents, symbols of perfidy, bodies of disgust, creep, and yelp, and crow. Bois's ceremony involves a universal confusion, a commingling of opposites, a collapsing of dichotomies. Metaphors regress to meanings and the objects that they signify. The vulpine treachery of witches reconverts them into foxes, and gender differences are obliterated by indiscriminate copulation: "the sorcerer and sorceress, in their intimacy, become one."[18]

Taboos normally structuring a world of antinomy and separation are violated as corpses are disinterred from their resting places in graveyards, and engage, not in the coupling of Decadent Luciferianism, but in carrion banquets consecrating incest and necrophagia. Cemetery desecration restores a primitive universe in which everything is eaten, everything excreted. Corpses undressed of shrouds are dismembered by their pillagers. Their intestines are devoured or are saved for later use as ingredients in kitchens or "the den of alchemists."[19]

Janine Chasseguet-Smirgel, in her analysis of Devil Religion, links perversions like incest, bestiality, and necrophilia to a metaphysical objective to undo divine creation, recreating original chaos from which new worlds can be fashioned. Judeo-Christian interdictions on intercourse with children, on mating with animals, on breaking body boundaries are violated so that everything coalesces and blends together. In Bois's picture of the country Sabbath, disorder reigns supreme. Words are retransformed into referents like stomachs reconverted into food. As Chasseguet-Smirgel suggests: "perversion represents a magical process aimed at a return to the state of indistinction, a manifestation of hubris, of man's desire to discredit the Father-Creator, and to shape a new reality from chaos."[20]

Bois's picture of the Sabbath is one where anything can happen and where anything can be said. It authorizes a liberation from rote thinking and bland expression. At the Sabbath, Schopenhauerian pessimists are gladdened by reawakened possibility. Touched by Pan's scepter, "every sick or melancholic human being reels blissfully to the beat of the cosmic dance."[21]

Representations of the Decadent devil are more colorful and animated when they are oriented along an axis of retrospection and nostalgia. Take the moribund Satan soon to be euthanized by science, the devil neutered by the imaginative sterility of his followers, and dress him in his erstwhile glory, in the multifariousness of the absurd. Infinite in the inchoateness of worlds still unmade, he is greater than a God constrained by the singularity of his Creation.

Bois himself asserts the regenerative potential of Satanic metanoia. Under the rubric of Criminal and Scientific Excuses for the Sabbath, he cites the fecundating benefits of disassembly and undoing. Like the nineteenth-century anarchists intent on assassinating presidents, on subverting social institutions, and exploding received ideas – seeking to re-establish a *tabula rasa* undefiled by law or government – Satanists sow confusion, throw "the bombs of their evil spells."[22] Driven, not by a hope in social engineering, but by ontological despair, they seek to rid the universe of what Bois calls "that human leprosy."[23] More beautiful than the building blocks of creation unbegun is the wreckage of an old world reduced to broken limbs and rubble. As Bois says, Satan forgives the cemetery when it delivers up the dead who, as vampires, enjoy a spurious life that allows them to kill again. In Bois's tableau, the devil subscribes to a Decadent aesthetic: "Ruins alone are beautiful, sorrowful, worthy of Satan."[24]

For Bois, the Satanist is a perverted double of the scientist who dismisses God. But whereas the Positivist heralds man's progress toward enlightened self-knowledge, the devil-worshipper practices science *à rebours*, seeing "man's origins as an animal, his reversion to the status of animal, whose instincts he retains and with whom he maintains an affinity."[25] For the anarchist who burns with ideological intransigence, for the writer outraged by the senescence of his art, "Satan is the great revolutionary working doggedly to transform creation."[26]

The Decadent devil

In fictional representations of the fin de siècle, the heroic, triumphant, demiurgic Satan of folklore has largely disappeared, replaced by a devil mirroring the Decadent himself. In J.-K. Huysmans's critical essay on Félicien Rops, nostalgia for the exuberant devil of popular narrative is evident in the author's praise for the erotica of Thomas Rowlandson. On the one hand, the devil is eclipsed by his priestess, "the terrible faun of Lust,"[27] who excites the writer's misogynistic loathing. Huysmans characterizes the demoness as "a fornication machine," recalling the "medieval concept of woman as an *instrumentum diaboli.*"[28] On the other hand, evidence of Huysmans's sexual anxieties are offset by his enthusiasm for Rowlandson's picture of "a surprising uproar of rutting crowds,"[29] an image recalling Bois's depiction of the country Sabbath.

Instigated by a devil who is either a participant or a witness, this debauchery evokes a Satanism that is riotous and festive – far removed from the devil worship Huysmans chronicles in *Là-bas*, where the celebrants are old and worn, pathetic and hysterical.

Bois's image of the jubilance of the open-air Black Sabbath suggests the retrospective yearning of the Decadents, whose sins are unenthusiastic and cerebral, who rarely couple in the moonlight but cultivate perversions of the mind. Huysmans seemingly deplores his contemporaries' intellectualized transgressions, and despite denying that vice belongs to the realm of medical investigation, he still classes morbid delectation as both a sin and a disorder: "Cerebral erethism, says science."[30]

What, in Bois, had been the implied homology between the devil and his worshippers becomes more overt in Huysmans's picture of fin-de-siècle evil, where lassitude, cynicism, arrogance, and ennui replace the robust loins and sweaty bodies seen in Rowlandson.

It is in Rops's work that Huysmans finds the weary Satanism of the Decadence – where the devil is personified as "a gentleman in a black suit."[31] The work of the Belgian painter heralded by Huysmans and admired by Péladan was most responsible for establishing the fashion of Satanism in pictorial art. The Satan of the Middle Ages, symbolized as the zoomorphy of man's sins – the surreptitiousness of cats, the lechery of goats – gives way in Rops to a debonair devil, ironic and disabused.

According to Huysmans, in Rops's watercolors, the devil is subordinated to a Lust Goddess, as man's prurience is projected as the object that inspires it. Rops's pictures suggest Decadent ambivalence about evil, locating sin in the devil, in man, and in the woman who arouses him. The terrible energies and infernal glory that were the appanage of Lucifer are re-gendered and resituated in the fin-de-siècle Sataness.

In "L'Enlèvement" (The Kidnapping), Rops harkens back to his own art's antecedents – showcasing, not the urbane devil resplendent in formal dress, but a more traditional embodiment of instinctuality and satyriasis. The elements of Rops's painting, reproduced in detail in Huysmans's commentary, recall Bois's crossroads Sabbath pullulating with monsters from nightmares. The lushness of Huysmans's word painting suggests the critic's excitation, as his imagination is disengaged from the picture he is contemplating and, unmoored, sets off in reverie about rituals of bygone eras. At the Sabbath, Huysmans imagines natural life forms all commingling: the mandrake root, valued as a narcotic and aphrodisiac which – with its resemblance to the human form – symbolizes a phylogenetic interface, "the point where vegetable and animal kingdoms meet, as Madame Blavatsky would observe."[32] Toxic beverages brewed from henbane, from selenaceous plants, philtres composed of menstrual blood, cats' brains, hyenas' bellies, orgies devolving into infanticide and sodomy show the overflow of Huysmans's text from the picture he is analyzing.

In Rops, the devil as a male figure is increasingly decentered. Like the believer who, in the fin de siècle, is marginalized by science, the devil is threatened by rationalism, subordinated to the demoness. Huysmans's meditations on Rops's art express Decadent insecurities about the obsolescence of the aristocracy, the discrediting of religion, the emasculation of men by the virago and the gynander. The Decadent obsession with the Androgyne seen in Péladan and Guaïta may derive in part from alchemy, a belief in the original bisexuality of God, but it also bespeaks concerns about man's diminishment and castration.

In another of Rops's plates, "Satan semant l'ivraie" (Satan sowing tares), the devil is no elegant wastrel in formal black attire, but a bearded peasant whose face is twisted into a rictus. Sower of sin, he fills the sky, straddling the Seine, but despite his malevolent enormity, he lacks the power to inseminate. The germinating force that promotes a harvest is not male seed but the *larves de femmes* he shakes out of his apron.

In Huysmans's response to Rops's painting, the devil is no chameleonic figure assuming the face and form of the people who invoke him. He is the proleptic incarnation of the Decadents' dying faith, their belief that when science kills religion, the devil will accompany it. While he towers over the city, the devil is ancient and emaciated, planting his skeletal legs over the unsuspecting populace. While the devil is the past – Decadent evil wasted into an osseous frame of futility – the future is the seed of women from which lust and evil spring. In Huysmans's essay, Satan is eclipsed by the Harlot of Revelation, "the poisonous, naked Beast, mercenary of the Darkness, the absolute serf of the Devil."[33]

Huysmans's writing confirms the aphorism that the devil exists, that Satan is strong, only to the extent that power is accorded him by man. Huysmans's gynephobic rhetoric identifies Decadent anxieties that man is most susceptible to evil's blandishments when they are embodied in woman.

Finally, in "Sphynx," evil's transitivity is evidenced by the devil-woman, as Satan is a just caricature of the ineffectual fin-de-siècle male, only able to reap the harvest of sin planted by his female counterpart. Sidling up to a Sphinx frozen in the hieratic dignity of centuries, a naked woman whispers, urging it to reveal its timeless secrets. On the other side, a monocle-wearing Satan waits passively to hear the information he is powerless to extract. Huysmans's appreciation of Rops's work may convey the author's anti-feminism, but it also shows the writer's sense of the shrunken majesty of Satan. Dismissed by occultists like Papus as a perversion of white magic, sanitized by scientists who classify it as a disorder, Satanism was threatened with destruction by analysis on all sides.

The devil as fantasm

The most thorough demonstration of the devil's representational pro-teanism can be seen in the conflicting images given in Huysmans's *Là-bas*, heralded as the canonical work on nineteenth-century Satanism. Recognizing the novelist for "giving currency to the Question of Lucifer," Waite credits Huysmans for "promot[ing] it from obscurity into prominence."[34] Yet Waite makes no distinction between Huysmans's text as a work of invention and as an empirical record of events witnessed first-hand. Apart from the issue of Huysmans's narrative veracity, his interest is in opposing the pageantry of medieval Satanism and the perfunctory sacrilegiousness of a contemporary Parisian Black Mass. The drabness of the nineteenth-century devil is a projection of Satanists and their literary investigators – as inglorious and banal as their sense of themselves. The devil called forth at Canon Docre's Black Mass reflects a fin-de-siècle worldview laundered of mystery. Because Huysmans's protagonist despises his countrymen's venality, he sees Satan and his partisans as petty and mean: a renegade priest wearing only black socks under his chasuble, pederast choirboys, their cheeks caked with make-up, the devil no more than an impossible symbol of materialism.

Because what Durtal witnesses is a dismally ordinary ceremony – ugly, common, blasphemous, and profane – the physical reality of the devil is never at issue. On the other hand, because Gilles's Satan is unascertainably distant, he gains in prestige, grandeur, and mystery. As Gilles's slaughter of children becomes more compulsive and nightmarish – as he fills his sepulcher-dungeons with skeletons and peoples the landscape with mothers weeping for their lost sons – the devil for whom this tribute is paid becomes more frightening and real. Because the historical record of this Satan is partial, the contemporary imagination finishes a picture that is at once gripping and vivid.

On the night the devil is summoned by a sorcerer in Gilles's employ, the Maréchal and another magician stand transfixed at the door, listening to the imprecations and howls that come from inside. And when the cacophony subsides and they enter, they find only the victim's mangled limbs and crushed head. The marauding Satan of fifteenth-century Normandy is as boundless as his worshippers' imaginative powers.

In *Le Temple de Satan* (*Satan's Temple*) Stanislas de Guaïta also comments on the compromised prestige of *le Satan fin-de-siècle* – a bogeyman eliciting hilarity and ridicule. If not consigned to non-existence, the nineteenth-century Prince of Darkness is more hesitant to reveal himself to scoffers and unbelievers. As Guaïta writes: "these days, the Demon shows some reluctance to manifest himself in person to an irreverent public, capable of laughing in his face, if he were to show it."[35]

Born in 1861 into a noble Italian family, Guaïta had first begun his research into esotericism as a student in Nancy, where he had taken up a study of metaphysics and the Kabbalah. Guaïta's own interest in diabolism had taken him from youthful attempts at versifying on Satanic themes to an immersion in the writings of Eliphas Lévi. Independently wealthy and therefore free to devote himself to esoteric research, Guaïta had steeped himself in theosophy and magic, acquiring an impressive breadth of knowledge. Freed by his personal wealth from suspicions of charlatanism, Guaïta had offered his home as a gathering place for the prominent esotericists of the day, successfully advancing himself as the deepest and most erudite thinker of the occultist movement.

Despite Guaïta's effort to establish his credentials as an historian of magic, he still devotes a long chapter in *Le Temple de Satan* to underscoring the sorry predicament of a devil reduced to the predatory machinations and opportunism of a pervert. Citing a recent work by the magisterially named Chevalier Gougenot des Mousseaux, Guaïta refers back to transcribed accounts of a recent manifestation by the devil. Seventeen young girls of problematic virtue had been persuaded to summon a stranger to their sexual frolics. Called forth by a male acquaintance reading from Albertus Magnus, a bon vivant of attractive mien had appeared inexplicably in the room. The devil, Guaïta writes, "had that day the face of a young man in his thirties, wearing a suit of an elegant cut, and having no more and no fewer claws than any flirtatious woman."[36]

The narrative recording the devil's 11-year liaison with one of the girls is followed by another story of his appearance at a séance, where he caused the skirts of buxom ladies to balloon and rise immodestly, and where he had touched them above the knee, as the chevalier writes discreetly.

More than the drollery of Guaïta's tales, the tone with which he tells them conveys the modern devil's plight, his displacement by nineteenth-century nymphomaniacs, his expedient incarnations as deviants and roués.

Guaïta concurs with Papus in assigning Satan certain impersonal, abstract qualities. Responding to the atheist who claims the devil manifests himself to the feebleminded, materializing in the fog of sickly imaginations. Guaïta echoes Papus in denying the existence of *un Diable personnel* [a personal Devil]. Embodying the defects of the gullible, Satan, as Guaïta reasons, "in his metaphysical form is Error, in his psychic form is Egotism, and in his perceptible form is Ugliness."[37]

The bulk of Guaïta's treatise consists of a history of religious myth, a cultural anthropology of postlapsarian evil. Paralleling *Au Seuil du mystère* (*On the Threshold of Mystery*), Guaïta's encyclopedia of occultism, *Le Serpent de la Genèse* (*The Serpent of Genesis*) traces the devil's avatars through the ages: the Zoroastrian Ahriman; Moloch, the cannibal idol of the Ammonites; the Hebrew monster, Leviathan; the Beast of Revelation, who with its prophet, is "thrown alive into the lake of fire that burns with sulfur" (Revelation 19:20).

Guaïta recalls the devil's invasion of the Ursuline convent of Loudun, describing the futility of exorcisms to drive the demon out: "Howls, contortions, obscene utterances and poses, an erotic furor unleashed without restraint."[38] While suspending judgment as to whether these phenomena were produced by evil forces – "Possession or hysterical demonopathy – "[39] the panoramic breadth of Guaïta's history of sorcery betrays a fascination with the Satanism occultists rejected as imposture. Epilepsy and hysteria may be plausible diagnoses, but for the Decadents, Satan is great, and medical etiologies are small.

The artist's devil

The final chapter in Guaïta's exploration of the Temple of Satan concerns manifestations of the devil through the medium of art. Guaïta's essay marks the convergence of Decadent aesthetics and epistemology, where Truth-as-Beauty displaces the despairing lessons of empiricism. For Guaïta, the dabbler in necromancy, the Magus-dilettante may be seduced by the arcane imagery and mystery of Satanism. Occasional tourists in the realm of devil worship, they may be captivated by art's shimmer, but "they limit themselves to the superficial picturesqueness of the grimoire; their teeth bite only into the skin of the forbidden fruit."[40]

Papus, Guaïta, Péladan, all self-styled occult masters, admonish the casual seeker to abandon his vain quest. The paradox of these propadeutic manuals of occult science is that they beckon the initiate and warn the curious away. The unique character of Decadent magic is to combine titillation and frustration, to offer the forbidden fruit that ultimately is withheld. It is like all of Decadent art that tempts with the sparkle of illusion, entrancing audiences with the incantatory beauty of its language while concealing what lies beneath, either mysterious truths or nothingness.

Guaïta identifies the devil operating in fin-de-siècle art as the principle of cunning, immorality, and nihilism. Invoking Baudelaire, founder of the poetics of nineteenth-century evil, Guaïta describes the poisonous blooms growing on the edge of the abyss, flowers that adorn the ravine wall and lead up to the pit. Heedless infatuation with black magic may lead the artist to perdition: "There is a fantastically ideal quality even in the mystery of abomination that has captivated people in all times."[41] The poetry of evil is spoken by the Great Seducer. It is the hypnotizing voice each artist recognizes as his own, imparting insidious messages of jadedness and surrender.

The devil is also skilled in cultivating flowers unique to each era, encouraging the Decadent fad of Satanism that mocked God and trivialized Satan, inducing artists to array with gorgeous imagery their vain ideas. The devil's dominion is apparent in the prevalence of cynicism, in the loss of what Baudelaire called *consciousness in acts of evil*. For Guaïta, the effects of the inflexible logic of Goetia are recognizable "as the progressive loss of man's moral sense, as the proselytizing power of the negative philosophies of free will."[42] What Péladan heralded as the approaching end of western civilization – *la décadence latine* – is the blasé fashion of transgression, casual vices indulged by Rops's monocle-wearing gentleman.

Guaïta discerns the devil's influence in the voguishness of Buddhism: the consecration of the individual's dissolution of the self, the equation of abulia with the ecstasy of ego-death, a celebration of "the suicide of one's true personality."[43] The perversion of religion whose practices are misconstrued, the confusion of weakness and passivity with Nirvana show the workings of the Evil One at the turning of the century.

Materialism, skepticism, immorality, unbelief – supernatural evil evidenced as a denial of the supernatural – lead Guaïta to idealize the naïveté of past centuries, to long for a restoration of magic practiced, not by wizards, but by children. In a catalogue of supernatural horrors committed through the ages, Guaïta concludes with an apostrophe to the person who regaled him with fairy tales: "Grandmother, tell us another story of the olden times."[44]

An unusual feature of the fin de siècle, this overlapping of fantasy and esotericism shows the Decadents' competing interest in occult sciences and folklore. The romanticizing of childhood, the privileging of imagination over knowledge, pervades the fin de siècle and explains the Decadent nostalgia for the past. In Huysmans's preference for the Middle Ages over the aridity of his century, in Jean Lorrain's evocation of the folktales recounted by his cook (*Princesses d'ivoire et d'ivresse* [*Princesses of ivory and intoxication*]), in Marcel Schwob's account of Monelle and her nomadic band of waifs, searching for the White Kingdom of comforting untruths, the Decadents display their love of innocence, their detestation of truth and fact. The Decadents are like the little girls nestling by Monelle around a campfire: "They wished for nothing more than perpetual unawareness. They wanted to devote themselves eternally to games. The work of life brought them despair. For them, there was nothing but the past."[45]

What else is Decadent diabolism with its pentacles and grimoires than a rejection of truth and work, than a re-enactment of childhood games? How else can one explain the wild success of Bataille's book, with its tales of talking apes and piano-playing crocodiles, than as the public's fondness for hyperbole, their penchant for escapism? Having established his credentials as an historian of esotericism, Guaïta ends his book by citing the benefits of unknowing. Schwob's proscription against self-awareness ("Know thyself not")[46] is echoed by Guaïta in the tribute to his grandmother, who had spoken "the hereditary language of the unintelligent."[47] A castaway on the beach of Decadent rationalism "where the waves of this brutal century wash up,"[48] the Decadents sought oases of miracles and horrors, in stories of Sleeping Beauty or accounts of witches' Sabbaths.

At the conclusion of Guaïta's volume, there comes a conspicuous shift in emphasis: from the historical, moral, and epistemological character of Satanism to Satanism as narrative and the strength of audience reception. Guaïta aligns himself with others of his contemporaries for whom the devil assumes reality as a function of his remoteness and the descriptive virtuosity of the authors recreating him. Since, in *Là-bas*, Durtal assembles the devil from archival debris, the evil he imagines is more creatively compelling than the evil he experiences. Similarly, in Bois's overview of necromantic ritual, Satan is more eloquent, more entertaining, and believable at open-air Sabbaths featuring sorceresses and dead babies. Even when engaging in the controversy over Satanism, the Decadents countered science less with arguments from religion – less with defenses of the legitimacy of occultism – than with the iridescence of their style. As Guaïta comments, "Art also has its magic – shadowy or splendid, beneficial or deadly."[49]

In the works of Eliphas Lévi, the century's greatest popularizer of hermeticism, authors are celebrated as belonging to a sacerdotal brotherhood, whose language reinforces the operational power of the *Logos*. It is "the creative Word that constitutes man's true resemblance to God."[50] One can easily imagine the writer's profanation of art's purpose, magnifying, not God's work, but the expressive cleverness of his epigone. In the wheedling tone of Satan-Panthée, Guaïta hears an echo of the writer's voice. Reflected in the weeping face of Satan, as Bois imagines him, is the wretched likeness of the outcasts and criminals who venerate him.

The final perversion of doxology seen in Guaïta's book on Satanism is the encomium he directs, not to God, but to the storyteller. Decadents – historically criticized for subordinating moral truth to style – do the

devil's work by instituting a religion of aestheticism. In preferring artifice to nature, "this mirror of divinity," the artist engages in a narcissistic
adoration of the image. When eurhythmy and grace no longer celebrate
the Creator, art abjures its sacred purpose and becomes a form of taboo
magic. "Substituting the discordancy of individuals' evil intentions for
the wise harmony of general laws," art, as Guaïta argues, "becomes
Satanic in its ugliness."[51]

In the Decadents' cult of the individual, in their practice of art for
art's sake – in privileging the image over the rightness of a principle –
Decadent art risks degenerating into self-worship and iconolatry. When
the Satan of Decadent literature no longer inspires respectful horror but
becomes, as in Bataille's book, a figure of curiosity and amusement, the
devil inhabits authors as their self-satisfied insouciance. This is the position taken by writers like Guaïta, who still contest the physical reality of
Satan. When the response to Huysmans's *Là-bas* is skyrocketing sales
and increased fame, Satan manifests himself in the materialism and
vanity Huysmans professed to despise.

In their treatment of Satanism, the Decadents were pulled in two
directions, pandering, on the one hand, to public hunger for sensation-
alism, disseminating, on the other hand, information on the meaning
of occult teachings. Papus may strike a doctoral tone when he describes
the devil as Non-being, but the Satan who thrived in the literature and
pictorial art of the fin de siècle existed more intensely as the vividness
of the image.

In Denis de Rougemont's 1944 work, *La Part du diable* (*The Devil's
Share*), he characterizes the appeal of creative work as fundamentally
diabolical: "In truth the will to create, the need to write [...] coin-
cides deep down with the Luciferian temptation: to become like God,
to make oneself an author, to authorize oneself in an autonomous
world."[52] Along with pursuing the demiurgic project to compete with
God as a creator, the Decadents neglected the idea in preference to its
expression. Shifting emphasis from God's domain of material reality
and moral values to the human realm of artifice and stylistic ingenuity, they succumbed to the devil's lure and began to worship what
they fashioned. This, as C. G. Wallis writes in a review of Rougemont's
book, is the "dialectical diabolism" inherent in the act of writing:
"to forget the thought in developing the image or trope in which it
must be expressed, to lose sight of what is signified and see only the
symbol one is using."[53] A clever thought that teaches nothing, a gra-
tuitously elegant turn of phrase: these are demon spawn, the artist's
offspring, a father's pride. For the Decadents, the Creator's child is not a

deferential author. It is the art work whose progenitor loves the devil as himself.

J.-K. Huysmans's *Là-bas*

The establishment of the Decadent devil as a product of the creative imagination – a projection of the artist who worshipped Satan as his work – can be traced back to the conditions in which turn-of-the-century diabolism flourished. Repelled by the explanatory aridity of scientific methodology, the Decadents rejected a model of the world as a cold, inhuman mechanism and proclaimed instead the existence of mysteries not susceptible to any analytical elucidation.

It was against this backdrop of epistemological discord and philosophical strife that fin-de-siècle authors began recording instances of Satanic activity, as they sought to confirm the veracity of supernatural phenomena and justify their awarding the devil a special place in their works of art. In 1887, renowned psychiatrist Jean-Martin Charcot had complained that in contemporary art, manifestations of hysterical neurosis were presented, not as illness, "but as a perversion of the soul due to the presence of the demon."[54] In response, J.-K. Huysmans, in his preface to Jules Bois's *Le Satanisme et la magie*, denounced the shortcomings of psychology in explaining genuine manifestations of evil. Whereas, in earlier centuries, as Huysmans elaborates, "demonologists had confused certain hysterical episodes with Satanic phenomena," in the present day, "doctors attribute to hysteria incidents that belong more properly to the domain of the exorcist."[55]

Huysmans argues that, in an effort to distinguish the insane from those possessed by the devil, medicine had adopted an absolutist posture and, in so doing, had blinded itself to incontrovertible evidence of Satanic activity.

In support of his assertion, Huysmans furnishes numerous accounts of desecrated sanctuaries, sacrificial murders, sacrilegious acts: the 1891 assassination of a Trappist monk, the violation of Notre-Dame de Paris by an unnamed woman who had absconded with two ciboria containing consecrated hosts. According to Huysmans, thefts of the Eucharist had spread to the four corners of the country: "In la Nièvre, in le Lorient, in l'Yonne, tabernacles had been forced open and the Eucharist seized."[56] Since no ascertainable financial motive could be found for these transgressions, Huysmans concluded that they could have only been an attack on Christ's body and that the stolen hosts were intended for use in works of black magic.

By the time that Huysmans prepared his comments for the preface to Bois's book, his name had already been indissolubly linked to contemporary Satanic practices. The notoriety Huysmans garnered from the publication of *Là-bas* had gained the attention of writers throughout Europe, including occultist Alfred Waite, who cites extensively from Huysmans's text as evidence of the rise of devil worship in France. Describing Huysmans as "the discover of Modern Satanism," Waite proclaims: "Under the thinnest disguise of fiction, he gives in his romance of *Là-bas*, an incredible and untranslatable picture of sorcery, sacrilege, black magic, and nameless abominations, secretly practiced in Paris."[57]

Seeking to establish a parallel in nineteenth-century Paris with medieval Satanism and the atrocities committed by the legendary Gilles de Rais, Huysmans had learned of the exploits of Abbé Louis van Haecke, prototype for the figure of Canon Docre in *Là-bas*, a charismatic figure who reportedly had confided his knowledge of devil worship during the author's visit to Belgium. Beginning in 1889, Huysmans's acquaintance with Joseph-Antoine Boullan, successor to Eugène Vintras, the mystic prophet and founder of L'Ordre de la Miséricorde [the Order of Mercy], had also afforded the writer access to a secret world of necromantic practices. Huysmans had become embroiled in warfare with another secret faction led by occultists Oscar Wirth and Stanislas de Guaïta. Already, in 1887, the two had collaborated in writing an exposé denouncing the master's arcane doctrine. Wirth, having professed admiration for Boullan and gained his confidence, had betrayed Vintras's successor, while Guaïta had accused Boullan of engaging in "adultery, incest and bestiality," of promoting the practice of "incubism and onanism."[58] After appointing themselves Boullan's judges and pronouncing summary judgment, the two set about enforcing the sentence of death. The occult warfare between the rival camps had been ongoing for two years when Huysmans first made contact with the controversial cleric. Soon thereafter he found himself involved in a mystic battle of spells and counter-spells, during which he complained of being attacked by hostile spirits emanating from the astral plane, feeling himself beleaguered by invisible forces, experiencing hallucinations that affected both the author and his cat.

Huysmans's successful entrée into the forbidden world of nineteenth-century Satanism had earned him the fame and money he deprecated, sometimes unconvincingly, in his novel. And despite the invisible enchantments exchanged between the warring factions, both regarded Luciferianism and the sacrilegious acts it authorized as less dangerous than science that discounted the devil's existence altogether.

When, in his preface to *Le Satanisme et la magie*, Huysmans marshals evidence to prove the resurgence of Satan worship in France, he attacks a devil who privileges body over spirit, promoting materialism of the kind Huysmans saw enshrined in Zola's fictional corpus. This was a devil who, to Huysmans, consecrated a value system and advanced a perception of reality that seemed patterned on positions held by Positivists themselves.

Indeed, in *Là-bas*, the first mention of diabolic influence comes in a comment on the nature of capital, whose capacity for self-multiplication is seen as monstrous and infernal. To Huymans's protagonist and alter-ego, Durtal, money contaminates its user, perverting its function as a symbol, and occulting the physical reality it overvalues and replaces. Possessions, hyper-invested because of their temporary renunciation, become more desirable, more entangling because they are unavailable. The most modest and virtuous pauper, undefiled by attachments, comes by money and then is tainted by greed that thrives on dispossession. Unlike language, sublimating reality into beauty and significance, money does not purify the world by ridding it of objects. Instead, by abstracting material reality into value, price, and number, money exacerbates consumers' hunger for the things for which it substitutes. In Huysmans, money talks, and the things it takes away are made present by covetousness whose eloquence is diabolical.

An examination of the link between the evolution of Huysmans's faith, the post-naturalist novel's movement toward greater purity of expression, and the triumph of Christian mysticism over the influence of the devil reveals the effects that Satanism had both on Huysmans's fiction and religion. Whereas the devil claims to reward the poor with pleasures and possessions, it is the Catholic artist's work that lifts him out of the realm of sensuality. Not promising material satisfaction but matter's transmutation into intelligence, divinely inspired creation becomes, in Huysmans's later works, the true instrument of redemption.

However, following other fin-de-siècle figures for whom art itself became Satanic, Huysmans's characters had to learn the dangers of diabolical aestheticism. Captivated by the beauty of the artifacts he fashioned, the artist risked succumbing to the sterile worship of himself as their creator. Only when the work was recognized as a means of communion with an audience could the writer escape the cult of self and resume his true task, producing art that enlisted readers in the magnification of the Creator.

Satanism and materialism

From the beginning of *Là-bas*, Huysmans's protagonist intuits that the devil manifests himself as the human tendency toward iconolatry: the writer's adoration of his text, the materialist's enslavement to his wealth – attachments that turn the sinner from an appreciation of the divine and encourage his obsession with objects that are acquired or manufactured. The worship of false gods brings no happiness or satisfaction, as Durtal realizes in his rumination on the Midas touch. A poor man's house whose cleanness is evidenced by its vacancy, is soiled – as is his soul – when it is affected by acquisitiveness. Vice, which had been starved of opportunities for indulging it, is fed by money, which Durtal calls "the greatest nutrient imaginable for sins."[59] Despite replacing objects, money sustains an economy of self-replenishing materialism. The parthenogenetic agent of its rebirth, "it breeds all alone in a bank vault."[60]

Huysmans, whose artistic ideal was of bodies spiritualized into nothingness, was appalled by money's fecundity, its ability to fuel materialism. As Durtal reasons, "either money, as master of the soul, is diabolical or it is impossible to explain."[61]

Despite their affiliation with warring camps, the occultist Papus shared the view Huysmans imputes to Durtal: that Satan inspired the unbeliever's cult of money: "On earth, the Adversary's true priest is the atheist-materialist, for whom all spiritual forces manifest a mental weakness tending toward mysticism. The ascendancy of these people, who believe in nothing but the need to satisfy their appetites in any way possible, will be characterized by a cult of force and violence considered as the only law, by a love of money considered as the only good."[62]

Implicitly, Huysmans treats money like language, as a symbolic system endowed with magic power. Yet Huysmans's experience of Satanism is that, like money, it reversed the power of literature – and that, as a counter-aesthetic – it re-embodied what artistic intelligence ennobled. Unlike Grünewald's Christ, whose crucified flesh is converted into radiant spirit, the Satanist's tormented soul refocuses him on worldly pleasures. Huysmans's eschatological art proclaims the coming of the Paraclete, its succeeding the era of the agony of the Redeemer incarnate. As history's confusion yields to fiction's order, so space will be evacuated of succubi and larvae, and the world will be transfused with divine glory, love, and light.

After Zola's opus, whose effect "had been to turn literature into an embodiment of materialism,"[63] will come the intermediate epoch of "naturalisme spiritualiste" (Spiritual Naturalism). This will pave the way for the supersession of all art, made obsolete in a messianic time of mystical inexpressiveness. Then, Durtal believes, there will be no more formulaic adultery novels, no more stories of sex and madness. Then writers and consumers, once separated by the book, will be able to experience the transparency of communicating face to face.

In Durtal's analysis of the diabolical toxicity of capital, he refers to money as the exchange medium for the forsaken and dispossessed. Whereas Durtal characterizes capital as an obese idol squatting in the shrine of the cash box, Canon Docre vilifies Jesus as the "favorite vassal of the banks."[64] What, for Durtal, is an investor's god, a trickster turning commodities into banknotes, is identified by Docre as Christ, the lackey of the rich. Docre accuses Jesus of violating the spirit of the covenant, offering his disciples only the counterfeit currency of misery: "You were to have redeemed man, and You have not. You were to appear in Your glory, and instead You sleep."[65]

In Docre's lexicon of blasphemy, redemption means conversion into cash, worshipping a devil who endows the penniless with wealth. Durtal despises money as an illusory instrument of happiness, seeming to empty the world of forbidden objects and desires but in reality only hiding them behind a "black veil" of the word "capital." For Durtal, capitalism is materialism without matter, an ideology all the more virulent because it conceals the object of worship. Unlike language, which destroys the things it resurrects as meaning, money is fat with commodities whose consumption is just postponed.

For Huysmans, the Satanist is a materialist exiled from a world saturated with satisfaction. Unlike him, the Catholic artist imagines life purified of excess, in which the ringing of church bells drives out malignant spirits. Space for him is empty, not seething with unseen larvae, not permeated with the destructive energy of spells and counter-spells. Ideas perfectly expressed, material elevated into literature cease to exist, and when Baudelaire or Balzac dies, their souls do not inhabit a transitional zone where they are available to imbeciles who contact them at séances. Death brings extinction, a purifying disappearance. There is no reintroduction of cadavers into an economy of necrophagia, no dismal reincarnation, no activation of the food chain: "it seems to me one life is enough," as Durtal opines. "I'd rather have nothingness, a hole, than all these metamorphoses."[66]

Huysmans's picture of a Satan who consoles embittered paupers is the same as the one that Jules Bois gives in the volume Huysmans prefaced. A versatile essayist, playwright, and proto-feminist, Bois devoted much of his career to examining elevated states of consciousness and investigating manifestations of the supernatural. Already in 1894, the year before the publication of *Le Satanisme*, Bois had patiently researched the covert practice of devil worship in *Les Petites Religions de Paris* (*The Little Religions of Paris*).

Despite professing concern over Bois's religious views, Huysmans praises his book as an indispensable tool for those seeking to arm themselves with knowledge in order to defend their faith. "While he may not profess the most orthodox ideas," Huysmans writes of Bois, "he is at least an ardent and committed spiritualist who has alerted the church's explorers of the need to map out the countries of Lucifer."[67]

Indeed, Bois's description of the first of the Three Satans is the same as that evoked by Docre in his attack on the Christ of plutocrats. Bois professes horror for "the Satan of profanations, enchantments, spells, and shameful love."[68] It is this Satan whom Bois refers to as "the most desolate of Anarchists", the devil who presides over necromantic rituals, and who is "the god of Gilles de Rais."[69]

For Bois, the Satan of the Lost offers a poisonous compensation. Benighted souls who adore matter are rewarded for their sacrilege with material satisfactions. Yet, in *Là-bas*, Huysmans shows that the gift of riches can be spoiled, as it is in fairy tales, when the beneficiary experiences the disappearance of his appetite. *Là-bas* offers a miscellany of moralistic lessons on the disappointments of the dreamer whose fantasies come true. Handmaiden of the devil, Madame Chantelouve awakens Durtal's dormant sexuality, but when he finally possesses her, he is disenchanted and disgusted. The imperturbable bachelor whose ideal of femininity had been the virtuous Madame Carhaix with her steaming cider and beef stew is roused to life by the demoness with her volcanic lust and icy skin. Part succubus, part maenad, Madame Chantelouve does the devil's work – re-appropriating a romance once sublimated into conjectural narrative, then re-embodying it, as in Zola's novels of insanity and rutting. The teleology of Catholic authorship takes flesh and refines it into insight, transmuting the desultoriness of historical data into the ordering and intelligible structure of fiction.

In Durtal's relationship with Madame Chantelouve, this relationship is reversed, when a love affair initially pursued as a distant exchange of letters is reconverted into a collision of bodies that scratch and sweat and pant. Flattering words written on feminine stationery and addressed to Durtal, the author, turn into animal grunts of passion heard by Durtal, the fornicator. When Satan is seen in Huysmans's novels that address the question of evil, he is summoned by the prurience of the hero's sexual fantasies. As Jean Borie writes: "It is by the intensity of the author's erotic imagination that Huysmans's Devil manifests himself."[70]

It is in space emptied of the desired object that Satan first appears: lines of text written in Madame Chantelouve's myrtle green ink, the vast halls of Tiffauges where Gilles, his debauched cohorts, and his alchemist advisors gorge themselves on salmon, beer, and peacocks – where, "in that womanless castle" they sink into "monstrous dreams."[71]

Solitude unfilled by women, indigence unrelieved by the provision of physical necessities are filled by the Evil One and the material satisfactions that he promises. Citing unnamed "professors of mystical eroticism," Bois claims that the experience of succubacy "depends on auto-suggestion," and that "a subtle form of onanism" affords "the illusion of possessing whomever one wants, living or dead, provided one has a clear enough image of them."[72]

In *Là-bas*, Durtal sees Madame Chantelouve as infernal because she is nothing that becomes something, an epistolary mystery vulgarized and explained as sacrilege and perversion. Durtal's mistress is never experienced as more bewitching and seductive than when she is a figment of her lover's imagination, "a non-existent being, a chimera invented by his brain in a moment of crisis."[73] But by bringing her to life and introducing her into his bed, he puts the fantasy to death and refrigerates the heated image, turning intercourse into a diabolical celebration of necrophilia. Despite her ember eyes and burning lips, Durtal finds himself "embracing a corpse, a body so cold that it froze his own."[74] In Huysmans, possession is simultaneously financial, sexual, and demonic: the man whose Midas touch turns the desired object into gold, bloodless, inorganic, metallic, and cold, is like the lover whose sated lust turns a woman into the cadaver of his indifference. The succubus, writes Bois, is a desire "dressed in flesh that haunts," having the color, shape, and smell of "an actual being."[75] Diagnosed in the psychiatric idiom for which Huysmans professed antipathy, invoking demons, inviting succubi requires only morbid ideation.

The Satanist's aim to reincarnate what is rarefied as spirit opposes the literary project of changing historical accident into explanatory narrative and the lover's mission to refine his lust into dialogic romance.

Satanism and the body

Central to Satanic liturgy is a desecration of the Eucharist, literalizing the symbol of Communion as spoiled food or poison sustenance. In *Là-bas*, Huysmans's focus on the species of the Eucharist, his interest in Christ's body as present in consecrated bread, reflects the emphasis on the materiality of the sacrament in the teachings of Eugène Vintras.

Described by Robert Baldick as "the aging miracle-worker of Tilly-sur-Seuille,"[76] Vintras had propounded the doctrines cited by Durtal and his fellow spiritual questers in the final chapters of *Là-bas*. It was Vintras who proclaimed the advent of the era of the Paraclete, the Third Reign preceding the return of Christ in glory. Purporting to be a reincarnation of the prophet Elijah, the visionary Vintras claimed to administer bleeding hosts in which mystic words and images appeared. Abbé Boullan, who succeeded Vintras as leader of the sect, instructed Huysmans in the principles of Dolorist reparation, whereby Christ, whose continued suffering was manifested in the bloody Eucharist, was linked to consumers of the hosts who participated in the Passion.

In his preface to Bois's book, Huysmans cites as evidence of the devil's cleverness his ability to inspire people to deny the fact of his existence, asserting that Satanism thrives on the difficulty one has in convincing the public of its danger. Whereas the devil works like money by hiding his material reality, the writer destroys that reality by exposing and denouncing it. Concurring with "the old axiom from Magic, that once a secret is divulged, it is lost,"[77] Huysmans endorses Bois's attempts to ventilate the obscene truths of Satanic ritual: "the Spirit of Darkness lives in the muddy night of the soul, and he is paralyzed, rendered powerless once a spotlight is thrown on him."[78]

This is the obliterative goal of Huysmans's literary project as a whole: to annihilate the squalid realities of life by converting them into text. For Huysmans, Christ is revealed through his emancipation from the flesh, as the Savior's corpse is found to have vanished from the Sepulcher. During the era of God, the Son, sinners are redeemed by martyrs' suffering. This age will end when Vintras' hosts are healed and when Christ is freed from his prison of food. Until then, the Messiah will be thwarted by evildoers who re-concretize Him as symbol – who deny his transcendence, not by discarding "round wafers of bread," but by defiling and violating "the very flesh of Christ."[79]

In *Là-bas*, Satanists opposing the soul's ascendancy over the body invert high and low, and, like Docre, tattoo the Cross on their feet. They relocate from the aerie in which the ringing of church bells is a tintinnabulary exorcism that purifies the air of larvae. They descend into the bank vault where they adore the god of capital. Or like Gilles, they go down into crypts where they murder Christ again by violating innocence through the sexual immolation of little boys.

Durtal observes in Grünewald's painting the moment that Christ is finally liberated, escaping from scourged limbs and ulcerated flesh, refined and purified into the creative power of the Logos. The celebrants of Black Masses who purport to attack Christ in the body are more accurately described by Huysmans as "abbés Verbicides" (priests who murder the Word).[80]

Là-bas marks a new stage in Huysmans's religious thinking, since – while Huysmans's fictional counterpart, Durtal, may dream of a spiritualized alternative to Zola's physiology-based naturalism – he also acknowledges that creation necessarily entails embodiment. In addition to housing clean, inchoate thoughts in the debased, democratically accessible idiom of the people, books also behave like bodies in being circulated among readers who soil sublime ideas by passing them through their minds. Artists once sequestered in the ethereal realm of inspiration are compelled to re-descend to the squalid milieu of the bookstore. Obliged, "once their book is in print, to see it exposed to the filthy gaze of the masses," they experience publication as "a rape of the little they are worth."[81]

Passages like these show Huysmans's Christological identification with a martyr who suffers in a body devoured by his disciples. J. Hillis Miller explains how the sacrament of Communion enacts the fate of the writer whose work is "broken, divided, passed around, consumed by the critics."[82] Huysmans's aesthetic is therefore not ascensionally oriented along a vertical axis; it does not represent the artist disincarnated as the beauty of his creation. Having risen as Spiritual Naturalism, art is reappropriated by its audience when the text, as tortured body or bleeding host, is eaten by its readers.

In this way, *Là-bas* describes the homology of the mystic and the Satanist, both condemned to suffer in the flesh that they simultaneously exalt and vilify. However, unlike the Satanists who deny the Resurrection by sexualizing Christ's body and impugning his divinity, the Dolorist adopts a different system of positional inversions, showing the High Man who comes down again in the communion with his followers. This is what the astrologer Gévingey tells his listeners in Carhaix's bell-tower, when he explains the meaning of Dr. Johannès's celebration of the sacrifice of the Glory of Melchizedek, where the officiant's robe is adorned with a symbol "in the form of an upside down Cross." Like the Hanged Man represented in the Arcanum of the Tarot, the inverted Cross "signifies that the priest Melchizedek must die in the flesh so that he can live again in Christ, assuming the power of the incarnate Word who was made man and died for us."[83]

Unlike the embodiment of the Word as flesh and blood the faithful consume, the Satanist's aim is to intellectualize desire and invent new transgressions of the soul. This is what Huysmans, in *Certains*, identifies as the singular vision of Félicien Rops who, in his series *Sataniques*, captures lust that goes beyond the physical. As Huysmans remarks, the devil is manifested in desires that transcend corporeity – that illustrate morbid delectation whose effect, Huysmans says, is to "spiritualize ordure."[84] Abstention from sinful acts promotes a monstrous inflation of guilty impulses, a truth that Rops communicates in his illustration for *Le Vice suprême (Supreme Vice)*. There, the author, Joséphin Péladan, describes the ultimate in evil in terms like those Huysmans uses in his analysis of Rops: "To adore the demon or to love evil; these are concrete or abstract expressions of an identical act. There is blindness in instinctual satisfaction, there is madness in the perpetration of sinful deeds, but to conceive of or theorize evil requires a calm operation of the mind. This is the Supreme Vice."[85]

The semioclastic crimes done by worshippers of Satan elevate physical acts of violence to the level of the metaphysical. Diabolical infanticides, like the theft of consecrated wafers, are attacks on bodies as well as attacks on purity as symbol. The murderers who cut a child's throat, drink his blood, or eat his heart seek to rematerialize the sacramental meaning of the Eucharist. They do what Léo Taxil accomplishes on the level of blasphemy-as-ridicule when he calls Communion bread "Jesus grub."[86]

Satanism and the restoration of chaos

In opposition to the anti-spiritual objectives Huysmans ascribes to Luciferians, he proposes his own work as a dialectic of raising and lowering, the creative sublimation of art's material and its subsequent re-embodiment as textual sustenance. At the same time, he contrasts Satanism's movement toward chaos and incoherence with the unifying principle of literature that replaces contingency with meaning. In her commentary on the demiurge, Janine Chasseguet-Smirgel contrasts the processes of divine creation, which emphasize ordering, naming, separating, and structuring, with the anarchic aims of Sade's hero, whose objective, she says, is "not to annihilate things but to dissolve and metamorphose them after breaking down the molecules."[87] In opposing God, who replaces nonsense with intelligence and who gathers disparate entities into recognizable forms, the Satanist seeks a restoration of randomness and fragmentation. By shattering whole bodies into constituent parts, by privileging atomization over totalizing perfection, the Satanist tries to compete with God and so "entertains a belief in the possibility of creating a new kind of reality out of original chaos."[88]

In *Là-bas*, Durtal is advised that Satanists fill the air with invisible malignancies, evil particulates, deadly, unseen agents targeting the victim of a spell. As Gévingey explains: "Space is inhabited by microbes. Is it any more surprising that it should be teeming with spirits and larvae?" Like vinegar and water, "which are saturated with animalcules," air also seethes "with beings that are more or less corporeal, with embryos that are more or less fully developed."[89]

For psychiatrists like Charcot, the man who believes himself attacked by evil spirits may suffer from a paranoiac horror of the infinitesimally small. But the person targeted by a bewitchment or a curse feels he is besieged by criminal thoughts and murderous intentions.

Like archival minutiae which are the by-product of history and which the fictional biographer rearranges as his narrative, larvae are hostile thoughts collected by a spell-caster and directed by his will toward a single destructive goal. Negatively complementing Huysmans's picture of the devil-worshipper – assembling spiritual pathogens into a deadly force governed by his intelligence – the biographer/historian collects the existential debris of time, scattered documents that coalesce into a coherent explanation of the past. As a convert who chose Christian teleology over an impression of life's adventitiousness, Huysmans was repelled by the senselessness of raw experiential data. Opposing the devil, who embodies meaninglessness, Christ symbolizes suffering made purposeful.

Joanny Bricaud describes the aftermath of Abbé Boullan's quarrel with Stanislas de Guaïta, who allegedly targeted Huysmans, the renegade priest's confederate, with spells that were transported by swarms of unseen larvae. Despite celebrating a sacrifice to the Glory of Melchizedek, Huysmans for years reported being terrorized by invisible assailants, feeling himself pummeled "on the head and face with fluidic fisticuffs."[90]

To Huysmans, spiritual evil was represented by small things, bits of sinful ideation, unfocused thinking, guilty reverie. Without discipline, work, or prayer to illumine or eradicate them, these fragments of iniquity came to saturate the spiritual plane. Bois describes these larvae as "human wishes or dreams shaken out of their astral sheaths, crumbs of thoughts, the detritus of anger and hate."[91] Inconsequential and disorganized, these unformulated impulses are largely harmless, suggesting only the moral pusillanimity of their sources.

Bois elaborates on what he terms "the ridiculous terror of larvae" by citing extensively from the writings of Charles Berbiguier, who complained of harassment by malicious *farfadets*, goblins who stole his tobacco box and garter buckles, inflicted flea bites and induced sneezing. Huysmans is similarly disinclined to dignify small sins, feeling a greater affinity for the Satanist whose rebellion was majestic and who aspired to greatness in his wickedness just as saints aspired to greatness in their sacrifice. Unlike imps diffusely pullulating on the astral plane, heroic evil is ordered by intelligence and clarity. "The Devil," as Bois says, is "the collectivity of larvae,"[92] multiplicity made unity regimented by design.

Art and alchemy

Throughout *Là-bas*, Durtal continues to remark on the gemmation of exceptional malefactors and visionary Christians, describing Gilles himself as high and low, sublime and monstrous, never common: "from the most exalted mysticism to the most aggravated Satanism, it is only a short step."[93] Durtal's meditation on the sinisterly occult properties of capital may shed light on Gilles's passage from Christian soldier to raving butcher, performing hecatombs in the dungeons of Tiffauges. Illustrating Durtal's apothegm about the diabolical influence of money, his research on Gilles shows how materialism had corrupted the Maréchal. Bibliophile and collector of priceless art treasures, Gilles had squandered a fortune in dressing a sumptuous table and decorating an opulent chapel. Unstinting in attempts to satisfy the appetites of the body and the soul, he had assembled a vast library containing precious Latin manuscripts, attracting to Tiffauges a princely entourage of clergymen whom he had outfitted in rare surplices and sacerdotal ornaments.

Yet Gilles's profligacy had not been directed just at fulfilling his own desires. Instead, with his legendary hospitality, he had welcomed poets and pilgrims on whom he bestowed his largesse and whom he showered with rich gifts. Gilles's profligate generosity had evidenced a self-cancelling materialism, as he disposed of wealth as carelessly and feverishly as he acquired it. As money destroys the objects it changes into the symbol of itself, Gilles exchanged symbolic riches for the plenitude of possessions, then recklessly consumed them or gave them away to others. Unlike the speculator growing fat on wealth whose enjoyment he puts off, Gilles had practiced an indulgently ruinous asceticism, spending everything, consuming everything until his coffers

had been emptied. In the mystic who renounces the material satisfactions of this world, in the writer who destroys the reality that he
transforms into beauty, in Gilles, the madman, whose extravagance
betrays a metaphysical revolt, Huysmans identifies the spiritual brethren
whose stories he narrates in *Là-bas*.

Yet Durtal is careful to observe that Gilles's first dabbling in alchemy
had not been motivated solely by the debtor's panicked desperation.
While in his demonic invocations and holocaustic human sacrifices,
Gilles conducted alchemical experiments to regain the riches he had
dissipated, his initial occult studies aimed at his spiritual ennoblement.

Indeed, as is thematically developed in the novel, alchemy acts as a
metaphor for the competing goals of Satanic ritual and Christian mysticism. On the material plane, it transforms vulgar substances into gold;
on the level of literature and religion, it turns confusion into knowledge. In the imprecations he directs at Christ as enemy of the poor,
Canon Docre invokes the rights of the indigent to pleasures and possessions. Yet Docre's Satan is like the bank vault god who produces wealth
exchanged for virtue.

In the tradition of Paracelsus, whom Durtal praises in the novel, the
gold the alchemist manufactures is a symbol of a symbol – a catalyst
that does not multiply what the experimenter has but that effects a
purifying change in what the experimenter is. Manly Hall provides a
summary of alchemy's higher aspirations, saying that, through art, "the
mental body of ignorance" is purified by being "*tinctured* with understanding [...] through faith and proximity to God," adding that, in this
way, "the consciousness of man may be transmuted from base animal
desires [...] into a pure, golden, and godly consciousness."[94]

For the Satanist, and for Gilles, gold is wisdom's body re-materialized.
This is what explains the devil-worshippers' rejection of transcendence,
their insistence on the abject physicality of a Redeemer hypostatized
as adulterated food mixed with menstrual blood and semen. Desiring
pleasure and satisfaction, they maintain that the body is all there is.

Conversely, as spiritual alchemy, Christian art is operational, engaging
in the dynamic interaction of material reality and human intelligence.
Driving out the larval swarms of fetal dreams and ambitions aborted by
laziness and cowardice, it refines the body of ignorance into the light of
understanding.

In Bois's taxonomy, there are three Satans: one for the poor man, one
for the lecher, one for the self-exalting intellectual, all joined by their
subordination of others to the self. These people make no commitment
to refine themselves into better beings but wish to cheapen the external

objects they take in and assimilate. The Satanist, as Bois writes, "believes that his miserable self is the only truth, he cries out that the universe is nothing but a pale reflection of himself, while before him, the universe rises up in its splendid mystery."[95] Even in Durtal's pre-conversion state, he sees the writer as an artifex, his text as the crucible in which reality is not paid for but embellished and redeemed by elegance.

Art and communion

The final difference that Durtal discerns between the Satanist and Christian has to do with the former's isolation and the latter's selflessness and solidarity. While the greedy man wants to acquire goods and the lecher desires to possess women, the Catholic artist bestows his writings on others and so works in imitation of his Master. He is unlike the Magus, Mérodack, in Péladan's *Ethopée*, a gloomy, imperious figure, lonely in his contemptuous aloofness.

Forgoing the pleasures of sex and the solace of friendship, the Magus contemplates the spectacle of human depravity with Olympian disdain. Bois also describes the Magus as an anti-social figure: "he is truly alone, at once superhuman and inhuman, unfortunate and inaccessible. Without a wife, without pleasures, without weaknesses, he is only eyes untouched by emotion or sleep, only a mouth that never smiles, only his hands and his intelligence."[96]

It is in Huysmans's study of superhuman evil and divinely inspired self-abnegation that he first shows his hero joining in a community of like-minded seekers. No longer is Huysmans's character isolated, like des Esseintes, in the opulently appointed sanctuary of his aestheticizing consciousness. Durtal is still an elitist who loathes the democratic crassness of his era, but even in the solitary work of authorship, he interacts with others with whom he shares a spiritual and artistic kinship. In *A rebours*, des Esseintes is so secluded in his sickly superciliousness that he is unable to produce anything: a work of art, a new idea, a fresh perspective on a memory. Des Esseintes's ambition to attain perfect autonomy is exemplified by his fantasm of the nourishing peptone enema, the desire to consume nothing and make nothing outside himself.

In *Là-bas*, Durtal initially presents himself as a descendant of des Esseintes, clinging to a fantasy of self-sufficiency, authoring literature intended only for his own enjoyment – defining himself, not as a child of God, but as the father of himself. Like the diabolical capitalist whose wealth begets more wealth, Durtal sires the book he takes as his bride.

Literary creation begins as forbidden endogamy, a refusal of Christ's self-sacrifice for a fallen humanity. Durtal himself describes his authorial activity as transgressive and taboo, boasting to Chantelouve and his wife of inventing the new sin of Pygmalionism which, he says, achieves a synthesis "of cerebral onanism and incest."[97] While professing reluctance to pimp his book by displaying it in bookstore windows, he also incubates the fantasy of violating the daughter of his soul. After fathering his work on Gilles, Durtal entertains two options: either compromising the virginal integrity of his textual offspring by marketing it to the public, or keeping it for himself, refusing to set it free. The work on Gilles becomes another aliment-as-excrement, self-administered like the peptone enema, affording solitary pleasure.

Durtal's denial of art's function as communion marks the moment in *Là-bas* when the appeal of Satanism is the strongest. Beyond acting as a ritual profanation of innocence, the devil-worshipper's immolation of children – disemboweled and sodomized like Gilles's victims – stands as a symbolic rejection of the independent externality of the other person. Before he can grow and mature, the child is slaughtered, dismembered, his body parts eaten and incorporated by celebrants of the Black Mass. Devouring one's progeny, raping the daughter of the soul enlists the help of the devil, who encourages the criminal in the adoration of himself. Pygmalionism, as Durtal theorizes, is a refinement of incest, since it involves no actual intercourse, since the child is exclusively the father's product, "the only one he could have sired without the flesh and blood of another person."[98] There is even an adumbration of Huysmans' sadomasochistic hagiography of The Blessed Lydwine (*Sainte Lydwine de Schiedam* 1901), the pleasure he takes in enumerating her physical and spiritual torments: "Suppose an artist paints a saint with whom he then falls in love. That would involve a crime against nature as well as a sacrilege, whose consequences would be enormous!"[99]

This onanistic pleasuring of the self through the medium of art is presented in *Là-bas* as the ultimately Luciferian perversion. Withheld from interaction with undiscriminating readers, texts are unassimilated to the "ochlocratic art" that Péladan abominated. But having listened to Durtal's explanation of Pygmalionism, Chantelouve dismisses the possibility of inventing a new sin, saying "the book of vices and virtues is an edition *ne varietur*."[100] He refutes Durtal's assertion that the Pygmalionist is master of his work, claiming that, in the relationship of text and author, it is the former that retains control.

By projecting parts of himself into the body of his work, the artist performs a self-bewitchment, becoming the object of his own spell.

Transposition of a self objectified as artwork is analogous to the sorcerer's modeling of the *Volt*, the talismanic doll, the wax effigy of his victim on whom his hostile thoughts are trained. The book is a repository of the author's larval fantasies, the crumbs of his ideas, pieces of his soul. Like the figurine of an enemy fashioned with fingernails and hair, it is a metonym that its creator has endowed with magic power. This spell-casting is evident in Huysmans's identification with the Satanist, the mystic *a rebours* whom he later would repudiate. It is seen in Huysmans's embrace of the fame and fortune *Là-bas* won him, in the denunciation of these vain things that he expresses in his novel. It is apparent in the intellectual pride that joins him to his work, and in his recognition that his work is what spiritually bonds him with his audience.

Là-bas enables Huysmans to identify and overcome temptation. Indeed, as Chantelouve remarks, the Pygmalionist is less the rapist of his soul-child than the object of the malevolence that his work directs at him. Pygmalionism "is nothing more than a refined expression of succubacy,"[101] which, like art, involves the embodiment of obsessions, giving form to larval thoughts that the imagination brings to life. At first, the author's relationship with his work is onanistic, allowing him the illusion of possessing an idea "provided that he has a clear image of it." It is the artist who is captivated, transfixed by his creation, the author held in thrall by his text's seductive power.

So, notwithstanding his misgivings, Durtal accepts that he must complete his book, that the textual child, having reached maturity, must be released into the world. While creativity retains the value of an alchemical transmutation, refining the stuff of life into the gold of its expression, the finished work is a false god whose blandishments must be resisted. Pygmalionism is iconolatry that is Satanic in its effects, causing the artist to worship his artifacts as a monument to his genius.

Conclusion

Là-bas describes the successful attempt to overcome the lure of succubacy, allowing Durtal to exorcise the chimera of Madame Chantelouve, as he rejects the ordinary uncleanness of her reality as a woman and retains her only as the harmless embellishment of his narrative.

Durtal learns that Satanism requires a denial of transcendence, enchaining its practitioners in a realm of base desires. Born of angry poverty, it engenders no new life and ends with no rebirth. As capital hides greed's dirty truth behind the black veil of a word, Satanism conceals its aims with the pageantry of its liturgy. As Durtal learns, evildoing is irreconcilable with creation: no new vice can be invented. Sin's book is an edition *ne varietur*.

Satanism only codifies this incomplete creation, narcissism that never culminates in parturition and delivery. Unlike the Christian who rejoices in the nativity of Jesus, the Satanist delights in the persistence of disorder, "the distress of an enormous Fetus that never becomes the Child."[102]

Like Huysmans's writing of *Là-bas*, his prefacing of Jules Bois's book shows the author moving between the realms of experience and fiction, as Durtal navigates between historic research and literary invention. What distinguishes reality from imagination, religious faith from science, is a belief that elevates the seeker onto the plane of the transcendental. At the conclusion of *Là-bas*, Durtal and Huysmans's conversion is uncompleted, but when he finishes his book and acquiesces to its publication, it is as if he already models his artistic practice on the celebration of Communion. He participates in a modest version of the Eucharistic feast when he leaves his bachelor's quarters and climbs up into Carhaix's bell-tower, joining friends and commensals in conversation and beef stew. Huysmans's characters predict the victory of Christianity over Satanism, anticipating the dawning of the Third Age of the Paraclete, when man's emulation of Jesus and suffering the Passion will give way to disincarnation during the reign of the Holy Spirit. Then Lucifer's dominion, the cult of pleasure and materialism – symbolized, as des Hermies says, by the heart's resemblance to the penis – will be succeeded by an era when only the pure can reproduce. As Gévingey explains, citing the doctrine of Vintras: "The action of the Paraclete will extend to the generative principle. Divine life must sanctify those organs which henceforth will procreate only the elect, those exempt from original sin, those beings no longer needing to be tested in the furnace of humiliation."[103]

It is as if the novel's final chapters foreshadow the growing maturation of Huysmans's faith, anticipating the time when his isolation in a body will be over. When fulfillment of the messianic promise absolves literature of naturalism, there will be no more opposition of high and low, of flesh and spirit. But until then, Huysmans's author will have to embody his thoughts as bread, suffering in the textual body of which his audience partakes. As inspiration's alchemy purifies a writer's subject into meaning, the divine alchemy of Dolorism requires he feed readers with his body. Huysmans's novel marks a break in the evolution of his art, an emergence from the Thebaïd of succubacy and solipsism. Huysmans's hero no longer couples with the daughter of his soul but fathers works of literature that bond him with his brothers. The Satanist materialist may convert pleasure into banknotes, but the Catholic novelist, of whom Durtal is the prototype, sacrifices his art as the son whose suffering brings a redemption of the world.

2
The Hoaxer

After enflaming public curiosity with his lurid blockbuster *Là-bas*, J.-K. Huysmans went on to abet the fin de siècle's most accomplished hoaxer, Léo Taxil, by publicizing stories about the secret Luciferian sect of Palladism, an entity whose existence Taxil had fabricated. Rewarding readers with a frisson of sacrilege, the pleasurable horror of debauchery, Huysmans incorporates into his laudatory preface to Jules Bois's *Le Satanisme et la magie* an exposé of the cult that allegedly flourished in the forbidden lodges of nineteenth-century Freemasons.

Unlike Satanists, whom Huysmans describes as solitary agents, Palladists, he says, joined together in an army preparing for the arrival of the Anti-Christ. A worldwide force of evil, they had established a hierarchical order which, like the church, possessed an "anti-Pope, a curia, a College of Cardinals" that together formed "a parody of the Vatican court."[1] With a liturgy and prescribed rituals, Palladism was an inverted mockery of Christianity: Catholicism *à rebours*, as Huysmans writes, alluding to his 1884 Decadent masterpiece. Describing the perpetrator of this massive fraud as a blasphemer whose anti-clericalism was as contemptible as it was grotesque, Huysmans contributes his considerable influence to perpetuating the mystification which marked the culmination of the Satanism craze of the fin de siècle.

Nineteenth-century occultism: freemasonry and the devil

The reason to analyze the climate in which Léo Taxil raised up his towering imposture is that it yields an understanding of the cultural conditions that fostered interest in the occult. Certainly, the church had found in Satanism a more familiar nemesis, a less threatening antagonist than it had faced in its war with Republican politicians and scientific rationalists. By inspiring a precautionary dread about the spread of

Luciferianism, Taxil had tapped in to existing fears among the conservative Catholic faithful, appealing to their Anglophobia and anti-Semitism in enlisting support for his campaign against the Masons.

What were the cultural conditions that nurtured a hoax whose preposterousness extended to tales of demons appearing as piano-playing crocodiles leering at female listeners, accounts of Lucifer taking disciples on intergalactic voyages to Sirius? What unique traits and motivations enabled Taxil to create a fiction so cleverly concocted that it would fool the Pope himself? What reasons did Taxil's audience have for investing in his magisterial travesty? What prejudices did it play to? What appetite for entertainment did it satisfy?

The Catholic reactionaries drawn to the occult in the fin de siècle were altogether different from their predecessors from the Romantic generation. As Eugen Weber writes in his study of nineteenth-century superstition, messianic thought in the aftermath of the Revolution had often been coupled with a utopian socialism that espoused "a chiliasm of hope."[2] Drawing its source material, as Weber says, from Swedenborg and Saint-Martin, Romantic occultism expressed "fashionable themes of eschatological thought: a new last age, the end of days, the cult of woman as redeemer."[3] Despite differences in ideological orientation, these same beliefs informed the thinking of the Decadent mystics, whose apocalypticism was nonetheless considerably more pessimistic. On the one hand, fin-de-siècle Catholics regarded Positivism as their enemy, since for empiricists, God was only an archaic vestige of a bygone era of magic thinking. On the other hand, because of the historic link between occultism and utopian socialism, Catholics viewed their left-wing counterparts as practitioners of black magic, "revolutionaries who disestablished the church, persecuted the Pope, executed the king, were clearly *suppôts de Satan* [instruments of Satan]."[4]

Huysmans's preface to Jules Bois's book begins with a recurrent Decadent trope: that in a scientific era where religion had been supplanted by psychiatry, where Satanism had been diagnosed as a disorder, and evil had been pathologized, cases of possession were classified under reassuring etiological labels. Huysmans's comments underscore a common worry among Catholic believers that, if devil worship was seen as the product of mental aberration, then the whole of institutionalized Christianity could be discredited as delusional. According to Huysmans, the faith that healed could be healed itself by science.

In Huysmans's rebuttal of criminologists and Charcot's disciples at the Salpêtrière, he cites sacrilegious acts that could not easily be classified as civil offenses. The violation of sanctuaries and theft of consecrated

Hosts could not be explained, as Huysmans reasons, except as acts of demonolatry. Communion wafers which, for the unbeliever, held no commercial value had been stolen, while gold ciboria and pyxides were left untouched. Attacks upon Christ's body as Eucharistic bread were "acts of execration" that led one inevitably to conclude in "the certain existence of Satanism."[5]

Given the Decadent Catholics' investment in the material species of the Eucharist, it is not surprising that demonophobia drew on fears of assaults on Christ's body. Thus, in Taxil's portrait gallery of Palladism's leaders, he notes a fondness for displaying amulets containing consecrated Hosts used for ritual defilement. One such talisman, engraved with Luciferian hieroglyphs and symbols, bore the image of a pontifical tiara being vomited on by a Chinese monster. As Taxil says, it had contained a hidden cavity fitted with needles which, when closed, impaled a Host, thereby re-enacting the nailing of Christ's hands and feet.

The tone of Huysmans's preface conveys the Catholic preference for fighting the mysterious abominations of Satanism rather than refuting the principles of atheistic rationalism. What Weber sees as the Restorationists' tendency to disparage the values of the revolutionaries – their belief that "democracy looked like demonocracy"[6] – could have easily led to mistrust of an order like the Freemasons, with their embrace of democratic values and their tendency toward secrecy. Long disapproved for their advocacy of religious tolerance, the Masons had come under attack by the church in the final decades of the nineteenth century. In Pius IX's epistle, *Scite profecto*, published in 1873, the Vatican for the first time explicitly linked Freemasonry to Satanism. In 1877, an order promulgated by the *Grand Orient de Paris* rescinded an article declaring the Masons' obligation to believe in God and the immortality of the soul, reinforcing long-held impressions of the Order's promotion of unbelief. Finally, in Leo XIII's 1884 encyclical, *Humanum Genus*, laying out the Pope's broad understanding of Masonic doctrines and objectives, he had urged the faithful to combat its deleterious teachings. Leo's message described a Manichean struggle between Christianity and Luciferianism, combatants willing to defend the church and enemies wishing to return to paganism. In concluding his encyclical, Leo had admonished all the bishops of the Catholic world to unmask "the iniquity of Freemasonry and to expose it in all its somber truth."[7] Against this backdrop of anti-Republicanism, anti-rationalism, and anti-secularism, Catholics came to see the church as an imperiled and besieged institution, allowing Taxil to resurrect the familiar hobgoblin of Freemasonry as a vehicle for perpetrating his hoax.

Taxil, the prankster

Biographical studies of Léo Taxil may explain the origins of his anti-clericalism, yet they fail to account for his virtuosity as a peerless hoaxer. *Né* Gabriel-Antoine Jogand-Pagès in Marseille in 1854, Taxil adopted his nom de plume as an early expression of insubordination, rejecting patronymy in a way that extended from the family head to church elders. A refractory student, Taxil was placed by his father in the hands of Catholic educators; however, attendance at a Jesuit school was hardly an unusual occurrence among Taxil's artist contemporaries. Recalling the misadventure that befell the young Octave Mirbeau at the school of Saint-François Xavier in Vannes (an incident transposed in Mirbeau's autobiographical novel *Sébastien Roch* [1890]), the alleged sexual abuse of a student by a predatory teacher might have kindled the anti-Catholicism of two otherwise dissimilar writers. While supplying little probative detail, Michel Berchmans makes this argument by innuendo, explaining that Taxil's animus toward priests came from experiencing "the indiscretion of a chaplain who took in hand something more than the spiritual interests of his pupils."[8] Yet Taxil's denunciation of the Vatican and church officials does not single out the pedophile as the most dangerous malefactor but instead encompasses a broad arraignment of the clergy as pan-sexual deviants and hypocrites. Before implementing the Palladism hoax, Taxil had penned *Les Amours de Pie IX* (*The Loves of Pius IX*), a catalogue of Papal excesses, had described Leo XIII, who would later welcome the supposed penitent back into the bosom of the church, as guilty of poisonings committed during his pontificate. More tellingly, as Alfred Waite points out, Taxil had authored a book on *Contemporary Prostitution*, which Waite characterizes as a "collection of revolting statistics upon, *inter alia*, the methods, habits, and physical peculiarities of persons who practice pederasty."[9]

Like the judge-penitent Jean-Baptiste Clamence in Albert Camus's *La Chute* (*The Fall*) Taxil coupled the practice of confession and incrimination, mystification as gratuitous perversity and as a hygienic regimen for establishing fact. As Weber writes: "Taxil enjoyed Voltaire, whom he often cites in his *Confessions*, notably when it came to justifying the art of deception, which the two practiced with consummate skill. 'Lying, wrote Voltaire to his friend Thiérot, 'is a vice only when it is harmful. It is a great virtue when it is beneficial. One must lie like the devil, not timidly, not just for a little while, but boldly and all the time.'"[10] Taxil's recourse to pseudonymy as an instrument of self-authentication, his use of fraud in campaigns of unmasking reveals a dialectic of deception and exposure – concealing the truth in order to make its final disclosure more dramatic.

In admitting authorship of what he calls "the most fantastic practical joke of modern times,"[11] Taxil establishes his bona fides as an accomplished charlatan. Beginning with youthful pranks, he describes the great shark hoax that had sown panic in the coastal city of Marseille in 1853. Deluging the desks of Marseille's editorial offices, letters of alarm had reported sightings of voracious sharks terrifying bathers and intimidating fishermen. Explaining the proliferating swarms of bloodthirsty predators in the waters of Marseille: a Corsican vessel's accidental jettisoning of its cargo of spoiled smoked meat. In response to public panic, a certain General Espivent had assembled 100 intrepid citizens to man a tugboat and clear the harbor. But when they reached the site, not a single shark was seen. And at the postal addresses from which the letters were sent, not a fisherman was found who might have reported the danger.

Taxil acknowledges that General Espivent, the dupe in the matter, had previously suppressed publication of Taxil's lampoon, *Marotte, journal des fous* and had therefore been the target of what its designer called "an inoffensive act of vengeance."[12]

Sharks or devils – bodies of diffuse anxiety, fears coalescing as a child's nightmare terrors – Taxil's inventions materialize what lurks in the subconscious, inadmissible nemeses and forbidden desires. A narrative elaboration of hallucinations, which are themselves the product of a wish or a fear, the hoax re-presents a fantasmatic absence.

The second of Taxil's early fabrications also involved inducing visions of something not there. Here again, the hoax elicits a creative response from the victim, confirming reception theory's foundational principle that fiction, in its attribution of meaning, originates as much in consumers as in producers of works. One fine day, Taxil explains, excited announcements began circulating through the scientific community relating the discovery of a submerged city at the bottom of Lake Léman, between Nyort and Coppet. Citing apposite passages from the *Commentaries* of Julius Caesar, historians had identified a settlement constructed at a time when the diameter of the lake had been smaller. Now swallowed up beneath the waters, the sub-lacustrine village became a magnet for scholars and curiosity-seekers. Boatmen taking tourists out to the center of the lake spread oil over the surface of the water to facilitate vision. Visitors told of seeing underwater intersections and thoroughfares, and a Polish archeologist proclaimed his discovery of an equestrian statue.

Taxil's mystifications, thriving in a fin de siècle in which miracles were common, in which bewitchments were performed, and in which the dead were contacted at séances, drew on the popular disposition toward auto-suggestion. Infestations of sharks, apparitions by Asmodeus, cartographic explorations of submerged Roman towns – all are fictions concocted by a master-impostor and cultivated and completed by an imaginative audience. Abhorrence of reason on the part of Catholic intellectuals, the prevalence of superstition among the uneducated and credulous, the timely resurgence of supernatural evil for the church to combat: all created a climate hospitable to the emergence of Palladism. There was money to be made, there were books to be written, there were jokes to be told on the subject of Satan. As Papus writes in his essay of demystification: "The Black Mass imagined by Mr. Huysmans laid out the path to follow. One could exploit in every possible respect people's terror of Lucifer."[13]

Palladism: The history and doctrine of an imaginary cult

In his detailed anatomy of the origins of Palladism, Alfred Waite enumerates the central elements in Taxil's great hoax. According to Waite's chronology, Palladism, as an offshoot of Freemasonry, had been established in France as early as 1737. Already initiating women designated as Companions of Penelope, Palladism had expanded the membership of Freemasons to include androgyne orders.

Thereafter, Waite comments, the historical trail of Palladism had grown faint until, having been reconstituted in Charleston, South Carolina, it had flowered again as the Scottish Rite of Perfection and Herodom under the leadership of legendary politician, man of letters, and esotericist Albert Pike, elected Grand Master of the Ancient and Accepted Scottish Rite in 1859. Operating secretly and independently from the Order of Freemasons, Palladism had effected a radical schismatic break with its founding organization, as it proceeded to implement heretical changes: establishing a central directorship, formalizing its religious aims, and propagating what Waite calls its "transcendental teachings."[14]

Initially impervious to campaigns of debunking, Taxil's master-narrative had strengthened its credibility by integrating elements of historical fact, incorporating the well-known figure of Pike, establishing ties and enlisting the collaboration of Monseigneur Léon Meurin, Archbishop of Port Louis in Mauritius and author of *Freemasonry: The Synagogue of Satan*, a farrago of episodes of outlandish deviltry liberally interlarded with anti-Semitic rants.

Marianne Closson has chronicled the growing anti-Jewish senti-
ment pervading the fin de siècle: the association of Freemasonry with
Satanism as part of a worldwide Jewish conspiracy, paranoid prejudice that reached a level of paroxysmal intensity with the conviction
of Alfred Dreyfus for treason in 1894. Meurin's somber divagations
about the Kabbalah and its underpinning of the secret body of Masonic
doctrine – his assertion that the head of an occult group known as the
Patriarchs of Judea was none other than the "famous unknown head of
the Freemasons"[15] – came in an era that had already witnessed publication of a host of polemical exposes and fictional depictions of malignant Jewish schemes threatening France and the church. Taxil himself
deplored anti-Semitic prejudice, calling *la juivomanie* (Jew-mania) the
manifestation of "a new form of mental alienation."[16] However, he
showed no reluctance in welcoming the support of bigoted fanatics and
propagandists like Meurin in perpetrating his merry prank.

It was in part as a result of the publication of works like Meurin's that
the association of Kabbalism, Freemasonry, and Satanism crystallized in
nineteenth-century popular consciousness. Huysmans's description of
Palladism as Catholicism *à rebours* had been illustrated by the rhetoric,
apparel, and ritual practices of Canon Docre in *Là-bas*, where the renegade priest, naked under a chasuble adorned with an inverted cross, had
officiated at a Black Mass while standing beneath a statue of a tumes-
cent Christ. Genuflecting when required by liturgy, Docre seemed to
be presiding, as Huysmans's protagonist, Durtal, says, over a simple
Low Mass.

But apart from its symbolic and ceremonial inversions, Palladism, in
its ritual and dogma, involved more than a profession of obedience
to, and adoration of, the Evil One. Jesus, whom Docre had decried
as deaf to the cries of the hungry and poor, is identified as the true
monster, "Abstractor of stupid purities, cursed Nazarene, feckless king,
cowardly God."[17] Conversely, Lucifer is honored for rewarding the
abused and humiliated, for empowering them with the capacity for violent retribution: "Satan, it is you that we adore: God of logic, God of
justice."[18]

In Taxil's exposition, Palladism is structured by a rigorously
Manichean binarism, following Zoroastrianism with its conflict between
Ormuzd and Ahriman. In the beginning, Adonai, true God of darkness,
had dethroned Lucifer, God of Light, expelling him from heaven. While
hallowed by Christians as the principle of clemency and righteousness,
Adonai reigns over an accursed world of suffering and turmoil in which
the misbegotten raise up their cries of just petition. At the same time,

Lucifer, champion of the destitute, remains the true *Dieu bon* who, at the end of days, following the coming of the Anti-Christ, will re-ascend to his rightful place as the sovereign of the universe.

With its antipodal positioning of warring factions – the wrongly dispossessed against the unjustly triumphant – Palladism mirrors the cosmology of the Catholic mystics of the Decadence, recalling Eugène Vintras's condemnation of the sclerotic hierarchy of an oppressive church, foreshadowing Léon Bloy's rebuking Christ for not returning sooner to save humanity. Waite argues that such "an instruction would [not] seem to recommend itself to a numerically powerful following."[19] But from Gérard de Nerval's affiliation with the chthonic gods living in underworld darkness to the Romantics' adoption of Satan as a heroic figure symbolizing revolt, the central doctrines of Palladism had already proved to be popular.

Building on this foundation – working in a climate of metaphysical anxiety and xenophobic fear-mongering – Taxil went on to finish the architectural masterpiece of his fraud – identifying Albert Pike as the Grand Master of the Supreme Council of the Ancient and Accepted Scottish Rite headquartered in Charleston, locating other directorates in Washington, Montevideo, Naples, Calcutta, and Port Louis, producing such a wealth of detail that the truth of Palladism seemed to many incontrovertible. "Even if one remembers that it is only a mystification, even if one keeps his mind alert, there emerge from these pages such minute facts, such detailed anecdotes and citations that one has the impression they are true. No doubt Hacks and Taxil were accomplished hoaxers, but they were also, in their own right, genuine novelists."[20]

Docteur Bataile and *Le Diable au XIXe siècle* (*The Devil in the Nineteenth Century*)

While Taxil continued to publish journalistic revelations of the alarming pervasiveness of Luciferianism, the primary vehicle for propagating the Palladism hoax was a serialized exposé by Charles Hacks, writing under the pseudonym of Dr. Bataille, that appeared from November 1892 to December 1894. With Taxil's public renunciation of Freemasonry and conversion to Catholicism, he had earned an audience with Pope Leo XIII, who hailed the repatriation of the reformed prodigal. Taxil's embrace of his childhood faith had been all the more dramatic since, in the first confession to his spiritual mentor, Taxil admitted to having murdered an entire family, a crime so exorbitant that his confessor believed it to be true. The anti-Masonic tracts that Taxil began penning shared the same thematic emphases as his earlier anti-clerical writings, the only difference being that "Freemasonry had replaced the church as the site of debauchery and vice."[21]

Notwithstanding the hoaxer's success in duping this most prestigious victim, Taxil had felt the need to eclipse himself behind other professed antagonists of Palladism. In order to secure the collaboration of Hacks, an old school friend working as a ship's doctor when Taxil rediscovered him in Paris, Taxil had taken Hacks into his confidence, explaining the foundation and history of the swindle, finding in his comrade an amateur of occultism already conversant with popular beliefs in demons and werewolves. As a counterweight to Taxil's sometimes laborious exposé of Masonic ritual, he had solicited the doctor's assistance in presenting Palladism in the form of an extended travel narrative: "publishing rituals doesn't offer the same interest as narrating adventures that have been witnessed first-hand, especially if these adventures are full of magic mumbo-jumbo."[22]

While Taxil had assumed responsibility for supplying the technical details, drawing up the identities and histories of its innumerable proponents, he asked Hacks to flesh out these elements in an exotic travel phantasmagoria: descents into dungeons swarming with reptiles and spiders, journeys into jungles, a visit to a munitions plant in a secrete site beneath Gibraltar. It was the genre complementarity of Hacks's serialized novel and Taxil's exhaustive analysis of Palladism's doctrine and institutional structure that ensured the believability of the improbable fabrication.

As Closson rightly comments, readers of nineteenth-century popular romances readily accepted the effacement of boundaries between reality and fiction: "already accustomed to works whose novelistic and ideological stakes were inextricably intertwined," they were familiar with stories informed by a political agenda: "pro-military, pro-clerical, anti-clerical, anti-Semitic: readers so unused to the distinction between fiction and information – especially when, in the fin de siècle, such information rarely aimed at objectivity – certainly contributed to the success of Léo Taxil's mystification."[23]

The divergent audiences for which Taxil tailored his imposture, from the Vatican court to consumers of what Waite calls the "penny dreadful," show the genius of a mystifier purveying both propaganda and entertainment, purportedly earnest religious treatises and action melodrama. Like the Polish archeologist predisposed to make an important finding – seeing at the bottom of Lake Léman the statue of a horseman – Taxil's readers: cardinals, anti-Semites, lovers of potboilers, interpreted his fiction as a dream, as cautionary or reassuring, as fulfillment of a wish or as defense against a fear.

Bataille's *Le Diable au XIXe siècle*, undertaken in 1890, is presented as a diary of the experiences of a ship's surgeon on board the steamer *Anadyr* on its return voyage from China. The chance acquaintance with an Italian passenger, Gaetano Carbuccia, once hale and happy, now haggard and prematurely aged, is the pretext for Bataille's introduction to the terrible mysteries of Freemasonry. Carbuccia, persuaded by a friend to seek initiation into the Masons, had – upon payment of 200 francs – acceded to the status of 33rd grade, subsequently becoming Grand Commander of the Temple, Sublime Hermetic Philosopher, member of the New Reformed Palladium, and associate of the Society of Re-Theurgists. In Ceylon, reports Carbuccia, he had participated in a true Luciferian ritual, during which the fallen Angel of Light had manifested himself in human guise. Induced to appear by the offering of the three skulls of mummified missionaries, he had heaped imprecations on Adonai and blessings on Baphomet. Accompanied by claps of thunder, Lucifer appeared in his effulgent nakedness, complimenting worshippers, encouraging them to persevere. Bataille's theatrical effects overshadow the venality of the confraternity, willing to invite to the most solemn ceremony and grant the highest rank to an unknown outsider, in return for a small price. Indeed, Bataille – committed to exposing the blasphemous truths of Palladism – had obtained the 90th Misraim grade himself for 500 francs, thereafter gaining access to the most secret Masonic enclaves and obtaining instruction in their most arcane practices.

In Taxil's own revelations of recondite Masonic ritual – the induction of female members into the Order of Penelope – he underscores the disparity between pompous ceremony and vulgar motivation. Lengthy re-enactments of Greek myth or Biblical drama precede the sexual initiation of the fledgling Masonic Sister, staging the story of Judith and Holofernes, for example, as a dramatic aperitif for ensuing orgies.

Thereafter, Bataille, fortified with good intention and equipped with the passport of his lofty insignia and grade in the Masonic hierarchy, proceeds to travel throughout the world, penetrating into the most impregnable Palladian sanctuaries and Luciferian lairs. In Bataille's inaugural encounter with the supernatural, he repairs to a hut at the heart of the desert, greeted there by a vampire bat, a cobra, a black cat, and an ape fluent in Tamil. Attended by impotent fakirs and a partially mummified disciple of Satan, a pythoness 152 years old is burned alive on a coconut-fiber altar amidst chanting, screaming, and praying.

Bataille's experiences of Masonic diabolism are frequently accompanied by discoveries of animal polyglottism, universal semiosis, a boundless hermeneutic in which small things hide immeasurable meanings. Bataille and Taxil often work with a familiar principle of the occult: that everything signifies more than it seems, that nothing is plain, monosemic, or evident. Phylogenetic gradations of intelligence are wiped away when apes speak languages unknown to the subject, when nothing is gibberish, and Abracadabra opens locked doors. In the world of the occult, outsiders are always disadvantaged by their status as the uninitiated. Lost and amazed – wandering in a labyrinth of unreadable hieroglyphs and unanalyzable wonders – the neophyte is handicapped both by his ignorance and interest. Obsessed with knowing and despised for his ignorance, he is told there is a secret and wants to know what it is. Thus, Bataille's narrative is freighted with picturesque detail signifying nothing – hiding from readers the secret that Lucifer is destroyed by indifference to the fact of his existence.

Rewarded for his participation in the mysterious Ceylonese auto-da-fe, Bataille is given a winged lingam, itself an omnibus signifier of untranslatable esoteric power. A representation of the Hindu goddess Shiva, a lingam in Sanskrit means a mark or sign. A signifier of significance, a tautological expression of its importance, the lingam, unsurprisingly, is also a figure for the phallus, a passkey, a sign of recognition among members of the priestly elect.

Continuing his voyage to Pondicherry, Bataille encounters his next mystical guide, Ramassamiponnotalmy-palé-dobacha, bearer of the lingam of his onomastic phallus, whose length is all-important and whose size is what matters. When asked where he comes from, he says "From the eternal flame." When asked where he is going, he answers "To the flame eternal."[24]

Cryptic palindromic utterances whose conclusion returns to the beginning recall the ouroboros, the serpent biting its tail, symbol of self-regeneration and cyclical recurrence. An image of completeness, perfection, or infinitude, the circle is also a zero, the numeric of worthlessness; "a reunion of opposites,"[25] it is pregnancy of meaning that at the same time denotes insignificance.

Palladism and taboo

Bataille's vagabond narrative also incorporates familiar elements of fantastic transgressivity: violations of taboos eliciting disgust and disapproval. As Janine Chasseguet-Smirgel writes of devil religions, the ordering solar god of taxonomic clarity operates by naming and dividing: darkness from light, sacred from profane, waters from the earth, male from female, the heavens from the underworld. On the other hand, devil religions, of which Palladism is a model, work to restore an original state of undifferentiation, namelessness, and confusion, as in the institution of androgyne lodges within the order of the Freemasons. Bataille's Luciferians also follow the example of Sade in seeking a return to chaos or *anomos*: that which is without a name, a teleology, or structure. As Chasseguet-Smirgel says in comments that could apply to Bataille: "Subversion of the law, the parody of a religion devoted to the worship of God, seeks to reverse the way leading from indistinctness to separation and demarcation. Here we are very close to the [...] religions of the devil. A black mass is a parody of the sacrifice of Christ. In it the cross is placed upside down, or facing the wall; the mass is said backward and the Tetragrammaton is pronounced the wrong way round and is accompanied by sexual orgies."[26] Interdictions on incest, necrophilia, and bestiality are broken, and old laws are defiantly overthrown. If not culminating in the re-ascendancy of Lucifer to the throne of heaven, a restoration of the state of unity preceding creation of the world manifests itself, as Mircea Eliade says, "in a supreme act of regeneration and an enormous increase in power."[27]

Of course, along with exploring the Palladists' demiurgic ambitions, Bataille's narrative exploits "the Grand Guignol dimension of these anecdotes,"[28] moving from an examination of metaphysical revolt to an indulgence in gratuitous exercises in the comic and grotesque. Boundaries between life and death are blurred by representations of unending decomposition and temporal stasis. In Pondicherry, Bataille takes part in a ceremonial invocation of Baal-Zeboub, a ritual showcasing fakirs "in advanced stages of putrefaction." As Waite writes: "Most people are supposed to go easily to the devil, but these elected to do so solely by way of a charnel-house asceticism and an elaborate system of self-torture. Some were suspended from the ceiling by a rope tied to their arms, some were permanently distorted into the shape of the letter 'S'," and the holiest of holies had "legs covered with gangrene, ulcers, and rottenness."[29]

The Satanic rituals that Bataille describes elicit laughter or revulsion yet still draw on the rich resources of cultural anthropology and archetypal symbolism. In one of the Seven Temples of Sheol, a celebration of the sin of Eve re-enacts the Biblical origins of the *felix culpa*. But rather than formalizing in the Exile the separation of the Creator and the creature, the Grand Master and Vestal couple dialogically, in words whose explicitness compels Bataille to censor them.

The Fifth Temple consecrated to the Pelican, symbol of Christ's self-immolating generosity, is a site profaned by a Masonic discourse on the virtues of promiscuity. Bataille then visits the Temple of Rosicrucianism, historically associated with the Freemasons. As Manly Hall remarks: "It is probable that Rosicrucianism is a perpetuation of the secret tenets of the Egyptian Hermes, and that the Society of the Unknown Philosopher is the link connecting modern Masonry, with its mass of symbols, to ancient Hermeticism, the source of that symbolism."[30] Yet Bataille's description contains no elucidation of the Rosicrucian mysteries, only alluding to more Vestals, more mummified fakirs, and more yawning sepulchers. Taxil credits his collaborator with considerable knowledge of esotericism, but Bataille's travel narrative seems aimed at atmospherics and theatrical effects, and offers no initiatory detail about the historic link between Rosicrucianism and Masonry.

From Pondicherry, Bataille continues his tour of Palladism, traveling next to China, which, the doctor says, is the entryway to hell, a land whose inhabitants, despite their innocent appearance, are temperamentally Satanic and iniquitous by birth. Here Bataille pauses to remark that no matter what exotic place he visits, no matter what diabolical sect he studies, devil worshippers across the world "belong to one and the same secret, demonic religion."[31] In this way, Bataille illustrates a common feature of ethnocentricity: the demonization of the stranger, a tendency to homogenize those most unlike ourselves, to find in alterity an element of sameness, to perceive in alien races and cultures a uniform unreadability. Among Chinese and Indian Satanists, there is the same use of intoxicants, the same exorbitant cruelty, the same magic reanimation of the dead, oracular skeletons, zombie cannibals, mummies still susceptible to torture. Those who most resemble us are agreeable to look at. They are distinguishable by little differences in physiognomy and behavior. Those different from us are collectivized by fear and incomprehension. Asians, Jews, and Africans all resemble one another and serve the Evil One. Thus, Taxil, taking his cue from Occidental prejudice, gathers outsiders "into the same group. Thus, Hindu fakirs, Chinese, Jews, Protestants, carbonieri, Russian or French anarchists, independent or organized Satanists like Guaïta or Péladan are all devil-worshippers whether they belong to secret Palladian Lodges or not."[32]

It was precisely because of the Masons' proclivity for secrecy that they appeared uncanny. Considered threatening, they came to constitute an umbrella organization for all foreign and outlawed belief systems. What Chasseguet-Smirgel sees as a unifying practice among those defined as Satanists – the desire to restore an original state of muddle and confusion – aims at an erasure of primary ontogenetic boundaries, those separating us from them and formalizing a system of integration and exclusion. Classifications are swept away. Fraternal incest re-establishes a prior genetic indivisibility. People become animals, and the dumb begin to talk. What was outside is assimilated and then expelled again as excrement, and cannibalism incorporates us into the triumphant other. As David Frankfurter writes, this "signifies the Other's most profound danger to us [. . . .] In antiquity, ritual expression meant sacrifice, the central religious act by which a community achieved reciprocity with the supernatural world by transferring some body or substance. But sacrifice often implied – in the imagination of the Other – transgression of humanity, ecstatic states when such barbarians would come together and, through frenzied dance, lose their reason and engage in bestial acts of violence." Sacrifice suggested "what 'they' might do to 'us.' Ritual might then imply the deliberate mockery or inversion of human [...] customs, and then [...] an alternative supernatural world, a dangerous and chaotic one, reciprocity with which might bring real and destructive powers into the arena of the human and domestic."[33] It is no wonder, then, that in a fin de siècle dominated by millenarian fantasies, by fears of the looming extinction of Occidental culture, by apocalyptic expectations of the coming of the Anti-Christ, there should have been such a proliferation of spectacular conversions, when renegade outsiders were joyfully repatriated into a Catholic community that felt fragile and imperiled.

In China, as Bataille reports, the ceremonial counterpart of the initiation of neophytes is the ritual slaughter of missionaries sent abroad to convert the godless heathen. As invocations of the devil are often Masses recited backwards, the Chinese sacrifice that Bataille witness involves the manufacture of a Jesuit dummy on which devotees inflict imaginary torture. Next, inverting the Passion, they enact the crucifixion of a pig. The ritual murder and consumption of an actual missionary – one who tries to proselytize outsiders and assimilate them as Christians – ends with an anthropophagic banquet like that in Voltaire's *Candide*, where the cannibal Oreillons chant "Mangeons du Jésuite" (Let's eat some Jesuit).

Bataille's voyage next takes him to more familiar western climes – to Charleston, headquarters of the International Masonic order. There he meets the legendary Albert Pike and the infernal hierophantess Sophie Walder, who instructs the doctor on the hierarchy and member demons of the underworld. Here Bataille relinquishes his role as narrator to Taxil, who, from the outset, had taken charge of explaining the organizing principles of Palladism. It is therefore Taxil who supplies the architectural diagram of the Charleston temple, with its subterranean labyrinth at the center of which is the chapel of Lucifer.

Taxil describes the triangular sanctuary containing the tremendous idol of Baphomet, a room containing a statue of Eve that can be animated by a Masonic Sister and that becomes the demon Astarte who kisses the chosen Mistress of the Temple.

Despite admonitions to the Pope by Monseigneur Northrup, bishop of Charleston, the Vatican remained unconvinced that the Masonic directorate was Taxil's invention. Indeed, one of Taxil's accomplices had denounced Northrup as a covert Freemason, further discrediting Taxil's accuser in the eyes of church officials.

Gibraltar's monsters

Taxil also claimed authorship of the episode relating Bataille's visit to Gibraltar, arguably the most spectacular tale in the doctor's sprawling, 2,000-page adventure-romance. An English territory, Gibraltar was a natural site for debauchery and demonolatry, since to the French, the British were perennially the most insidious outsiders, similar in appearance to civilized Catholics from the continent, yet also exceptionally depraved and given to all manner of perversion.

Ante-chamber to the underworld, Gibraltar was like Charleston's subterranean temple: criss-crossed by mazes of tunnels, housing alveolar workshops in which devilish business was transacted. "The particular characteristic of Gibraltar," writes Taxil, "is to be like a giant stone sponge, a human beehive with thousands of openings, riddled from side to side, from top to bottom, with cavities, holes, grottos, and gulfs all interconnected by a tangled network of corridors."[34]

In Taxil's axial structuring of evil, Gibraltar is the place of repression, the underground where transgressive acts are perpetrated out of sight. Encounters with the monstrous require a defamiliarizing of the landscape, trips to a terra incognita where Leviathans lurk beneath the surface, descents into cellars, mines, and crypts where guilty impulses are buried alive.

Unlike the monster of hyper-semiosis, the creatures toiling in the subterranean laboratories of Gibraltar are the shocking bodies of equivalency, between what they do and what they are. The metalworkers, smiths, and metallurgists producing obscene Palladian amulets and statuary are embodiments of their *praxis*, incarnations of their work site. Subconscious, subhuman, subterranean, subliminal: they are ugliness so shameful that it is unspeakable and invisible.

In the Luciferian laboratories of Gibraltar, Taxil observes the arcane science of an alchemy *à rebours*. Rather than expediting the refinement of base matter – acting, like the alchemist, "as the brotherly savior of Nature," assisting her "to fulfill her final goal, to attain her 'ideal', which is the perfection of [her] progeny – be it mineral, animal, or human – to its supreme ripening" as gold,[35] Palladian toxicologists perform a science of regression, reversing the maturation of substances, returning them to the undifferentiation and formlessness of monstrous primordialism.

In the enormous stone sponge of Gibraltar, beneath a giant fuliginous statue of Baphomet, workers shape infernal stuff with monstrous implements, as agent, tool, material, and design all coalesce into an evil whose exceptionality begets a failure of description. Sublimations that make man bipedal, articulate, and beautiful are undone as workers turn back into hairy beasts that grunt and howl. Demonic industry engenders demonic laborers whose work is overseen by a goat-faced foreman named Tubalcain, "the ancestor of Hiram, according to Masonic legend, the diabolical patriarch of iron and forges, the older brother of Vulcan from pagan mythology."[36]

Finely executed work brings a raise in salary, an increase in the alcohol ration given to cynocephalic brutes. Poisoned with the devil's elixir of unrepression, they are released from their work cells to cavort and rave on the Gibraltar coasts amidst the devastation of hurricanes. Drooling alcohol and sweat and crime, they join together in "an infernal sarabande of circling creatures who hold hands, whirling in the midst of clouds, torrents of rain, and lightning bolts."[37]

The dance of revelers evokes images of the traditional witches' Sabbath held at country crossroads at midnight. Here again, Taxil draws on a Satanic economy of limited archetypes and plethoric meanings. When evil moves toward the absoluteness of malevolent intention and expression, it devolves into chaos, hybridization, the disintegration of named entities into excrement and confusion. Stability and coherence give way to centrifugality and vertigo, as riotous creatures spin in circles, and the witness's nominative and analytical powers are submerged beneath the *unnamed and the unnamable*.

Since there is no human language adequate to convey the hideous work of the Palladians, they evolve their own idiolect, the infernal lingua franca of Volapuk. Like the universal tongue pre-existing the destruction of the Tower of Babel, it represents, Waite says, "an irreligious attempt to produce *ordo ab chao* by a return to unity of speech."[38]

Among Gibraltar's bacteriologists – scientists who are human, articulate, evolved – there is no animal instinctuality, no whirlwind dance beneath the moon. Here chemists creating solutions that spread cholera and typhus live in cells that are tastefully decorated to give an illusion of refinement. Yet they, too, are depersonalized by the abolition of their names, as they are designated by two letters of the secret alphabet of thaumaturgy. Patiently cooking and breeding new bacilli, seeds of the apocalypse, they work in up-to-date facilities, not over dusty alembics, but with test tubes and glass vials, the latest in laboratory equipment.

In Taxil's description of Palladian research into epidemiological catastrophism, he preys on fears about the unholy alliance of the scientist and the necromancer. The medieval wizard, draped in his black robe adorned with anchors and half-moons, is telescoped into the toxicologist with his white coat and gleaming instruments. What Eliade refers to as the soteriological purpose of alchemy, accelerating the pace of natural processes, purifying base matter, is perverted by the Satanist who seeks the confused state of the *nigredo*. For the true alchemist, matter is crucified in the retort and, like Christ, is then reborn in higher, nobler form. "Initiatory death and mystic darkness thus [...] possess a cosmological significance; they signify the reintegration of the 'first state', the germinal state of matter, and the 'resurrection' corresponds to the cosmic creation."[39] However, in Gibraltar, *material prima* is not tortured and broken down in preparation for its aurefaction and ascent into perfection and immortality. Rather, secret knowledge is applied in developing killing microbial cultures which can wipe out an entire population of several thousand.

Taxil's picture draws on Catholic concerns about science as the true enemy of faith, unlike devil worship that legitimizes the religion it endeavors to destroy. The secularizing influence of medicine, chemistry, pharmacology is harnessed by Palladians, who use science in the service of the demonic. Replacing the faith that heals is the laboratory methodology that exterminates.

Yet Taxil does not persist in exploiting the paranoia of the devout, but in an effort to prove his axiom that "human stupidity knows no limit," follows his mapping of Gibraltar's catacombs with tales of séances and invocations that return the narrative to the domain of the burlesque. Historians of the fin de siècle who have studied Taxil's hoax delight in retelling the episode of the calling up of Moloch. Taking the form of a winged crocodile that sits smiling at a piano, it vanishes from before the astonished onlookers, but not before emptying bottles of pale ale, gin, and whiskey arrayed on a table.

Another favorite is the story of Albert Pike's successful summoning of Lucifer – called up by reciting from a grimoire in Latin, Greek, and gibberish: *"Lumen de lumine!...Rex!...Pater!...Athanatos!...Tibi sum!"*[40] Materializing in the room, the Prince of Darkness admonishes the caller that he does not enjoy being raised from the netherworld for nothing: "Ask me for something," as Lucifer orders Pike. The ensuing voyage to Sirius, covering 52 million leagues, takes Pike to another universe, of which Lucifer is the architect and in which Adonai reigns only over the unknown planet Oolis.

Taxil's *Soeurs Maçonnes*

At this point, Bataille's narrative gives way to Taxil's delineation of the structure and ritual of contemporary European Freemasonry, beginning with the struggle for succession after the death of Albert Pike. Taxil devotes much of his narrative to highlighting the starring role of the Masonic Sisters, assigning pride of place to the diabolical feats of two leading Luciferian priestesses, Sophie Walder and Diana Vaughn, both products of Taxil's mendacious creativity. Taxil's fabrication of these she-devils may well have come in response to the fin-de-siècle tendency to portray women as conduits of the supernatural and instruments of the occult. Against a backdrop of Catholic inflexibility in matters of institutional order and doctrinal orthodoxy, Catholic mystics had turned to cultivating an acute form of hyperdulia. Focusing on Mary, who warned of the approaching world's end, publishing treatises on medieval martyrs, they also accorded a central role to female visionaries in their fiction, as with the Satanic Madame Chantelouve in J.-K. Huysmans's *Là-bas*, and Clotilde Chapuis, advocate of mystic suffering in Léon Bloy's *La Femme pauvre* (*The Woman Who Was Poor*). So inextricably linked was supernaturalism with prophetesses and female oracles that Taxil's readers would have easily credited Mistress Templars with astral voyages and metaphysical revelations. To Taxil, the mysteries of Palladism were no more preposterous than those of Christianity: "Asmodeus transporting Miss Diana Vaughn to an earthly paradise is no more extraordinary than Satan carrying Jesus Christ himself to a mountaintop from which he showed him all the kingdoms of the world."[41]

While being entirely apocryphal, Sophie (or Sapho-Sophia as she is called by her occult soubriquet) is given a genealogical history that establishes her predisposition toward Luciferianism. Daughter of Phineas Walder, first an Anabaptist, then a Mormon, before ascending to the highest possible grade in the New Reformed Palladian Rite, Sophie had distinguished herself as a somnambulist and powerful Satanic medium. In a scene enlivened by a fantastic elaboration on the divinatory power of the Ouija Board, Sophie is put into a trance by an expert magnetizer and given questions traced with an iron rod on her naked back. Then a serpent encircling her neck like an ophidian collar forms letters along her spine with the coils of its tail, mystic phrases responding to the queries posed by onlookers. Sophie's function as an oracle draws on the fin-de-siècle stereotype of women as preverbal beings, unguided by intelligence. Moved by somatic impulse, by inexpressible intuition, Sophie's body, like those of hysterics, is a text on which occult messages are inscribed.

Besides channeling communiqués from denizens of the underworld, Sophie played another role in which she was also denied autonomy – as the matrilineal vehicle for the coming of the Anti-Christ. Wombs and lips delivering the flesh and word of Lucifer, Taxil's women are gestational containers of beings they are incapable of fathoming.

Taxil's self-deflating comedy often interrupts portentous reports of cosmic warfare, announcements of the coming Armageddon and the enthronement of Christ's nemesis, with anecdotes that strain the credulity of his most committed readers. The same vacinatrix who issues the following ominous message: "from me will be born, on the eighth day of the month of Paophi, in the year of the True Light 000896, a daughter who will be the grandmother of the Anti-Christ"[42] also receives from Sister Hebe, goddess/nymph of foolishness, a bottle of holy water which, if drunk, induces the vomiting of flames. Encircling the bottle is a typed note greeting Sophie, a message ending with the salutation: "Long live joy and fried potatoes!"[43]

On the one hand, Taxil pushes the limit of his *joyous mystification*, astonished at his audience's taste for incoherence and absurdity. On the other hand, the Palladism hoax provides a platform for analysis of the mentality from which the fin-de-siècle occult craze arose. A universe whose majesty had been impoverished by science, a church desiring to fight an enemy less impalpable than empiricism, a public hungry for the transcendental, craving entertainment and escapism – titillating horrors, guided tours of hell – gave hope that the end would be announced with the pyrotechnics of an apocalypse, not the refrigerated boredom of entropy and exhaustion.

Diana Vaughn, high priestess of Palladism

Taxil's history of Palladism contains another story of waywardness, transgression, repentance, and redemption, one vindicating the church's power to recuperate and save. Different from the unregenerate

Sophie, the other Masonic priestess, Diana Vaughn, seemed to re-enact Taxil's own inspirational drama of the reformed prodigal. While Sophie had been "a myth," as Taxil confided to Bataille, Diana, who assumed a prominent role in the hoax, needed to be physically present, available to church officials wishing to verify her existence and confirm the sincerity of her spiritual rebirth: "since at a given moment, this Luciferian was to undergo a conversion, it was necessary to have a flesh and blood woman in case she needed to be introduced to someone."[44]

As Taxil explains, it was the professional necessities of his work that had first put him in contact with Diana, a stenographer employed in Europe by a manufacturer of American typewriters. Lively, intelligent, cosmopolitan, quick-witted, Diana had impressed Taxil as an ideal collaborator, and to his delight, he had found that, once apprised of his plan, Diana enthusiastically offered her cooperation: "corresponding with bishops and cardinals, receiving letters from the Sovereign Pontiff's personal secretary, telling them all kinds of impossible stories, informing the Vatican about sinister Luciferian plots filled her with indescribable mirth, and she thanked me for including her in this colossal mystification."[45]

So convincing was Diana in her role as a Grand Palladian Mistress that after an announcement of the appointment of Adriano Lemmi as newly elected Pope of Freemasonry, certain Italian members of the secret order – most notably Domenico Margiotta – reported having already made the acquaintance of the Luciferian priestess and of having met her in 1899, at a reception at the Hotel Victoria in Naples.

A dupe enlisted to serve as co-author of Taxil's deception, Margiotta himself produced a detailed and engrossing anatomy of the secret society: *Le Palladisme: Culte de Satan-Lucifer dans les triangles maçonniques* [*Palladism: The Cult of Satan-Lucifer in the Triangles of Masonry*] (Biblioteca Esotérica Herrou Aragón, 1895). There Margiotta expands on the imaginary liturgy and dogma of Palladism, documenting its history and derivation from Gnosticism, including versified hymns to Satan penned by benighted Satanists: "Christ is the force that inspires faith, the force deriving from perfection itself! But the God of real force, the God of true force, is Satan – Satan who personifies grandeur and extermination, Satan, the God of legitimate revolt!" As Margiotta concludes, "Satan is the other half, the complement of Christ. Together they form a single being, an identical whole."[46]

Implacable enemy of the usurper Lemmi, Margiotta had tasked himself with unmasking Palladism, refuting its teaching that genuine saints are those reunited with *le Dieu bon*, or Lucifer, living with him forever "in his kingdom of eternal fire."[47]

Margiotta was among those hailing Diana's conversion and the ensuing collapse of Palladism. With his elaborate exposition of a secret Palladian alphabet modeled on the alphabet of the Magi of Alexandria, with his explanation of the doctrine of metempsychosis and his reproduction of Satanist prayers, Margiotta had demonstrated that the best perpetrators of hoaxes are often victims themselves.

As for Diana, Taxil acknowledges that after assigning her the lead role in his mystification, her influence and popularity had soared, especially since, after having played the sorceress, she professed to be a penitent. As Taxil had won the trust and support of the church by confessing to murder, Diana convinced the Vatican of her sincerity when she denounced Masonry as an abomination, rejected Lucifer, and embraced her childhood faith. Earlier, Diana had seemingly exhibited independence and piety by refusing to impale a consecrated Host on a dagger, as Sophie Walder had commanded her. Declining to participate in the symbolic murder of Christ – "to kill Him palladically"[48]– she had shown she was not beyond redemption, promising to serve as a future crusader against the iniquitous Palladian cult. As with other reformed sinners, the more heinous the wickedness, the more glorious the redemption.

In her *Mémoires d'une ex-palladiste* [*Memoirs of an Ex-Palladist*], Diana describes a miraculous colloquy with a statuette of Joan of Arc. Pledging never to write or speak a word disrespectful of the Virgin, beloved of Joan, Diana had seen materialize before her eyes Baal-Zeboub, Astaroth, Moloch, and Asmodeus, still cloaked in their customary guise as angels of light yet with faces contorted by rage. Calling Joan to defend her, Diana had heard the air rent by the roaring of lions, and the demons, reverting to their true forms as monsters with hooved feet, horns, and tails, had disappeared into the blackness while issuing the imprecations of the damned.

Accounts of such apparitions, combined with Diana's devotion to Mary, offered Catholic skeptics powerful testimony of the sincerity of her conversion. The 1895 publication of Diana's saccharine *Novena of the Eucharist* further ingratiated her to clerics proclaiming that only divine intervention could have saved the erstwhile Masonic Sister from the infernal mechanism in which she was caught. Alternating volleys of incredulous denunciation and admiring acceptance greeted Diana's many devotional writings. Humbug or miracle: church officials wavered in their evaluation of Diana's spiritual awakening until Taxil exposed the fraud that he had masterfully concocted, in which he was ably assisted by an American typist and an imaginative ship's surgeon.

At an 1897 gathering of the Geographic Society, in a speech entitled "Palladism Vanquished," Taxil broke the news that finally put the controversy to rest. Taxil's explanation of the motives that inspired him to undertake his imposture is maddeningly simple, evasive, and imprecise. Claiming that his youthful aversion to Catholicism might have been unfair and misplaced, he claimed to have sought to win the church's favor by infiltrating the Masons and exposing their diabolism. More often, Taxil remarks on his inveterate tendencies as a joker, pleads for audience approval of his innocent love of fun, admits to a certain perversity in deceiving the public for no reason, and claims that playing tricks and lying are proclivities of his countrymen: "one is not a child of Marseille with impunity," he maintains.[49]

No doubt the same demiurgic impulses imputed to Masons and Luciferians – the wish to topple institutions whose rules structure and divide – appealed to Taxil as much as it did to the Palladists he invented. There is an anarchic intent in Taxil's deflation of popes and generals, an anti-authoritarianism impelling him to castrate fathers with ridicule. Just as monumental and elaborate as the body of church law is Taxil's towering structure of untruth that effects that law's subversion.

Taxil's campaign treats Catholicism and Satanism equally – as massive systems characterized by inflexibility, pomp, and dogmatism. No less pretentious than the ceremony and hierarchical stratification of the Vatican are the rigid order and stylized depravity of the secret Masonic androgyne lodges.

In *Les Soeurs Maçonnes* (*The Masonic Sisters*), Taxil describes the ritual induction of the *Sublime Ecossaise* (the Sublime Scotswoman) whose virtue had been eroded in ascending the many grades of the Masonic sisterhood. While re-enacting biblical scenes in the initiation pageantry – while answering questions posed by lodge officials with ostentatious titles (President of the Aeropage, Grand Elect Knight Kadosch), the inductee is initiated into the mysteries of wantonness. A secret vocabulary is learned, canticles to Venus are intoned in "a hodge-podge of declarations and chants, with low-cut costumes and theatrical scenes of dissolute behavior worthy of the most disreputable café-concert."[50]

Like magic, whose clavicles are mysterious and unalterable, the Masonic celebration of the initiate's induction foregrounds the disparity between grandiose ritual and vulgar aim. Here Taxil's mystification has as its purpose to demystify.

Conclusion

Today, Taxil's hoax still impresses historians of the fin de siècle with the intricacy of its detail and its astonishing longevity. Similarly, Taxil's conversancy with the tenets of Satanism, his giftedness as a fabulist whose romance adventure spanned the world highlight the authenticity of a talent used in the fabrication of a counterfeit. Yet as with every mystification enjoying plausibility and appeal, the artistry required belongs equally to the audience. As reception theory teaches, fiction is personalized by consumers: embodiment of an image and visualization of a setting are imaginative acts that singularize a text according to the reading subject. So Taxil's hoax, in persisting both as a fabrication and its disassembly, is meaningful in accordance with the predisposition of interpreters.

As Closson notes, Taxil's hoax explodes the myth of Jewish Luciferianism, yet the enormity of the fraud also helped to reinforce its credibility: "one reader has reproached Taxil for 'creating the issue of the devil in the way that Edouard Drumont created the issue of the Jew.' This disturbing suggestion invites us to ask ourselves about the consequences of the Taxil affair. Did it forever cover with ridicule this type of allegation? Or did it sow enough suspicion in people's minds that it contributed to the myth of a Judeo-Masonic plot that has itself become a form of modern demonology?"[51]

Among others, Huysmans comments that the devil shows the greatest ingenuity in persuading intelligent people that he does not exist. What could be more diabolical than confessing to having authored the myth of Palladism? Zombi fakirs, serpent writings, trips through space with Asmodeus are make-believe made comical at the audience's expense. Having fooled the Pope the first time by pretending to disaffiliate from the Freemasons, did Taxil fool him again by convincing him that his imposture was authentic?

In his book *Aesthetics of Fraudulence in Nineteenth-Century France*, Scott Carpenter claims that mystification serves to inculcate incredulity. "This corrosion of authority leads the victim of a hoax to experience a loss of footing – that well-known experience of having the rug pulled out from under one's feet. This is, in short, the great function of mystification: it drives cracks in the edifice of authority; it promotes a potentially creative instability, pushing its victims to become ever more critical and ever less inclined to take authority for granted."[52]

Whether the Palladism hoax spread the myth of Judeo-Satanism or whether it undermined the same myth with derision and hyperbole, it sensitized the public to the urgency of the controversy. The infallibility of the Pope, the inerrancy of the scientist: such assertions of authority are undermined by merry hoaxers. The majesty of the truth lies in the capacity to invent it, in the institution of a belief system charged with propounding and defending it. The properties of the Philosopher's Stone, the wiles of the devil, the letters in the name of God: are these the initiate's secret knowledge or the projections of the gullible, the imaginings of a dimwit? When it ventures into the supernatural, the hoax performs its special magic. By weaving an illusion and simultaneously dispelling it, by propagating a lie and immediately retracting it, it does the trick of perpetually constructing what is here with what is gone.

3
The Magus

Huysmans's research into devil worship and expressions of interest in Catholic mysticism took place in an unusual cultural climate that fostered investigations into all forms of supernaturalism. It was against a backdrop of Republicanism, rationalist Positivism, and the increasing laicization of French society that interest in the occult began to flourish in the final decades of the nineteenth century. Among the educated, there was a growing belief that science was poised to identify the exact laws governing the origins and destiny of the human species. Findings in the domain of geology, astronomy, and paleontology seemed to set science in conflict with traditional Christian teachings, opening to question, as Jean Pierrot observes, "the vision of the origins and evolution of the world found traditionally in the Bible."[1] In opposition to this trend, occultists writing at the century's end heralded the superiority of supra-rational knowledge, the Gnosis that, in their view, was not attainable through reason and analysis but came only through spiritual illumination.

Recourse by artists to ancient occult teachings was also motivated by the liberalization of institutions and enactment of democratic laws. Monarchists' receding hopes for a restoration of the true king combined with Catholic nostalgia for a return to conservative doctrine. From these reactionary impulses emerged the Naundorff imposture, allegations by the self-proclaimed heir to the French throne that he was the true Louis XVIII, an avatar of the God who was unrecognized and disowned, "an example of the Lord's Anointed suffering in ignominy, the great man thrown down from his high seat."[2]

In the works of Joséphin Péladan, the obsolescence of the aristocracy as a social class resulted in the cultivation of a new meritocracy of *aristes*: visionaries, poets, craftsmen, priests, composers, and hermeticists whose privilege and entitlement derived from the superiority of their genius.

In the domain of politics, the cabinet of Jules Ferry implemented policies that were anathema to the right. Liberalization of laws governing the press prompted Péladan's fulminations against journalism, a profession, he wrote, "in which one smokes and drinks and sees lots of people, and which would resemble prostitution if only it were held in higher regard."[3]

Foremost among Ferry's educational reforms was the establishment of a system of public schools independent of the church, another secularizing measure perceived to be part of the government's overtly anti-clerical positions. While often criticizing the inadequacies of Catholic instruction, the occultists wrote their own works of mystical pedagogy, manuals for an intellectual elite destined to become the prophets, seers, and Magi of the future.

The head of the church himself, Pope Leo XIII, did nothing to help bolster the failing spirits of the monarchists forming the core of the occult brotherhood. In his 1892 encyclical to the faithful, Leo discouraged Royalist resistance to Republicanism and dashed hopes of Vatican support for monarchical restoration. Urging Catholics "to desist from attacking the Republic, to accept the existing form of government, and to concentrate upon obtaining from it in constitutional manner the repeal of the laic laws."[4] Leo's message only stiffened the resolve of the clergy and nobility to pursue their existing agenda.

The January 1889 election of General Georges Boulanger, an impassioned adversary of the monarchist cause, further disheartened the intellectual aristocracy who turned increasingly from politics to the timelessness of mysticism and magic. At the conclusion of J.-K. Huysmans's *Là-bas*, raucous cheers of "Long live Boulanger" had risen up from the street, while, high above, in the bell-tower of Saint Sulpice, Huysmans's elite cadre of astrologers, doctors, novelists, and bell-ringers lamented the decline of Occidental civilization and expressed impatience for the dawning of the era of the Paraclete. One can only hope for better things, as the physician des Hermies opines, for "this century does not give a fig for the coming of Christ; it adulterates the supernatural and vomits over the otherworldly."[5]

However, despite their disaffection with science and their predilection for esotericism – despite yearning for the stratified society of a bygone age – fin-de-siècle occultists often made common cause with the same church officials who condemned their writings as heretical.

In place of an aristocracy of birth, they proclaimed an aristocracy of enlightenment. And in place of magic as a practice of initiatic exclusionism, they affirmed the superiority of the wisdom they acknowledged must be shared with the people they once despised.

Intellectual and spiritual nobility, formerly defined by privileges withheld, was henceforth demonstrated by generosity bestowed. Pervading the practice of magic was the principle of *noblesse oblige*. As they modeled themselves on a Messiah who had embraced the pauper, the prostitute, and the pariah, the Decadent occultists came down from their high places, proclaiming "that the Gospel, the absolute type of perceptible light, can and must be preached and heard by all men."[6] Modifying the esotericism that had turned them within, they accepted the faith redirecting them toward their less gifted and advantaged brothers. *Latria*, or worship as service, turned the knowledge jealously guarded by the few into a new Gospel that would henceforth be preached to the many.

However, it was only gradually that the fin-de-siècle occult movement began to embrace the idea of selflessness and service. Indeed, the inclination of Decadent writers had always been to celebrate the unique genius of an exalted subject. In the domain of epistemology, art, politics, and social theory, fin-de-siècle France had hitherto witnessed a consecration of the exceptional individual. Rejecting Emile Zola's science-based belief in optimism and social progress, the Decadents viewed with scorn the agitations of the masses. Despising the collectivity – reviling the ochlocratic expression of its will – the Decadents recoiled from social action with a moue of contemptuous disgust. While endorsing a theocracy structured by divine principles, administered by a priesthood of illuminati like themselves, the reactionary Decadents approved of secular authority only when it was concentrated in the hands of a superior, highborn ruler. As Joséphin Péladan admonishes his disciple in *Comment on devient mage*: "Governing a people must be the duty of one man: Royalty."[7]

As the king was the hereditary depository of wisdom, grace, and power, the Magus was the descendant of an immemorial line of wonderworkers. Accountable to no one – detached from society and its convulsions – the Decadent Magus assumed the task of ascetic self-perfection. Like a sovereign, the thaumaturge was autonomous and alone. But while a monarch administered to an often restive and unenlightened populace, the Magus accepted few disciples and acted principally for himself. Maximizing his difference from a passion-roiled vulgus, the Magus dismissed the chimera of romantic love and patriotism, enslaving bonds that subordinated him to mistresses and nations. As Péladan says: "Magic expresses the power of ipseity."[8]

Despite the self-ennobling rigor of his initiatic discipline, the Magus in Decadent literature is often pictured as ineffectual, endowed with a prescience that brings no ability to affect the future. The exclusiveness of his coterie of visionary brethren precludes interaction with those who are virtuous but weak. The enlightenment of a king benefits the collectivity of his subjects, but the Magus is selfish in his quest for knowledge that is private and inaccessible. Etymologically suggesting his inward orientation, his esotericism directs him toward the refinement of himself.

In his 1895 study, *Le Satanisme et la magie*, Jules Bois comments similarly on the aloofness of the Magus. Denied the solace of affiliation, love, and friendship, the Magus, as Bois describes him, appears inflexible and inhuman. Unlike his diabolical counterpart, the sorcerer or wizard – rooted in the telluric world of instinct, flesh, and nature – the Magus ascends to a rarefied plane of contemplative impassivity. "When, out of pity, you lower your head, heavy with eternal thoughts, toward ephemeral humanity, you cause your doom. The cry of desire, the sob of mercy, the gesture of consolation bring your undoing."[9]

This is the paradox of fin-de-siècle white magic: the need to reconcile the flamboyance and exhibitionism of the Magus – a self-dramatizing personage like Sâr Péladan – with the impenetrable hermeticism of the doctrine he espoused. While disseminating knowledge steeped in a history of secrecy, the Magus-author simultaneously aimed at concealment and disclosure. Discouraging the profane and proselytizing the elite, he accompanied his sibylline messages with coy gestures of explanation, setting himself above the world while deigning to address it. The publication of occult treatises suggests this contradictory objective: soliciting the curiosity-seekers whom the author warns away, promising hidden truths to a public deemed unworthy of receiving them.

The fin-de-siècle hermeticists who styled themselves as authors differentiated the privileged information they enveloped in cryptic language and the book itself, which was made available to an undiscriminating public. Turn-of-the-century occult literature problematizes the importance of itself as product. Is the work of art the strengthened character, the enlightened mind of an adept? Is it the elevation of the writer's status through the bestowal of his knowledge? Is it the text which, in beckoning readers, passes outside the initiatic dialogue?

On the one hand, the Magus/artist, in communication with an audience, is able to escape the isolation to which his superiority relegates him. His literary work stands as evidence of a transformation: proof he has completed an alchemical refinement, whereby he dies to an old self to be reborn in his disciples. The Magnum Opus culminates, not in the manufacture of an artwork – gold which, on the material plane, confirms the transmutation of base substances – but in a resurrected self which is benevolent and selfless. In his instruction manual, Péladan assumes this Christological role, suggesting that an author's masterpiece is not a work but his soul redeemed: "man has the power and the obligation to create himself anew, in accordance with what is good. One asks what the object of life is. For a man who thinks, it can only be the occasion and the means to remake the soul that God has given him: to sculpt it into a work of art."[10]

The sacrifice of an old identity, the second creation of oneself: Péladan's language suggests a marriage of occult theory and Catholicism, reconciling New Testament doctrine with the highest aims of alchemy. As Manly Hall remarks in referring to the Bible: "[U]nless the elements first die, the Great Work cannot be achieved; [...] unless a man be born again, he cannot see the kingdom of God."[11] On the one hand, the Magus's goal is the apotheosizing of himself, ascending to a higher plane in the manner of a divinity. On the other, it is celebrating a communion with his followers, distributing himself as the gift of knowledge he confers on those who seek it.

Following the spagyrical step of breaking down the base material, the initiatic process begins with disassembling the apprentice, burning away impurities left by a regimen of social conditioning. Like baptism, which rids the soul of original sin's uncleanness – like fire which refines the substance at the bottom of the crucible – the lessons of the Magus eradicate his disciple's existing flaws: "Magic removes from the individual the scoria that education left on his personality."[12]

Péladan deplores the fact that magic, as spiritual aurefaction, had been perverted by subordinating principle to technique, substituting the tricks of magic and the material benefits they bring for the thaumaturge's higher aim of sanctifying himself as a work of art. So instead of practicing hermetic pedagogy that offers the initiate wealth and fame, promising to transform talismans and charms into gold, Péladan teaches his follower to become the king of soul and body.

The scientist

While fin-de-siècle occultists renounced magic as showmanship, the performative aspects of their discipline received the most popular attention: clairvoyance, telekinesis, magnetism, divination. In the tradition of Paracelsus, who combined physics and metaphysics, the fin-de-siècle occultist foresaw the convergence of conflicting doctrines. In the coming hour, man would witness a synthesis "of the opposing fields of human knowledge, the solemn reconciliation of two enemy sisters: Science and Faith." So predicted Stanislas de Guaïta in an article in *Initiation* in 1890.[13]

Writers like Jules Lermina, in *La Science occulte* (*Occult Science*), argue that esotericism was in no way incompatible with materialism. In his argument, Lermina rejects the traditional body/spirit dualism, suggesting that the soul is merely matter in a subtler form. Other Decadents adopted the Darwinian principle of evolutionary progress, positing that the development of the human species would result in the emergence of more enlightened beings.

Investigations into the phenomena of electricity and magnetism also prompted interdisciplinary research that had crossed traditional boundaries. Belief in astral bodies, magnetic fluid, magic volition was often underpinned by scientific theory bridging the visible and invisible world, illuminating what Jean Pierrot calls "hitherto unexplainable phenomena, the doubling of the medium, the power of suggestion, the ability to act on bodies at a distance."[14] While wishing to rehabilitate their studies with an aura of scientific legitimacy, writers like Papus and Péladan expressed ambivalence about the theatricality of magic. This is only one of many paradoxes characterizing turn-of-the-century occultism: (1) the incompatibility of the Magus's reclusiveness and secrecy and the self-dramatizing ostentation of a "mystic impresario" like Péladan; (2) the occultists' condemnation of materialism and rationalism and their interest in reintegrating the physical and metaphysical; (3) the self-exalting superiority of the Magus and his recognition of the value of service and instruction; (4) the wish to reconcile magic as an art objectified as works and the primary goal of the Magus to effect his rebirth on a higher plane.

The most influential occultist of the century, Eliphas Lévi, was the first to try to resolve these conflicts, endeavoring to create a harmony between empiricism and mysticism. Lévi's "true greatness," as Alfred Waite asserts, "centres in his bold attempt to establish a harmony between religion and science by revealing to reason the logical necessity of faith, by proclaiming to faith the sanctity of natural reason."[15]

Né Alphonse-Louis Constantin, Lévi was born in 1810 in modest circumstances as the son of a shoemaker. At first destined for the priesthood, Lévi had been a seminary student at Saint-Sulpice, before exposure to the occult writings of Swedenborg and Fabre d'Olivet caused him to abandon the church in 1838. Study of the Kabbalah, adoption of the prevailing Symbolist aesthetic helped to shape Lévi's evolving and uniquely personal brand of esotericism.

However, the capital event that allegedly turned the fledgling Magus to an immersion in supernaturalism was the manifestation, by Appolonius of Tyana, to Lévi and fellow-occultist, Edward Bulwer-Lytton, during a discussion on magic the two were pursuing one evening in London in 1854. As Bulwer-Lytton, in the aftermath of this miraculous apparition, went on to develop the Rosicrucian theory that led to the establishment of the Order of The Golden Dawn, so Lévi, in the interval between 1853 and 1863, produced books on magic that would inform the thinking of the leading occultists in fin-de-siècle France.

As Waite argues, Lévi's proposal to map a confluence of rationalism and magic led him to posit the existence of a vital force or subtle energy, which – following Lévi – fin-de-siècle hermeticists often associated with magnetism. They believed that this force, when subjected to the Magus's will, was capable of effecting seemingly miraculous phenomena. Variously described as fluidic emanations, astral light, the alchemists' Azoth, it was described by the Austrian von Reichenbach as *Od* which, in Sanskrit, means "all-penetrating." It is this energy that operates on the boundary between the natural and supernatural world, between the human and divine, and which Reichenbach sees as the point "where the demarcation between body and spirit disappears."[16]

Virtually indescribable, this agency enables the Magus to intuit the correspondences between the material realm and a higher world. In language both imagistically rich and laboriously obscure, Lévi characterizes this energy as "a universal plastic mediator, a common receptacle for the vibrations of movement and the images of form, a fluid and force which may be termed [...] the imagination of nature."[17] Despite the difficulty of articulating the properties of this force, Lévi anticipates his successors in stressing the Magus's ability to harness it, to guide it with his will, and re-create himself in the Creator's likeness. As Waite summarizes: "To know how to master this agent so as to profit by and to direct its currents is to accomplish the *magnum opus*, to be master of the world, and *the depository even of the power of God.*"[18]

However, when entrusted to the hands of the ignorant, this energy can become a force leading to perdition. Like all esoteric powers, it depends on the enlightenment of its user, and so can induce in the unwise hallucinations, madness, violence. It is the tempter of Genesis that causes suffering and exile. It crowns the initiate but enslaves the fool. "It is a serpent but also a nimbus." To master it, as Lévi writes, "we must set a foot upon its head."[19]

The exclusiveness of the priesthood of fin-de-siècle Magi is reinforced by such messages of admonishment and dissuasion. Stanislas de Guaïta, in *Au Seuil du mystère*, notes the inauspiciousness of dilettantism, frivolous dabbling in the occult. Like Lévi, he decries the spiritualists' evocation of the dead, which he sees as motivated by greed and discredited by charlatanism. He remarks that even the most experienced of esoteric researchers may succumb to crippling acedia, undergoing periods of depression: "Even an adept like Eliphas confessed, after a curious attempt at necromancy made in 1854, to having felt a profound and melancholy attraction to death, without, however, being tempted to commit suicide."[20]

The Avant-Propos of Guaïta's book serves the complementary purpose of cautioning seekers of hidden knowledge moved by ambition, pride, or lust, and reproving unbelievers who equate magic with gullibility. Submitting his treatise to the derision of the uninitiated, he suggests his teachings can be unriddled only by those whose interests are sincere. Guaïta does not dismiss the value of magic as performance, since a virtuoso's demonstrations may prove convincing to the skeptic: "The experimenter who calmly says: 'My heart has only to beat faster: the invisible force that noisily moves furniture is an odic current subject to my control. The human form that comes together in the vapors of these scents is just a fluidic coagulation, a colored reflection of my mind's dream, a creation of the Azoth produced by the expression of my will.'" Such an actor, Guaïta says, need not be denigrated as a showman, a commercial medium staging séances to entertain the credulous. Such a one incurs no blame; instead, "he deserves the title of Adept."[21]

Whether fictional characters or prospective apprentices in the occult sciences, fin-de-siècle initiates are directed toward primal causes, seeking to discern first things and understand cosmogonic origins. Study of the Kabbalah focuses on identifying Creation's building blocks. Having poured over the Book of Splendor, Péladan's Magus/hero, Mérodack, pursues his initiatic program and so "asks numbers for their laws, asks letters for their esoteric secrets."[22]

Returning to the oldest Kabbalistic text predating even the *Zohar*, the Decadent occultists immerse themselves in the *Sepher Yetzirah*, the Book of Formation translated by Papus in 1888. A foundational text or incunabulum, the *Sepher Yetzirah* proceeds from the nameless state of being, referred to as *Ain Soph*, to the ten properties of the created universe formed by letters, sounds, and numbers. It is the Sephirotic Tree which, as Eliphas Lévi claims, offers the key to man's diversity, knowledge of God, the world, and the self. Mystical wisdom obtained from study of the Sephiroth leads back from the created world to the Creator, from material reality to generative principle: "Examine all things by means of the ten Sephiroth. Restore the Word to Its Creator and lead the Creator back to his Throne."[23]

The Decadents' intuition of a looming end of things motivates their quest for origins. Thus, the search for primary substances, the original elements of Creation, syllables in the utterance by which God produced the world leads Guaïta to infer an onomasiology of the divine. Seeking the hieroglyphic meaning of the four letters of the Tetragram, he divides *Jéhovah* into *Iod*, God as the masculine principle of creation, the Scepter in the Tarot, the Sulfur of the alchemists; *Hé*, the feminine element of fertility, the Cup in the Tarot, alchemical Mercury; *Vau*, the conjugation of male and female, the Sword in the Tarot, the Azoth of the alchemists; and *Hé*, the fecundity of nature, completion and fulfillment, the Coin in the Tarot, the Salt of the alchemists. Following the Kabbalistic principle of letters containing endings and beginnings, the components of God's name spell out the enactment of his work, letters associating "the idea of God with the idea of the universe as finality."[24] Likewise, Papus, in *Le Tarot des Bohémiens* [*The Tarot of the Gypsies*], uses the elements of the sacred name to interpret the meaning of the Arcana: Kings, Queens, Knights, Pages, to which he assigns Pythagorean numeric values, commenting that this first word confers on the person who pronounces it "the key to all human and divine sciences."[25]

The occultist's circular itinerary is represented by the Kether, the Crown, from which God's names all emanate, and by the ouroboros, "prototype of the primitive wheel of the Zodiac."[26] These convey an inexhaustible dialectic, an endless chain of life and death orienting the occultist toward a mythical anteriority. The quest for an inexpressible beatitude, a prelapsarian innocence, contrasts with the looming menace of the apocalypse at the century's end. Edouard's Schuré's biographies of the prophets whom he calls *The Great Initiates* begins with the Aryan Cycle of Rama and concludes with the story of Jesus. Guaïta's history of esotericism seeks to position Decadent hermeticists along a continuum beginning with ancient Magi, suggesting an unbroken transmission of secret knowledge. There is an effort to connect a present moment, in which magic had been discredited, to a Golden Age of wisdom known to disciples of Solomon and Zoroaster.

The fool

Fin-de-siècle occultists also wrestled with the contradictory image of the Magus: the evolutionarily enlightened being in possession of timeless wisdom, and the delusional dupe whose secret knowledge was only bombastic, empty nonsense. They tended to identify with prophets who historically went unrecognized, ambiguous figures simultaneously dismissible and sublime, like Maître Janus in Villiers's *Axël* whose name suggests his complex status.

In the Tarot, the Arcanum signifying epistemological origins is the Zero Card, the Fool Card, in French *Le Bateleur*, a figure whose youthful aspect situates him in an immemorial past – at the dawning of creation when confidence was wedded to intelligence. Read hieroglyphically, as Lévi writes: "His head and arms form the letter א; around his head, there is a nimbus in the form of ∞, symbol of life and universal spirit; before him are swords, cups and pentacles, and he raises toward the sky his miraculous staff."[27]

Other occultists like Papus have linked the Fool to Ain Soph, the Unknowable First Cause pre-existing God's manifestation as his Creation. The ambiguous representation of the figure, dressed in the jester's motley garments, suggests the Decadent occultist's plight, his being an object of derision. The Zero Card thus images the transitional status of the neophyte, his standing on the threshold between ignorance and wisdom. The juggler's costume is a bright illusion that misleads the uninitiated: "This world is a Mardi Gras – a pageantry of divine sparks masked in the garb of fools."[28]

However, the Card's significance may reside not in the image, but in the seeker's interpretation. To the profane, the Card is part of a deck used for amusement and distraction. The quest for knowledge is just a game when only fools decide to play it. "We must admire the wisdom of the Initiates," as Papus has remarked, "who utilized vice and made it produce more beneficial results than virtue."[29] To the serious student addressed by Papus and Guaïta, the surface image of foolishness conceals a message of grave import: that Truth is not in substances, but in the commitment to discovering it.

This is the reason for Péladan's campaign against spurious sophistication, the true foolishness of those imbued with social prejudice. The indispensable first step in "the creation of the self" is undoing a factitious persona that is a patchwork of erroneous ideas. The restoration of a zero state of innocence and receptivity is analogous to returning to the Kabbalists' Ain Soph, and is a precondition to the work of intelligent self-remaking. Having eliminated impostor selves and recovered the simplicity of being no one, the seeker undertakes the rebirth of his identity as a Magus. Thus, Lévi and others cite Christ's call to his disciples, his saying that those who follow him should become again like little children.

The alchemist

For the fin-de-siècle occultist seeking to transform the Fool into the Wise Man, there was a natural fascination for the secret science of transmutation. Adopting Christian teachings, alchemy described the Great Work of redemption, as the experiment also followed the death and resurrection sequence, with base substances being broken down, put to death in the retort, in preparation for their reappearance in the nobler form of gold. Matter's putrefaction is dressed in the blackness of *nigredo* before suffering's fire cleanses it and makes it subtler and more ethereal. Thus, in citing an unidentified philosopher, Jung states in *Alchemical Studies*: "The tortured thing, when it is immersed in the body, changes into an unalterable and indestructible nature."[30]

The idea of the Magus sublimating base desires, refining corrupted consciousness buffeted by accident and impulse, is often translated into the image of the alchemist's alembic. Commenting on Lévi, Waite describes man's will as the Great Arcanum: "The transmutation of the philosophical metals is not, from this standpoint, a chemical process; rather, it is a process of transcendental and mystical chemistry by the application of the [...] emancipated will."[31]

In fin-de-siècle occult writing, esotericism's cryptic messages are often described as relating to the initiate's moral education. Instead of acquiring secret knowledge enabling the adept to amass wealth and power, magic requires self-mortification, self-restraint, and self-control.

Péladan's goal is to controvert the rumor that the Society of the Rose+Croix was literally engaged in alchemical experiments. Clarifying his position, he admonishes his disciple: "the Philosopher's Stone consists in simplifying, reducing matter to its quintessence so that contingencies no longer affect us. Magic performs the ascetic operation of sublimating the palpable into the spiritual."[32] If occultism moves along a spectrum from elitism to humility, Péladan's teaching of self-differentiation may occupy one extreme, while on the other, antithetical to the individual's quest for glory, is the devotion to service that requires anonymity and self-effacement.

In J.-K. Huysmans's novels that deal with mysticism and Satanism, he also refers to spiritual growth as alchemical ennoblement. Taking the occultist notion of mortification and self-discipline, he describes suffering on behalf of others as transmuting sin into redemption. At the conclusion of his hagiographic narrative of the life of Blessed Lydwine, Huysmans characterizes the saint's torment as akin to the Magnum Opus. Enduring tumors, cancers, abscesses, weeping tears of blood that harden as stalactites on her cheeks, she offers her pain to hasten the emancipation of souls from Purgatory. "The formula for the divine alchemy of suffering is self-abnegation and self-sacrifice. After a period of incubation, the Great Work is accomplished. Out of the soul's retort comes the gold of Love that consumes despondency and tears." Lydwine's tortured flesh becomes a catalyst. As Huysmans writes, "the true Philosopher's Stone is this."[33]

In Huysmans's promulgation of the doctrine of Mystic Substitution, one sees how far the fin-de-siècle idea of alchemy had evolved. No longer does the adept withdraw into scornful isolation – immured in misanthropic pride in his anchoritic lodging: "a high-ceilinged, unadorned room, with its austere wood paneling."[34] Guaïta's guidebook of instruction for the followers of Saint-Just, Péladan's apprentice manual for the thaumaturgic neophyte still ostensibly address an exclusive audience of *aristes*. But the fact that these works are published at all presumes a dissemination of occult teaching, suggesting a reorientation from aloofness to collaboration. The magical asceticism that liberates initiates from the solicitations of the flesh becomes, in *Lydwine*, an embrace of sinners through expiatory self-abnegation.

The apocalyptic

The path of the initiatic quest ceases to be circular and repetitive and instead assumes a linearity that aims at eschatological completion. Fin-de-siècle temporality incorporates a sense of inevitable exhaustion, an irreversible decline toward hopelessness and entropy. Informed by a philosophy of catastrophism, the mentality of the Decadents had initially cast the future as a murderer of the present: "a hecatomb of possibilities that, one after another, are fulfilled."[35] This is why the Decadent occultists adopted a model of cyclical renewal, ancient knowledge perpetually re-transmitted by the Magi of the present day. This sense of history as a continuum, of magic as a confraternity of wise men, emerges as the central principle structuring fin-de-siècle encyclopedias of esotericism: Schuré's lives of the Initiates, from Krishna to Pythagoras, Guaïta's *Au Seuil du mystère* that moves from Hermes to Madame Blavatsky, from the Emerald Tablet to Tibetan Buddhism and the lessons of theosophy. There is no end or death but passages over thresholds of mystery, ascent to a higher plane and a return to mentoring and writing The knowledge of earlier visionaries is constantly re-acquired, complemented by insights gained from modern disciplines and new sciences.

In *Comment on devient mage*, Péladan acknowledges his indebtedness to his predecessors while still emphasizing the uniqueness of each practitioner of occultism. The ascetic regimen governing the neophyte's formation includes a program of meditation that structures daily life. The endpoint of the evolution toward spiritual perfection is completion of the initiate's self-awareness and self-definition. There is no ecstasy that collapses the walls of individual consciousness, no ego dissolution in the totality of things. The closer the student moves toward the light, "the more he is himself. Theosophists wrongly see evolution ending in a kind of collective Nirvana."[36]

Péladan's instructions signal the tension pervading fin-de-siècle occultism between the Magus's development as a member of a mystical elite and his desire to utilize his powers for the betterment of mankind. For Péladan, the initiatic process involves introspection and self-analysis that is literally dependent on dissociation from one's peers. At day's end, Péladan counsels the student to take leave of his acquaintances "in order to reclaim a personality diminished by their caresses."[37] The initiate is unlike the fool who has a plethora of experiences, yet never reflects on them, never converts their senselessness into meaning. For Péladan, self-study is like Lévi's application of the will, an alchemical transmutation of existential data into insights. Péladan distinguishes the mystic – beatified by surrendering to God – and the Magus, whose spiritual discipline entitles him to glory. Problematizing the value of catechistic writing like his own, he says that enlightenment does not come from studying others' works, but from authoring a unique self, from the "sculpting of one's soul."

Of all the fin-de-siècle practitioners of esoteric doctrine, Péladan was the most concerned with his pedigree as a master. He advises apprentices against immersion in the theory of their predecessors, warning that study of Eliphas Lévi brings only superficial knowledge. Learning the teachings of Paracelsus, Cornelius Agrippa, Heinrich Kunrath may create a learned man, but not a Magus, in Péladan's opinion. Wisdom is not acquired, not handed down from one's antecedents. It is produced anew as the unique achievement of every individual. "You must create your own magic, not because your efforts are motivated by vanity, but because you are seeking in yourself the originality of a work of art."[38]

The Catholic

Perhaps the most striking feature in the evolution of fin-de-siècle magic is the reconciliation of arcane practices, deemed heretical by the church, and the embrace of Catholic principles that require service to humanity. The Magus, once a lonely figure in his elevated genius, accepts the need to pass among the benighted masses he once disdained. Redefining initiatic knowledge that had been the exclusive property of the elect, the occultist becomes a proselytizer who, through the sacrifice of his pride, proves his superiority by sharing his privileged knowledge with the world. In Péladan, this becomes the missionary duty of the Magus, "our daimonic work, which is to serve as an intermediary between this world and the other."[39]

For Péladan, the development of a cadre of *aristes* had implied from its inception the principle of its transcendence. Four years later, in the preface to *Le Vice suprême*, Péladan's inaugural work of fiction, he announces magic's supersession by Catholic orthodoxy. Péladan resolves the traditional antagonism between occultists and Catholics – the former condemned by the clergy for heretical iconolatry, the latter taxed by hermeticists for anti-intellectualism. Péladan stipulates that Christ had supplanted the Wise Men who came to worship at the nativity: "The adoration by the Magi means that esotericism must cede to the Truth. What is true and fecund in magic is found in the words that Jesus spoke, and the Gospel annuls all the clavicles and grimoires because it supersedes them."[40]

Péladan had previously subscribed to a view prevalent among the Decadents: that religious education fostered uncritical submissiveness, acquiescence to church doctrine that bred incurious passivity. As Papus writes in defending magic against denunciations by the church: "At Saint-Sulpice, one does an admirable job of shaping the will and strengthening the heart. The education of the soul is conducted to perfection, but the mind is completely neglected. Worse than that, it is feared, and what is taught is ignorance."[41]

In his instruction manual, Péladan strives to achieve a working synthesis between the intellectual training required of the initiate and obedience to Catholic teaching expected of the faithful. He no longer makes a distinction between the mystic and the Magus, between the ego mortification of the saint and the apotheosis of an adept crowned in glory. Having schooled his students in the discipline needed for the re-creation of the self, Péladan acknowledges that they are shaped by forces more powerful than themselves: "In vain the selfish person wishes to raise himself up without dedicating himself to anything; the dilettante seeks to gain refinement without ever loving others. The highest stage in any journey can be completed only through an act of self-sacrifice."[42]

Following the ordering principles of much of occult teaching, Péladan's initiatic stages are based on God's three successive Kingdoms. According to Vintrasian doctrine, the era of the Paraclete – the Age of the Holy Spirit – following the Age of God, the Father, and God, the Son – will fulfill the messianic promise and usher in a time of spiritual perfection. According to Papus, these ages correspond to the tripartite organization of human beings: the physical body, "which supports all the elements constituting an incarnated man;" the astral body that animates them, and the psychic energies that move them – "the Mind, synthesizing in itself the three preceding principles, is enlightened by Intelligence and served by Will and thereby governs the entire organism."[43]

In Péladan's *Ternaire du Saint-Esprit* (*The Ternary of the Holy Spirit*), he begins with the time of God, the Father, when man was ruled by instinct, when humans had not evolved beyond their bodily existence. An era of commandments and punishments had served to regulate corporeal beings, dominated by sexual urges and homicidal impulses. Original sin, for Péladan, is nothing other than the state of incarnation: "Thus, in order to wipe away original imperfection, we must use our will so that we rise from the level of an organism to the level of a species, no longer limiting ourselves to living from sensations that are exclusively organic."[44]

Péladan's depiction of this early phase in the development of mankind becomes a pretext for more vituperation against jingoistic patriotism, the false god of the nation/state repudiated by the Magus, "the faithful knight of Providence."[45]

In *Le Vice suprême*, Father Alta, the spiritual confederate of Mérodack, tells his congregants that the age of spiritual crusades is not over: "One might answer me by saying that this is no longer the age of the defense of the Holy Sepulcher. But as long as there is a duty to fulfill, as long as there is a weak person to help, there is a place for the crusader. If civilization has taken away your sword, take up the pen. Raise your voice in order to magnify the Word of God in a work, as long as it is useful."[46]

Following the Reign of God, the Father, the age of instinctual repression, comes the age of God, the son, who teaches Christian love or *agape*. Until the Messiah returns in glory, the survival of man's spiritual being entails Dolorist suffering, by which the world's sins can be redeemed. For Huysmans, this continuation by the faithful of Christ's Passion enacts what Christian Berg refers to as a "victimal theodicy," whereby original

debt is liquidated, "offset by suffering and sorrow."[47] Péladan characterizes this era as one where mercy succeeds justice, and severity gives
way to humility – "harshness toward oneself must not be extended
to one's neighbor."[48] The ascetic rigor with which the Magus con-
trols his appetites is a personal manifestation of Christ's "voluntary
holocaust."[49]

Heralding the dawning of the era of the Paraclete is a definitive over-
throwing of ochlocratic rule. Tyrants will be cast down, the state will no
longer subjugate its citizens, and the church will no longer be guided by
the unlettered and superstitious. After the Father's Kingdom, grounded
in a discipline of the body – after the era of the Son that witnessed a flowering of brotherhood – comes the Third Age of the Holy Spirit crowned
by a triumph of intelligence. "Future saints will be theosophists and
geniuses; the power of the simple is no longer. The future belongs to
the sages."[50]

Esotericism, no longer required to disguise its majesty with gim-
mickry, stands revealed, and the Fool is superseded by the Arcanum
of the Magus. The card itself suggests the hierophantic role that he
will play: transmitting celestial knowledge, indicated by the right hand
pointing skyward, delivering it to the people, toward whom his left hand
is directed. The Magician, simultaneously oriented toward the heavens
and the earth, becomes a figure illuminating the occult principle of universal Analogy. As it is above, so it is below. *Quod superius sicut quod
inferius.*

Jean Pierrot cites the centrality of this fin-de-siècle occult tenet, as it
defines the operational role of the Magus as *microprosope*, "creator of the
smaller world."[51] The doctrine of Analogy, as Pierrot observes, informs
the theory of the Symbol, "which, through the interplay of vertical correspondences, makes each object in the visible world the material sign of
an invisible reality."[52] Likewise, the Magus/poet, armed with knowledge,
ascends to a plane of higher truth, before returning to the phenomenal
world where he disseminates his insights. The book of occult teaching
retains this referential property, revealing in material form, dressing in
the language of the tribe, a transcendental wisdom that is essentially
inexpressible.

Like Péladan, Jules Bois affirms that the ascendancy of the Magus
will coincide with the inauguration of the reign of the Holy Spirit. But
while Péladan boasts of descending from a line of Chaldean initiates,
while he insists on the formation of an apostolate of artist/geniuses,
Bois asserts that the future Magus will be divested of his pomp. Emulating Jesus, modeling himself on Buddha, he will behave with modesty
and renounce his self-isolating superciliousness.

Bois maintains that the wizard of the present generation is a show-man, a buffoon arrayed in necromantic raiment, an impostor enveloped in the clouds of his obscurantist jargon. To Bois, the self-styled successors to Eliphas Lévi enlighten no one, but only confuse people with their esoteric mumbo-jumbo: "the impostors who are descendants of this tempestuous writer are like shopkeepers in a shady pharmacy, comical curio merchants, professors of fluke and coincidence."[53]

The laughing stock that Guaïta feared the fin-de-siècle Magus had become emerges in Bois's account as a deplorable reality discrediting genuine occult research. The true visionary does not remain on the frozen summit of his mystic wisdom but comes down again to assume his role as prophet, guide, and teacher.

Edouard Schuré remarks on the essential meaning of Christ's work as Mage and mentor when, in his conversation with the Pharisee Nicodemus, he insists on man's baptism with water and fire. The Third Age of the Paraclete may see the adept's vindication, but until then, the sage must acquiesce to his imprisonment in the senses, as he commingles with the people to whom he prophesies of things to come. By interacting with the public, by accepting the fact of his incarnation, he rejects the Gnostic heresy and joins Christ in suffering the Passion.

Stripped of the opaqueness of secret symbols, the guiding principle of fin-de-siècle magic is to hasten man's rebirth as a more disciplined moral being. Right action, fraternal love disengage him from the flesh, enabling the "etheric, fluidic body" to clarify and grow lighter, allowing an escape from the dismal cycle of embodiments, establishing the "kingdom of glorified souls and pure spirits above and below, in heaven and on earth."[54]

The teacher

Here, the Decadent hermeticists justify the redemptive value of their teachings, books that elevate readers out of their instinctuality and automatism, that effect man's death to his animal nature and his resurrection as light and spirit. The magic catalyst, the Philosopher's Stone, is not the content of these writings, but their transformative capacity to change enslavement into freedom.

In Eliphas Lévi, this agent is referred to as *le Verbe*, the divine language of the *Logos* acquiring transitivity and power. "*In the beginning was the Word, says the Gospel of Saint John*," a word which, as Lévi says, "expresses at once both being and action."[55]

For Lévi and his followers, *le Verbe* is the agent of a magical transformation, liberating meaning hidden in the heart of experience.

Transmuting existential data into intelligibility and significance, *l'alchimie du Verbe* (the alchemy of the Word) effects a passage from flesh to spirit. Like Christ, "who put on a human body," "who clothed himself in matter,"[56] the substance dies in the retort to be reborn in higher form. Likewise, God, the Son, suffers so that he may reappear as *Logos*. If, as Jung notes, the "lapis may [...] be understood as a symbol of the inner Christ,"[57] that being may be freed when man undergoes a baptism by fire.

The fin-de-siècle occultist, in his attention to catalytic forces – poetic visions of the coincidence of the Analogic planes of high and low – emphasizes magic, not as wisdom to be possessed, but as energies to be released. Purification of the astral body enables decomposed matter to be regenerated. Poetry effects the rebirth of referents transmuted into symbols. These processes augur the end of the era of the incarnated Christ and the beginning of the age of the Holy Spirit when, as Huysmans's hero, Durtal, forecasts, there will be beings unstained by original sin, beings who will no longer need to be tested in the fires of pain and suffering.

Turn-of-the-century occultists, who focus on movement and transition, climbing and descending, passing between the upper and lower realms, saw their writing as raising up the ignorant, as bringing down knowledge from above. Even the dubious Vintrasian doctrine of "redemptive ascension" works on the Christological model of transmuting instinct, sin, and license into purification and self-sacrifice. Thus, as Guaïta reports in *Le Serpent de Genèse*, the great secret and foundational principle of the sect, is to work this transformation: "*It was as a consequence of a guilty act that the Fall in Eden came about; it is through an act of love performed in the name of religion that Redemption will be achieved.*"[58] Guaïta may condemn the rite for authorizing all manner of orgiastic excess – bestiality, adultery, incubism, and incest. But in its conception, ascensional redemption enacts the occultist goal of joining high and low, since one engages in acts of love: "with higher spirits, the elect of the earth in order to 'celestify oneself' ["se célestifier"] and with profane or inferior spirits, of an elemental or animal nature, in order to 'celestify' these fallen beings."[59]

While reproving Vintras's followers for their cynical acts of sacrilege, Guaïta patterns his own mission on a similar premise, moving along "Jacob's double ladder whose highest rungs are lost in the clouds."[60] Like God, who so loved man that he became flesh and gave his Son, the Magus/prophet is an archangel re-descending from the firmament to the world. These men come down, "like Moses, who, having seen the light, wears its reflection on his face."[61] Modeled on Christ, "son of the World," they bear witness to the truth and thereby create "the children of Heaven."[62]

For many fin-de-siècle esotericians, the requirement to do service inspired attempts to wed magic and faith. As Eliphas Lévi writes, knowledge and intuition, reason and devotion are the two pillars of Solomon's porch. Separate, Lévi writes, "they are one sustaining force, but joined together, [they] mutually destroy each other."[63] The objective of the Magus is to effect a synthesis of opposites, to overcome dualities, and thereby recreate the Androgyne.

Among the fin-de-siècle Catholics who ventured into occult studies, Villiers, Péladan, and Huysmans all ended by subsuming initiatic knowledge to orthodox Catholic teaching. Moving from grimoire to Gospel, they made professions of their faith, continuing their occult practices only when they served the interests of the church. Péladan advises his acolyte never to "leave the bosom of the church," adding that magic, the crown of faith, "would have no foundation without the edifice of religion."[64]

In *Le Vice suprême*, Péladan illustrates the alliance forged between the Magus and the priest, when, in an effort to stem the spiritual degeneration of western culture, Mérodack, the thaumaturge, visits the visionary Father Alta and, in the sacristy, the two embrace and pledge mutual cooperation.

The spiritual itinerary of J.-K. Huysmans follows a similar trajectory. After the early stirrings of religious hunger, the nostalgia for belief, revulsion for the material crassness of his era, Huysmans had been attracted to Catholicism by his love of iconography, by the moving simplicity of plainchant, by Chartres's soaring Gothic architecture. However, Huysmans's spiritual awakening was also sparked by his exposure to the secrets of sorcery and the rituals of Satanism. It was only after his descent *là-bas* – into the sordid underground of necromancy – that he was propelled *là-haut* in his quest for the immaculate and divine.

Like other contemporary artists, Huysmans was disheartened by the aridity of rationalism, but the course of his conversion had been slow, and faith elusive. It was his exposure to black magic, fictionally transposed in *Là-bas*, that had raised the skeptical naturalist out of his dissatisfied incredulity. In his dealings with Joseph Boullan, successor to Vintras, Huysmans had been introduced to demonomancy and bewitchment. Embroiled in occult warfare with Stanislas de Guaïta, he believed he was besieged by malignant larvae, subjected to invisible attacks, and so had learned of apotropaic magic that warded off spells cast by his enemies.

In *Là-bas*, there is an overlap of Catholic and occult practices that shows the author sensitized to supra-rational phenomena. Huysmans's protagonist, Durtal, is instructed by an astrologer in the techniques deployed in exchanges of spells. He hears of the ornithomantic use of tercels, sparrow-hawks, and falcons that alert a potential victim that a danger is approaching.

Ceremonial magic was embedded in Catholic liturgy, and cryptic biblical allusions appealed to Huysmans's sense of mystery. Enactment of the Sacrifice to the Glory of Melchizedek had warded off the evil spirits by which Durtal felt himself assailed, reminding Huysmans's character of the Genesis King of Salem, who, as Christ's precursor, had performed a variation on the Eucharistic feast. "He is without father or mother or genealogy, and has neither beginning of days nor end of life, but resembling the Son of God he continues a priest forever."[65]

Huysmans's experience with Satanism had persuaded him of a truth that Péladan advances at the conclusion of *le Vice suprême*, that evil is done aggressively, while good can only act defensively. Likewise, Eliphas Lévi, in his endorsement of Catholic doctrine, confirms that only religion can be a force for good, whereas magic is often misused, its teachings perverted and profaned, its techniques utilized for materialistic, selfish purposes.

The frequent fin-de-siècle supersession of magic by Catholicism is attributable in part to disenchantment with Positivism's clarity. The impenetrability of much of occult doctrine – the concealment of alchemical operations in theriomorphic symbols, the Kabbalists' assigning value to the relation between letters and numbers – is used to frustrate dilettantes and confound the profane. The unfathomability of religion, inhospitable to reason, expresses "a reaction against scientific literature and its insolent denials of the spiritual."[66] Rather than the orderliness of liturgy, the comprehensiveness of dogma, it was the majesty of mysticism that beckoned the fin-de-siècle seeker, drawing him to matters otherworldly and sublime. The intuition of analogies, the apprehension of correspondences afforded knowledge not obtainable through observation and analysis. "It was a matter of re-affirming the importance of certain aspects of the human soul, everything having to do with sensibility, everything affecting the imagination, everything that the evolution of western thought had tended to repress."[67] Exceptional states of consciousness – hallucination, synesthesia, hypnagogic trances – allowed glimpses of the beautiful that were only communicable in poetry. In its marriage of art and magic, fin-de-siècle esotericism ended by turning toward expression, communion, and disclosure – renouncing the concealment of knowledge etymologically suggested by the word *occultism*.

Villiers de l'Isle-Adam's *Axël* (1890) illustrates the false dichotomy encountered by the Decadents in their experiences with magic. On the one hand, there is the power conferred by learning the mysteries of Rosicrucianism, and on the other, the liberating submission to the requirements of Catholic faith. In his own life, Villiers had been troubled by the prerequisites for conversion: sacrifice of intelligence, blind conformity to church doctrine, acceptance of a life of obedience and penury, ascetic renunciation of the pleasures of the senses.

A native of Saint-Brieuc, Villiers was born in 1838 into an illustrious and increasingly indigent Breton family, and the material challenges he encountered in childhood only worsened over time, ending when Villiers died of cancer in a hospice for the poor in 1889. Villiers's aristocratic ancestry, his militant antipathy for Comtian positivism prepared the place he would assume in the fin-de-siècle occultist movement. Profoundly influenced by Charles Baudelaire, whom Villiers met in Paris in 1860, an impassioned devotee of Richard Wagner, Villiers evolved his own brand of turbulent Romanticism that would be further refined by his study and appreciation of the esoteric works of Eliphas Lévi.

Axël, Villiers's posthumously published drama, offers the fullest exposition of the author's belief in the magic power of personal thought and will. Opposing the masses' herd-like submission to the demands of objective reality, Villiers asserts the prestige of the Magus's superior intelligence, the acuity of his higher perceptions. Thus, in the drama, the postulant Sara is summoned by the Archdeacon to relinquish "the arrogant insistence on contemptible reason."[68] The profession of one's faith is both a suicide of the intellect, and the ultimate creative act, as the Archdeacon explains: "Isn't believing the same as projecting the object of belief and realizing oneself in it?"[69]

In Villiers's book, religious affirmation is like the Magus's self-engendering: authorship of a second self that is boundless and divine. As crucifixion precedes rebirth, an abandonment of the search for knowledge is a necessary precondition to spiritual awakening. Humility leads to exaltation. Renunciation bestows life everlasting. But like the fin-de-siècle occultist who rejected the immolation of the thinking self, Sara declines the Archdeacon's offer of Light and Hope and Life, choosing to complete alone the work of personal self-perfection.

For Axël, the tempestuous aristocrat in his impregnable forest castle, the appeal of supernaturalism involves initiatic training by the Magus, Maître Janus. The Rosicrucianism popularized by Péladan and Guaïta had appealed to Villiers, and references to the secret sect proliferate in his drama. During her conventual interment, Sara had poured over forbidden Rosicrucian texts. And when she escapes, she arrives at Axël's castle bearing a rose that had blossomed in the snow. Laying it over a cruciform dagger she was wearing on her belt, she comments on the Rose and Cross, and their ancient mystic symbolism: "a Sign that, long ago, had caused the proudest empires to crumble."[70]

In his interpretation, Alan Raitt asserts that these esoteric references are used atmospherically, suggesting at most a figural marriage of romantic love and spiritual suffering. But when combined with Villiers's frequent allusions to alchemical transmutations – when set in the context of a drama centering on the symbolic discovery of a fortune in gold – the Rosicrician thematic assumes a new and deeper meaning.

In his encyclopedia of occultism, Manly Hall reproduces an illustration of the Rosicrucian Rose from the foundational text the *Geheime Figuren des Rosenkreuzer*. Showing a rose, symbol of fecundity and purity, whose ten petals are open and separated, the picture, Hall says, suggests completion of the process of "spiritual unfoldment." In a manifest reference to alchemy, "the golden heart within the midst of the flower" corresponds, Hall adds, to the "spiritual gold concealed within [...] human nature." In a story concluding with the two lovers' suicide and the simultaneous celebration of their servants' nuptials, the idea of death and rebirth is conveyed by the setting of the last scene at daybreak, as the sunlight of a new dawn glints off gold coins rolling across the flagstones. In this context, Hall's comments on the mystical Rose assume a greater significance, since for the Greeks, the flower symbolized "sunrise," while in Apuleius's the *Golden Ass*, the donkey is cured of "his foolishness" – is able to regain "his human shape by eating a sacred rose given him by Egyptian Priests."[71]

In Villiers's text, Axël declines the role of the Magus and is instead disguised as a Fool, until he attains what he believes is the golden radiance of spiritual purity, rejecting material things and choosing death out of love. Villiers's novel unfolds in *The World of Religion*, *The World of the Occult*, and *The World of Passion*, and each realm requires of its adherents an absolute sacrifice of self and will. The theme of suicide informs each part of the narrative: the postulant taking the veil consents to her inhumation in the convent's in-pace, as she is asked "to crucify her mortal life by eternally re-enacting the divine sacrifice."[72] Likewise,

Janus entreats the initiate to renounce "the double illusion of Gold and Love,"[73] disengaging himself from time and Becoming, thereby escaping the curse of cyclical incarnations. Speaking in the esoteric idiom of the adept, he urges Axël to rise into the Increate and realize himself in his astral light.

Like Péladan, who had deprecated magic as technique, Janus urges Axël not to overvalue the material evidence of occult knowledge, not to equate it with protective pentacles, electuaries, potions constraining love, the Elixir of Long Life, "la Pierre Philosophale," the Magisterium of the Sun. The true Magus, Janus says, does not know passion. He is not entangled in attachments. Housed "beneath the veils of an organism, in a prison of relationships," he aspires to die "as an ascetic, of the death of the Phoenix."[74] So, like Sara, when Axël is called to profess his commitment to esotericism, accepting the Light, the Hope, and the Life, he, too, says no. As interment in the cloistered life had been presented as a form of suicide, so the vocation of Magus also entails self-annihilation, abandonment of humanity, a renunciation of affection, singularity's dissolution in the universal. The fruit of the Tree of Knowledge is cold, as Axël says.

Thus, when Villiers presents the climactic scene in which the lovers swallow poison, then fall to the floor, the suicide motif has already assumed a deeper resonance. Like magic, whose secrets are inexpressible, love is selfish, private, an expression of an impulse toward social suicide. Rather than death, what Villiers's text extols is the beautiful expression of a death wish, literature's surviving the morbidity of its material.

In the epithalamial duet that Axël and Sara perform together, they transpose their love into poetry. Speech assumes the poignancy and sensuality of lived experience, as Sara intuits that describing imaginary idylls in remote places is preferable to visiting them, to living a love doomed to disenchantment. She hymns a fantasy of a lovers' hideaway in Ceylon amidst vermilion towers enveloped by flocks of macaws with plumage the color of fire. She dreams of founding a new religion on the riverbanks of the Ganges. She imagines a strange and distant life together in the porcelain edifices of Yeddo. Villiers's text illustrates the alchemical power of *le Verbe*, refining lived events, sublimating them into poetry, transfusing the characters' deathly love into the vitality of its description.

Sara's sumptuous language issues an invitation to a banquet, cups of happiness to drink, bouquets of pleasures to pick. But Axël sees her words as putting to death the experiences they call to mind, saying that her dreams are too beautiful to come true. However, the fact that

Villiers's text survives the suicide of his characters shows the fate of turn-of-the-century magic, both as knowledge and expression. What Axël spurns as a compromise, a profanation of idealism – the banality of a life only servants need experience – emerges in Villiers's drama as a treasure of coins and diamonds, a valueless existence aurefied by purpose and sacrifice.

Conclusion

In Huysmans, the Dolorist martyr's gift is to live and suffer, not to hurry death that delivers her into ecstasy and silence. The Magus, whose superior knowledge raises him above the uninitiated, does not finish his formation until he comes back down, passing among the people to whom he imparts his wisdom. For Péladan and Guaïta, the ennobled sage is elevated, reborn as a teacher. The lesson of Christ's life as recounted in Schuré is that the Master, Son of God, accepts his mission as the Son of Man. For the Magus, the privileged self must die to be reincarnated as his servants.

In *Comment on devient mage*, Péladan still strikes his prideful tone when he predicts the evolution of a new art that will be loftier and finer: "literature, science, art: all must be raised above the level of the masses so that a new aristocracy may appear, that alone will be literate, that alone will be knowledgeable, that alone will be creative."[75] But by its existence, Péladan's text bears witness to his wish to disseminate occult teachings and expand the circle of initiates. As with gold, which is at once a metal and a symbol of higher consciousness, the occult work is an object which catalyzes spiritual growth. The Magus may remain enclosed in the austere solitude of his knowledge. The mystic may disappear into the blissful autism of his vision. But the Magus/mentor like Péladan, the author/convert like Huysmans leave behind their work as a treasure enriching those that find it. Glittering in the sunlight, it the gold produced by magic, flesh become *le Verbe*, experience resurrected as intelligence.

Joséphin Péladan: *La Vertu suprême* (1900)

Nowhere more conspicuously than in the writings of the eccentric Magus Joséphin Péladan is the link between Decadent art and occult theory more apparent. Opulent solipsism, nurturance of personal difference, cultivation of the exceptionality of a gifted individual: these are the structuring principles of a fin-de-siècle aesthetic that turned away from neighbors, peers, and brothers. By magnifying qualities that set apart a privileged subject, the Decadents celebrated uniqueness as both a stigma and a sign of election. In literature, Remy de Gourmont developed an overwrought style that strove for lexical singularity and expressive individualism. In philosophy, Villiers de l'Isle-Adam promoted the idea of *Illusionism*, the conviction that every person, confined to the prison of his consciousness, was free to create a world in harmony with his beautiful subjectivity: "Henceforth every consciousness would be locked inside its own representations, unable to decide if they corresponded to an objective reality or if they were nothing more than empty phantasms."[76]

From Villiers as well came a philosophical formulation of radical subjectivism that gained currency among his Decadent contemporaries. Propounded most explicitly in *Tribulat Bonhomet*, Villiers' view combined the Hegelian principle that "the essence of the real is by nature spiritual"[77] with Eliphas Lévi's view that the superior man shapes the world with his will, and that his intelligence extends onto the astral plane and into the world of the dead. Those influenced by Villiers saw religion as personally determined, asserting that doctrine no longer depended on the incontrovertibility of revealed truths but was indistinguishable from what each worshipper willed himself to believe. Since God was a divine concept, since the reality of that concept derived from "the will and intellectual perspective particular to each living being,"[78] the divinity was brought to life by the convictions of the faithful. However, Decadent epistemology became increasingly undemocratic, as artists retreated further into the shrine of their point of view. The reality of other people – deemed illusory and chimerical – was regarded as a matter that was both undecidable and uninteresting. Whereas naturalism advanced the view that knowledge was collectively shared and ratified, the Decadents turned to information sources that were private and exclusive.

The fin-de-siècle fascination with occultism reflected the Decadents' gravitation toward intellectual claustration, as the highest truths were seen as those attainable to the fewest, and articulation of those truths was the prerogative of an elite. Between Huysmans's des Esseintes (*A rebours* 1884), the embodiment of self-sequestering aestheticism, and Mérodack, Joséphin Péladan's model of thaumaturgic misanthropy, there is little difference in the characters' jaundiced outlook on the world. Both feel like exiles in a materialistic era of herd-like conformity. Both are vatic predictors of the coming cultural apocalypse, forecasting the shipwreck of civilization in a sea of ochlocracy and irreligion. Yet, whereas des Esseintes is made sick by his prideful isolation, feeling oppressed by being cut off from the metaphysical truths he intuits but cannot grasp, Mérodack is serene in his self-sufficient wisdom.

However, the development of Péladan's character follows the refinement of his views on magic, as he gradually abandons the Decadents' insistence on a self-immuring subject and comes to harness occultism to a commitment to work in the service of his brothers. A native of Lyon, Péladan (1858–1918) was born into a family given to occult pursuits and dire prognostications of France's future. An ardent Legitimist and self-styled disciple of Nostradamus, Louis-Adrien Péladan, father of the author, exercised an enduring influence on his son with his Catholic Illuminism and his predictions of an apocalypse soon to engulf Paris in a rain of fire and sulfur. Imbued with his progenitor's reactionary political views and prophetic mysticism, Péladan fils embarked for Paris in February 1881, making the acquaintance the following year of Barbey d'Aurevilly, who appreciated Péladan's fiction but deplored the obscurantism of his views on magic. In the capital, Péladan maintained a liaison with Henriette Maillat, the model for Huysmans's Satanic Madame Chantelouve, who appreciated the Sâr's visionary insights while complaining of his unremarkable virility. He collaborated with Stanislas de Guaïta in his esoteric research and became a member of the Occult Council of the Twelve of the Kabbalistic Rosicrucians, who banded together to deflect the mystic assaults ostensibly launched against them by the diabolical Abbé Joseph Boullan.

Undertaken in 1884, Péladan's multi-volume *Ethopée, La Decadence latine*, provided a forum for his singular theories on androgyny, sacred prostitution, and neo-Albigensian Gnosticism. As an art critic, a strikingly histrionic personage, a mystic pedagogue, and indefatigable novelist, the Sâr captivated the public with his vestimentary eccentricities, alienated his fellow hermeticists with his bombast and flamboyance, and deluged fin-de-siècle students of magic with writings at once preposterous and profound, comical and insightful. When Péladan died of complications of an alimentary infection in 1918, he had bequeathed on the public a breathtakingly diverse collection of sacred tragedies, treatises on theocracy, lovemaking, and politics, as well as some thirty volumes of occult fiction.

It is primarily by following the arc of Péladan's novels that readers can best appreciate the Sâr's evolving view of magic, as it changes from a sign of privilege and specialness segregating the adept from the uninitiated, to a set of skills used collectively for the betterment of mankind. In the different facets of Péladan's identity as a metaphysician and a showman, one can trace the development of his creative ideology. After projecting an image of an impenetrable and self-isolating sage, Péladan describes the Magus as increasingly interacting with the public, an audience sustaining him in the displays of his superiority. Both Péladan and his fictional avatars address a circle of cognoscenti: the politically enlightened, admirers of sublime art, a select community of Catholic brethren who share his ideas about religion.

The first stage in the Sâr's development as hierophant and teacher ended with a realization that the Magus not only accumulated secret knowledge but also needed to recruit disciples with whom that knowledge could be shared. The theatricality and flamboyance of the Sâr's controversial public image conveyed an awareness that the prophet's wisdom required disciples to appreciate it – intuition by the narcissist that he could not do without his mirror.

The second phase of the Sâr's career was marked by his development as an aesthete, and was defined by his activity as an art critic and organizer of Salons, which Ingeborg Kohn describes as "artistic extravaganzas that combined the visual arts, musical programs and theatrical performances."[79]

Yet when not confined to the domain of ostentatious exhibitions and performances – celebrating Wagner and popularizing elitist art – Péladan used his works as vehicles to voice his anti-Republican sentiments. An enemy of Jules Ferry and his policy of colonial expansion, the Sâr was similarly antagonistic to Pope Leo XIII, whom he saw as too tepid a partisan of the Royalist agenda. Péladan's positions on divorce, his denunciations of tauromachy, his belief that the Papacy need not be centered in Italy but that it should represent Catholicism worldwide were themes he incorporated into his polemical fictional works. In his later novels, Péladan's heroes embark on reckless political intrigues, ill-thought-out campaigns that inevitably meet with failure.

The derision that usually greeted Péladan's unsuccessful forays into public life no doubt caused him to refocus his proselytizing efforts. Not surprisingly, the final phase of Péladan's authorial development saw his heroes leave the treacherous world of political agitation in favor of the controlled domain of occult Catholic pedagogy. Notwithstanding the Sâr's profession of adherence to church orthodoxy, he defined his role as restoring the original purity of Catholic doctrine, returning the faithful to the integrity of the church's foundational principles. Until the end, Péladan perceived his role as an enlightened pastoral oracle, a visionary whose superiority was proved by the generous bestowal of his wisdom. But in his conception of the Magus as a missionary and a teacher, Péladan was finally able to embrace the idea of sacrifice and service.

In his fiction, Péladan ultimately shows how magic and religion combine in a syncretistic fusion, as the Rosicrucian brotherhood that his protagonist, Mérodack, establishes seeks to advance the Catholic principles that the church, as an institution, could not implement. From singularity to community – from individual impotence to group action – magic is increasingly utilized as a tool that ameliorates and instructs. Masters of arcane teaching still constitute an aristocracy, but they make common cause to promote art and thwart iniquity. Acting in imitation of Christ, the Magus accepts the noblest hardship in the immolation of his pride. Thus, Péladan's sage displays his greatness in acquiescing to his diminishment "for the highest expression of the will is to consent to pain and death even at the expense of one's dignity. There is nothing higher than self-sacrifice on behalf of an impersonal 'everyone.'"[80]

Magic as power

However, at the outset, the Sâr seemed disinclined to accept such fraternalist self-abnegation, and in the opening chapter of *Comment on devient mage*, he conveys no Christian self-deprecation. Despite denying the heterodoxy of his beliefs – despite professing submission to Catholic doctrine – the object of the Sâr's encomium is his own worthiness and glory. While Christophe Beaufils notes that Péladan came from "old Protestant stock"[81] and counted among his ancestors shoemakers, farmers, and hatters, the Sâr himself stressed his affiliation "with the sacred race of the Chaldeans."[82]

Already defining the Magus's role as both tutelary and sacerdotal, Péladan claims that studying occult tradition accomplishes a second baptism. While the sacrament washes away original sin, magic absolves the initiate of the blemishes of social conditioning, undoing the damage caused by a university education, by the homogenizing effects of military training, rescuing the neophyte from the ignominy of a career in politics or journalism.

Personality types governed by planetary influence and labeled with the names of the leading characters in the *Ethopée*, Péladan's students are divided by seven astral signs, determinants of temperament, special skills, and vulnerabilities. While describing the neophyte as a child of the constellations, Péladan claims that magic is a technique which, when mastered, can counteract "the malignant influence of a star that determines in an individual his irresistible propensities."[83] More than the forces of astrological predestination, what Péladan deplores are the baneful effects of socialization. In frequenting the racetrack, the brothel, the *café-concert*, the gaming table, Péladan's disciple succumbs to the lure of stupefying pleasures. It is in order to combat these deleterious influences that the Sâr lays out his program of magic as metaphysical hygiene, returning the catechumen to a state of innocence before undertaking his regimen of spiritual retraining. Péladan contrasts the world of men, with its vices and distractions, and the exclusive realm of the occultist, set apart by secret knowledge.

In *L'Occulte catholique* (*The Catholic Occultist* 1902), Péladan's decries magic's appeal as spectacle or show, satisfying a practitioner's desires to mystify and dazzle. He denounces the use of magic to enrich oneself and enslave another: "Grandier's enchanted Rose, Flamel's acts of transmutation: these are what sustained the Maréchal de Rais in his abominable undertakings and what continue to dazzle the minds of weak-minded people up to the present day."[84] But elsewhere in his writing, Péladan exalts the Magus as dramatic hero, whose displays of esoteric skills enchant and terrify his peers.

Despite pro forma condemnations of magic as performative virtuosity, Péladan uses his fiction to showcase the Magus's dramatic capabilities. Péladan's alter ego, the impenetrable Mérodack, exhibits an impressive array of arcane skills: harnessing magnetic energies to disarm an adversary, observing disturbances on the astral plane, using a clairvoyant to recount the details of a secret crime, performing insufflations to mitigate the trauma of a victim. After he disables a perpetrator, spell-casting prepares for Mérodack's fashioning an effigy or *Volt*, a wax figurine which, when violently manipulated, carries out the execution of the malefactor. Metonymy as magic – the manufacture of statuettes made with teeth and nails, the deciduous body parts of one's enemy – compels an evacuation of "the astral body of the bewitched, drawn out by impalpable threads, expelled by the winds of attraction."[85] Attacked with pincers, thorns, knives, shards of glass, or a headband encircling the skull, an evildoer is burned, impaled, or crushed – dying, as Jules Bois writes, "at the same time that the last vestiges of his wax double are melting away."[86]

While Péladan initially conceived of magic as skills that proved mastery and conferred election, his early works still adumbrate a realization of the limitations of occult power. Thus, the use of magic in *Le Vice suprême* expresses Péladan's opinion that the secret arts are practiced predominantly for apotropaic or retributive purposes, killing the wicked, exacting a belated punishment, exalting the unforgiving self of a brooding necromancer. Indeed, in Péladan's initial representations, the Magus is almost indistinguishable from the sorcerer, driven by hatred "to sacrifice the joys of life in order to repay evil with evil."[87] Scornful and self-glorifying, Mérodack is diminished by his narcissism, transfixed by the exceptionality of his knowledge and the scope of his powers. In his early incarnations, he is the opposite of the true spiritual seeker. As Péladan writes: "In the domain of magic, man seeks himself instead of God, and what he finds is often madness or another cause of his perdition."[88]

A disciple and admirer of Eliphas Lévi, Péladan studied the clavicles and grimoires in order to master techniques that isolated and protected. Control over what Lévi calls "the great instrument of magic" equips the thaumaturge with powers that are primarily defensive. Rather than multiplying his force for good, integrating him into a circle of adepts who propagate virtue, wisdom, and health, the mastery of magic and disposition of the Azoth combat the contagion of vice, thwarting the action of magnetic currents whose effect, as Lévi says, "is to attract and excite impressionable people with overwrought nerves and temperaments disposing them to hallucinations or hysteria."[89]

The Sâr's protagonist shuns the society of men and only mingles with the profane in order to fight the evils that infect them. In *Le Vice suprême*, Mérodack wishes to administer a Mithridatic inoculation against the tepid iniquity of his contemporaries and so chooses to live among princesses of sacrilege and artists of perversion. Succumbing to "his curiosity about evil," he can do no more than delay the impending collapse of western culture. In Péladan's inaugural novel, the Magus acquires strength only when he works in cooperation with a priest and when the two establish jointly a confraternity of geniuses and visionaries. As Rabbi Sichem, Mérodack's mentor, says: "However powerful he may be over individuals, the Magus cannot act on the multitudes unless he works with people of pure will, unless he forms part of a magnetic chain."[90]

Magic as performance

While Péladan's Magus admits reluctantly the need to work with other people, becoming a single link in the chain of enlightened beings, the Sâr himself was temperamentally ill-suited to a life of solitary occult study. Like Péladan's biographers, who describe him as a consummately public figure, historians of the Decadence comment on the Sâr's cultivated eccentricities. Péladan's abandonment of his view of magic as secret practice was surely in part motivated by his exhibitionist proclivities. Transposed as his persona, the Sâr presents an image of the Magus as an incongruously august figure with his striking features and strange apparel.

Mérodack's initial manifestation at a social gathering in *Le Vice suprême* is a moment of hierophanic drama, a *coup de théâtre* carefully orchestrated, eliciting wonderment and stupefaction among the disabused participants. With flowing, ebony curls veiling his forehead, with his hypnotizing gaze, his nose "with its gentle Judaic curve," with the red slash of his mouth, and his beard divided "in two points," Mérodack's entrance arrests conversation; "his appearance astounded the assembly."[91] Like Péladan himself, who produced astonishment in onlookers with his vestimentary strangeness, his hirsutism, and theatrical mannerisms, his protagonist constructs a persona calculated to produce the maximum effect.

Occultism, with its etymological connotation of hiddenness and secrecy, was not easily reconcilable with Péladan's grandiose extroversion. Many theories have been adduced for the Sâr's collaboration with Papus and Stanislas de Guaïta, who together founded L'Ordre de la Rose+Croix Kabbalistique in 1888. But one reason for what would escalate into Rosicrucian factionalism was the Sâr's refusal to be eclipsed by other prominent hermeticists. From the start, Péladan gravitated to more colorful literary figures – like his mentor, Barbey d'Aurévilly, the Constable of letters, prototype of the fin-de-siècle scandal-monger/dandy. Philosophical disagreements with Papus and Guaïta, who did not share the Sâr's commitment to a re-Christianized form of occultism, might have led to a falling out among the three notable adepts. Similarly, Péladan might have put off by Guaïta's role in the *affaire Boullan*, but most likely, he was motivated by a wish for greater visibility and fame.

Ingeborg Kohn suggests the Sâr was influenced by the popularity of Edouard Schuré's *The Great Initiates*, an occult treatise on the leading prophets and visionaries of history. Appealing to Péladan's messianism and hunger for publicity, the book might have prompted him to wish to present himself as the world's next spiritual leader. Having overcome his sense of oedipal inferiority on the occasion of Barbey's death, Péladan had noisily proclaimed his merit and preeminence: "No longer will I call anyone in this world Master," he had pledged. As Kohn writes, this was the moment for Péladan to "set up his own constabulary." An established figure in the world of esotericism, literature, and art, Péladan was ready to seek the notoriety he had desired for so long. "Why not as a *Grand Initié*," Kohn asks, "a prophet of his era?"[92]

Magic as art

It was this need for mirroring and approval that drove Péladan to combine art and esotericism. Indeed, as the founder of le Salon de la Rose+Croix, Péladan himself believed that the occult could attract the neophyte with the appeal of beauty and knowledge. Despite the Sâr's dubious taste, his vociferous excommunication of the Impressionists, his promotion of obscure artists with an indigence of talent, Péladan affirmed his role as a proselytizer whose responsibility was to strengthen the church and glorify the Savior, disseminating works that were other-worldly, elitist, and sublime. "In opposition to naturalism which was leading the West to its undoing, it was necessary to initiate a current of mystical art ablaze with Catholic fervor. Modern man had lost his faith, but the divine could still speak to atheists through the medium of a masterpiece."[93] This was the belief informing Péladan's establishment of a new brand of Rosicrucianism: since, across the Cross, Passion's symbol, lay the opening petals of Art's Rose.

Rigorous in its repudiation of nature and its celebration of spirituality as artifice, Péladan's aesthetic was enshrined in the exhibits of Rosicrucian art from which were banished all works of soul-degrading realism: "all ostensibly bourgeois subjects: historical scenes, military scenes, contemporary or rustic settings,"[94] as well as portraiture, humorous material, and canvases by women.

Despite its elitism, Péladan's conception of art as spiritual inspiration is what informs his changing image of fin-de-siècle magic, as it moves from a specialized body of knowledge, accessible to the few, to a means of uplifting the selfless in their crusade to spiritualize the many.

At the conclusion of *Le Vice suprême*, Father Alta admonishes his congregants not to lament the obsolescence of an aristocracy of birth or fortune. He claims that the modern-day Crusader wields a pen, and not a sword, affirms that as long as there are suffering people needing help, God's work is still unfinished.

Péladan's notion of art-as-magic effects a synthesis of faith and aesthetics, as creative work allows for a reconciliation of emotion and intelligence. Like Papus, who had complained about the anti-intellectualism of the church (*Le Diable et l'occultisme*), Péladan regrets the divorce between the Catholic's artistic sensibilities and his faith. Whereas Péladan lauds the mystic, guided by his conscience, not his intellect, he is saddened to see the church "show no interest in beauty."[95] This is why

Péladan idealizes the Magus for re-consecrating art used to usher in "the reign of God," for announcing the dawning era of the Holy Spirit, which would witness a second apotheosis of an adept functioning as a saint. Whereas religion had cultivated the soul and magic had disciplined the mind, the Magus will achieve a union assimilating the masterpiece and the miracle, likening "artists to priests, and the arts to sacred rites."[96]

In Péladan's conception of an aesthetic of holiness, he insists that the genius be an evangelist of Paracletism. Art will not be debased in order to appeal to the multitudes, expressing transcendent truths in meretricious imagery, dressing divine precepts in the cheap apparel of a common idiom, in order, Péladan says, to seduce "the rabble of humanity."[97] Instead, Catholic occultism will elevate an audience still incapable of appreciating it, touching them with a work "of so high an order that the people can sense it without actually understanding it."[98]

Over the course of Péladan's *Ethopée*, Mérodack assembles his band of Rosicrucian workers: sculptors of events, poets of dream, alchemists of history, those ready to advance their cause with unorthodox, forbidden weapons, willing to serve God "by what one calls from the pulpit the tools of the devil."[99] Yet Mérodack alone seems able to harness the essential energy, the telesma or "plastic mediator" of which Eliphas Lévi writes. However, his disciples, who are members of a modern-day guild of hermeticists, still use their art to influence what Péladan calls "second causes," actions whose consequences are manifested on the astral plane and whose effects, to the uninitiated, can often seem miraculous.

The disciples that Mérodack assembles adapt their work to sacred goals. For them, art is neither petitionary nor doxological. It is a blazon on the shield of the Christian warriors of the apocalypse, a tool used by those whom Mérodack calls "the hidden workers of the Holy Temple." Art affects what Papus describes as the higher levels of man's nature: "The Psychic Being that is guided by Instinct and that manifests itself to the Mind by Inspiration."[100] Guiding neophytes on their painful ascension to elevated consciousness, art ignites noble feelings that are ratified by the mind. As Mérodack advises his brothers: "We are conscious passions that assume mastery of unconscious passions. Using people's weaknesses, taking control of errant forces, we use our gifts to usher in the kingdom of the One who pardons everything that is conceived by intelligence and consented to by charity."[101]

In the final volumes of his series, Péladan shows that the Magus's noblest aspiration is the disciplined sculpting of his identity, sublimating the instincts, raising the mind toward God so that the soul becomes a masterpiece. Abjuring the showy feats of spell-casting, spirit summoning, the transmutation of base material, the thaumaturge returns to the arena where true occult operations take place – applying his will as the Philosopher's Stone that transforms directionlessness into strength, confusion into vision, and accident into destiny. Thus, the highest form of art is the perfection of the self: "All true magic is performed in the Magus. He is his own phenomenon, the object of his own conquest."[102] Yet this refinement of identity brings a realization that the Magus cannot rise to a higher plane unless he first engages with his fellow-men in an attempt to lift them up.

Magic as politics

While the Magus's talents are best utilized in the purification of his soul, Péladan shows that when his intelligence is directed outward and his arcane powers are trained on the world, his ambitions become misguided and his projects always fail. However worthy their objective and rarefied their skills, the Rosicrucian brotherhood that Mérodack commands is powerless to extend their influence into the realm of political intrigue. As Péladan remarks, the role of the Magus is not to change reality but himself: "Man becomes an angel by developing his highest faculty: ideality."[103]

In *Finis Latinorum*, Mérodack's ill-conceived conspiratorial effort to select the successor to Pope Leo XIII, to turn the church away from its missionary violence and democratizing values, had required the kind of Machiavellian practicality that is alien to the Magus. Plotting, after the expected death of Leo, to infiltrate the College of Cardinals and campaign for the installation of a pontiff willing to repudiate aggression and envisage the Vatican, not as an Italian entity, but as the center of a global Catholic community, Mérodack had reflected Péladan's own disagreements with church policy. Despite his professed acquiescence to Papal authority, Péladan had long voiced a wide array of complaints, advocating the abolition of bullfighting, arguing for a deprivileging of Judaism as the ancestral precursor of Catholic dogma, which the Sâr maintained owed as much to the Bhagavad Gita as to the Torah.

Apart from the fruitlessness of his plot, there is an unseemliness to the Magus's interference in matters of policy and church governance. As a follower of Mérodack proclaims in one of Péladan's more incongruous phrases: "there can be no possible copulation between our will and fatidic matters."[104]

Uncomfortable in the hothouse world of Decadent vice, Mérodack is also out of place in ecclesiastical cabals. More dignified and effective are his endorsements of the church as an instrument of irenics and ecumenicalism – not the church of Torquemada but the one recognizing the contributions of those "whom legend calls by divine names: Trismegistus, Orpheus, Moses, Manou, Zoroaster, those who bore witness to the light and revealed it to entire races."[105]

In proclamations like these, Péladan shows himself in agreement with Jules Bois's assessment: that the Magus should act as a prophet. Not becoming ensnared in campaigns to shape the force of destiny, he announces a future redeemed by spiritual prescience.

At the end of *Finis Latinorum*, Mérodack's brotherhood of illuminati see their plan miscarry for the most un-mystical of reasons. Identified by the Jesuits as a conduit to the spirit world, a certain Sister Marie de Gonzague of the convent of the Paraclete glimpses in a somnambulistic vision the dismal outcome of the Rosicrucians' machinations. Leo, whose demise was expected to be imminent, is seen to be alive for years into the future; Mérodack's covert work to elevate a successor is recognized as premature and pointless. The most impressive display of clairvoyance is exhibited, not by the Magus, but by an unschooled nun whose previous visions had been of her superiors' sexual indiscretions.

After being left to contemplate the ruins of their undertaking, Péladan's artist/magicians are forced to recognize the problematic wisdom of direct political action. Reorienting their efforts toward magic as personal enlightenment, they define art as inspiration, not as a platform for revolution. When Mérodack takes leave of his disciples, it is the thought of their company that consoles him, the confraternity of Oelohites that compensates for their fruitless undertaking. As the train carrying Mérodack departs from the station en route to Florence, his followers line the track and salute him as he passes. Their failed enterprise is only the manifest part of a hidden dialectic of occultations and appearances, the burial of seeds that one day will rend the earth, reborn as jewels: "*Gemmatus resurgam*," Mérodack's acolytes proclaim. While it may be unrealized in its execution, a noble project is still beautiful. Implementation may be unsuccessful and a justification still sublime. An action is still an art work irrespective of its consequence, and those who foretell a better future are poets of the Messiah. "Prophecy involves vision, not reason," as one avows. "as done by those who dream nobly, by those who strive heroically."[106]

Magic as teaching

When Mérodack summons his apostles to leave behind the secular world of intrigue, he defines their role as bridging the phenomenal and spiritual planes. To his followers, Mérodack explains that the Magus's work combines the eremiticism of the retreatant, the Dolorism of the martyr, and the performative virtuosity of the prophet. He describes a need to synthesize esotericism and religion, proposing that the hubris of the Mage be exchanged for the hybridity of the Catholic occultist. This new figure will be able to preach and pray, follow liturgy and decipher grimoires, uplift the heart and focus the mind, retreat into himself and then come out again, bestowing his insights on a community of seekers. As Mérodack and Father Alta are complementary halves of a mystic whole, the new Magus will perform a multiplicity of tasks that had once led men of God down different paths. Becoming "austere cenobites, monks who preach and teach," they will imprint *aristes* with the insignia of royalty and holiness.

To Mérodack, the adept is able to affect the future, not by tracing the bond between his physical and astral body, but by using his persuasiveness to inspire the thinking of his successors. Mérodack performs his greatest feats of magic in Péladan's first book, *Le Vice suprême*, when he uses magnetism to paralyze an attacker, charts an apostelematic map of his future, casts a spell on an evildoer. Thereafter, his role as figurehead is limited to assembling a group of acolytes whose later interventions will be more fruitful and effective. Mérodack compares himself to Moses, too infirm to reach the Promised Land, yet resolved to teach his followers how they themselves can complete the journey: "let us conclude that the hour has not yet come for our ideas to pass from potentiality into action."[107] The occult visionary may die and migrate to a shadow world while surviving as his word. As Péladan writes in a vindication of his role as an author: "writing prolongs discourse indefinitely; the abstract embraces the future as it does the present."[108]

In Péladan's later novels, the secret powers that were once withheld acquire value through their communication to another. How far Péladan has evolved in his depiction of the occult leader, a figure no longer isolated by narcissism and aloofness, a man whose goal is not self-aggrandizement, not the maximization of his difference. The highest purpose is not to glorify a being without peer but to work with those who serve a cause more deserving than the self; "*Non nobis, non nobis. Domine, sed nominis Tui gloriae soli.*"[109]

Magic as service

In his final novels, where he shows magic practiced, not in isolation, but communally, Péladan describes the initiate working with mistresses and colleagues. Women, earlier despised for ensnaring their lovers in a world of instinct, become inspirational helpers who refine man's intelligence and motivate achievement. In moving toward a view of magic as ministry and latria, Péladan advances his own ideas of sex magic and friendship magic. Once systematically anti-feminist, Péladan's later views include a conception of erotomancy that elevates the women formerly seen as base.

In *Comment on devient mage*, the advice given apprentices had involved minimizing contact with women. Desire, with its supervening sexual exertion and disappointment, had led Péladan to recommend that a woman be disembodied as an ideal, domesticated as a friend, evaporated as her perfume. The only worthwhile intercourse was the artist's conjugation with his work: "Art alone should satisfy your dreams. Live exclusively with masterpieces. Ask a woman only for her heart. Ask that she temper your sensibilities."[110]

Over time, however, as Péladan's views on magic became less elitist and exclusive, accommodating the possibility of comradeship and romance, the Sâr elaborated his unique idea of "sacred prostitution." Despite its condescension, Péladan's rehabilitation of the occult soulmate recognizes the intelligence and subjectivity of women acting in concert with the Magus. Péladan's notion of the mistress as sexual vessel and mystic weapon is encapsulated in his notion of *la fée* (the fairy) as the counterpart of *le mage*.

As early as *Le Vice suprême*, there is an occult explanation of desire's dynamic, with woman characterized as "an unconscious magnetizer who uses the law of sexual attraction." On the astral plane, desire acts an "an electric radiance," which, after targeting a woman, rebounds onto the person coveting her, causing what Mérodack calls, "a countershock."[111] Submitting to "her amorous servility," the woman becomes a magnetizer fully conscious of the occult energies she channels. Enemies of sublimity are crippled by the power of their guilty impulses, vanquished by women who see their vulnerability as "replacing a dagger with their love."[112] Placing themselves in the hands of their masters, Péladan's female characters become instruments of male magic, weapons cognizant of their destructive power. Practicing "selfless sexuality," the woman once patronized is raised up. No longer a blind, unconscious force of Schopenhauerian *Wille*, exiling man to the dark kingdom of instinctual automatism, women become helpmates and collaborators, "mystical lovers using their caresses, not simply as a source of pleasure, but as the instrument of the destiny of a doctrine – the source of pleasure for a despot who is all the more formidable since he is gentle, calm, incapable of cruelty, able to conceive of only the most elevated ideals."[113]

By the end of the *Ethopée*, Péladan has grown distant from his hero. While the author recognizes the value of comradeship and romance, Mérodack has not tempered his insistence that the Magus fortify his power by renouncing women's company. Summoning artists of the Gnosis, monks of the Ideal, he appeals to them to sacrifice desire to the perfection of the order. Péladan's own thinking reflects the schism within the Rosicrucian brotherhood, as Mérodack's followers reject his insistence on chastity and assert love's esoteric properties: "Love is an element of the Great Work," as one maintains.[114]

With the revalidation of sex, love, and partnership, Péladan's fictional corpus ends with the Magus's re-integration into the temporal world, as the initiate turns outward to serve humanity, not himself. Heroic and dehumanized, estranged by his absolutism from the brotherhood he founded, Mérodack alone clings to the notion of magic as uncompromising mysticism. Initially established as a separatist cult informed by the neo-Albigensian principles of abstinence, an embrace of death as deliverance from the body, the Rosicrucians renounce the ideal of Eros and accept the Christian notion of Agape, love of one's fellow man as strong as the love of oneself. From the untransmittable truths of occult teachings and the ineffability of private rapture, Péladan's works describe a descent back to the domain of service and solidarity, interdependence and communion with the fallen people one resembles.

As Denis de Rougemont writes, in this world, to love "is to shed selfishness and the desirous and anxious self; it means the death of the solitary human being, but it also means the birth of our neighbor."[115] What had been the marriage of Christ and the church, the visionary and his disciples, is re-enacted as the marriage of man and woman, the forging of a bond between friends. From magnifying the One, the unique being, *ipsissimus*, Péladan grounds his thinking again in the idea of a community of the faithful. Himself the author of a scholarly volume on Catharism (*Le Secret des troubadours* [*The Secret of the Troubadours*] 1906), Péladan models his own utopian order on the twelfth-century heretical movement, naming the fortress/sanctuary where Mérodack and his followers are housed after Montségur, the stronghold where the Albigensians had been headquartered. Mérodack also professes a Gnostic belief in the heterogeneity of earth and heaven, the soul's unhappy incarceration in a terrestrial body from which it seeks deliverance, an escape into the increate world of light, and a return to a prelapsarian state of spiritual unity. He, too, performs the ritual by which the Albigensians recognized one another, bestowing the Kiss of Peace, the

Consolamentum, by which they sealed their vow "to renounce the world, [...] to devote themselves to God alone, never to lie or take an oath, never to kill, or eat of an animal, and finally ever *to abstain, if married, from all contact with a wife.*"[116]

Thus, when Mérodack arrives at Montségur, "the Great Master, according to the Albigensian Rite of the Consolamentum, kneels in turn before each brother, kisses him on the mouth, and lifts him up again."[117]

Thereafter, the divergent practices of the two orders are more apparent. The Round Table, like that at which Arthur's knights assembled, is set with meat, along with the fruits and wine the brotherhood partakes of. Women, still banished from the company of the Elect, are evident in their embellishment of the castle, with tapestries sent by one illustrating the martyrdom of Saint Ursula, chasubles and sacerdotal ornaments provided by another, a bejeweled paten in the form of a rose and a cross at the center of which sparkled "an alchemical diamond."[118]

While resolving to abstain from procreation, the Rosicrucians are still forgiven for the sins of fornication and adultery because, as they claim, love inspires greater piety and creation, because it is "beautiful like a virtue" and strengthens "the striving for perfection."[119] When Mérodack invites his disciples to accept "The Way, the Life, and the Truth,"[120] they refuse, claiming that chastity murders art and that poetry is love's expression.

Along with indicating a moderation of his anti-feminism, Péladan's inclusion of women as artists' handmaidens confirms his view of magic collectively practiced as a religious aesthetic. The Magus who had worked alone with the alchemist's retort, who had poured over the hieroglyphs in the Arcana of the Tarot, becomes an artist whose special talents enrich the experience of his peers. Collaboratively authored, a magic artwork acquires a synesthetic fullness: the sculptor's clay is beautified by the poet's sense of eurhythmy; a writer's novel is structured by a musician's sense of a leitmotif from Wagner. Symmetries and tonalities create a universal harmony manifesting the analogy of the earthly and divine.

Fellow-artists become more than visionaries working together side by side. They are elements which, when combined, form something whole and indivisible, like the predestined gender complements which together form the Androgyne. Each artist sees his brother as one who mirrors and completes him: "the companion of his thought after being the companion of his soul, the brother of a work inspired by sacred ambition."[121]

On the social plane, this synergy produces art that is more complex, purer, and higher, greater than the sum of its components. On the theological level, it models the dynamic interplay of the will of man and the grace of God. Like his counterpart, Stanislas de Guaïta, Péladan's Magus climbs up and down Jacob's ladder, materializing his inspiration as a sacrament shared with consumers: *"the spirit clothes itself to come down and undresses to rise up."*[122]

For Péladan, the work of art serves a referential purpose since, as a body, it evokes a spiritual perfection that it only partially manifests. Like the woman who, in the *Ethopée*, is honored and respected, it is a terrestrial thing inspiring longings for the sublime. The axial orientation of Péladan's work, moving from magic to religion, abandons the incommunicability of Ain Soph for the accessibility of literary language. Likewise, horizontally, it abandons the exclusivity of arcane knowledge in order to embrace the exotericism of art as a proselytizing agent. Péladan proposes that in the coming era of the Holy Spirit, there will be a conflation of the saint and thaumaturge who form *une aristie nouvelle* and carry on the soteriological work of Christ. He echoes Huysmans in proclaiming that art aims at reflecting God's glory, reproducing "the divinity even in its feeble mirror." While it diminishes the uncompassed majesty of Creation, art still strives to achieve perfection, becoming "identical to God himself." Mérodack also refers to his brothers as "profound mirrors" who capture the divine light and reflect it in "the radiance of a masterpiece."[123] Who among us, he asks, would be the shadow of himself "without the book, the monument, the statue, or the painting?" Since illumination comes from God, "let us become luminous; let us work."[124]

Conclusion

Ingeborg Kohn, in tracing Péladan's career trajectory as a creator and an occultist, notes the pivotal moment when the Sâr first sought a reconciliation of art and magic. Collaborating with Papus, Jules Bois, and Stanislas de Guaïta, Péladan had initially adopted a brand of Rosicrucianism indebted to Eliphas Lévi, who, Kohn says, "based his occult system on the Kabbalah, Swedenborg, the *Corpus Hermeticum*, and the Tarot."[125] However, for numerous reasons including his friends' distaste for the Sâr's flamboyance and the exchange of spells between Huysmans and Boullan, Péladan had turned away from the secrecy of esotericism and had sought instead to harness creative work to a campaign of Catholic reform. "With the founding of *L'Ordre de la Rose+Croix et Kabbalistique* in 1888, there began a new period in Péladan's career, characterized by an intense search for spiritual values, and for ways [...] to achieve a new synthesis between religion and art."[126]

As with Mérodack, Péladan's advocacy of a spiritual aesthetic largely came to nothing. With his mania for Wagner, his bombastic manifestoes, and preposterous persona, he earned the ridicule of his detractors, not the reverence of his acolytes. Péladan's Salons were responsible for showcasing the Decadent sensibility of Fernand Khnopff and for promoting painters who imitated Gustave Moreau and the Pre-Raphaelites. But over time, critics concluded that Péladan championed art that was derivative, and excoriated him for his fatuousness, pomposity, and snobbery. As Kohn wonders, with Péladan's "meridional expansiveness, overbearing nature, effusive mannerisms, and florid [. . .] prose, [..] how could one take the Sâr seriously?"[127]

Yet in his fiction, Péladan was unique in proposing a synthesis of Catholic orthodoxy and occultism as the goal the Magus strives for. Having begun by embracing magic because it proved superiority and conferred power, Péladan had then shown himself dissatisfied with occultism's emphasis on secrecy. Temperamentally disposed to theatrical self-display, the Sâr had gravitated toward a version of magic that assigned precedence to spectacle. An outlandish public figure, Péladan had also stressed his conviction that the Magus's greatest work of art was the perfection of his soul.

Péladan's exhibitionism had led him to take on the work of art critic, arranging the Salons at which his own person was on display. The impulse to involve himself in public causes and social actions had prompted fantasies, illustrated in several of his novels, to conspire to affect affairs of state and set the course of Vatican policy. But the meticulousness and secrecy required of these machinations had been beyond the Sâr's abilities, resulting in the miscarriage of his plans. Ultimately, Péladan's view of magic as privilege and duty had caused a reconciliation of esotericism with a view of Catholicism as service. Péladan's hero may insist on inhuman principle and purity, but the author himself professes greater fraternalism and compassion.

At the conclusion of *La Vertu suprême*, Mérodack – having alienated his disciples by requiring of them the abstinence practiced by their Albigensian forebears – sets out in the twilight with the gloomy gait of Ahasuerus. Intransigent, uncompromising, arrogant, superhuman, he re-enters the immaculacy of his solitude. But having founded the brotherhood and promulgated an ideal of initiatic art, he embarks in a night illuminated by a star of hope and promise: "grandson of the Magi who

came to Bethlehem," he is a witness and a precursor.[128] Having celebrated exceptionality, Péladan elevates the Magus as a genius whose
superiority is isolating, then shows him exiled from the world, as his
work is completed by his followers.

As an expression of the fin-de-siècle goal of the self refashioned as a
masterpiece, the Magus in Péladan had initially become his own ideal.
Lofty, uncommunicative, he had left the realm of literature in order to
immure himself in a fortress of knowledge shared with no one. Yet in
choosing to act as a mentor, a pedagogue, and prophet, Péladan's character finally puts magic to use in the service of other people. In submitting
to the authority of the church, he acknowledges that revelation supersedes occultism's secret knowledge. Noting that his predecessors had
worshipped at the scene of the Nativity, he proclaims: "The adoration
of the Magi marks the abdication of esotericism to the Incarnation of
the Truth."[129] Like his Decadent peers, Péladan foresaw the approaching
world's end, had foretold the imminent extinction of a vitiated western
culture. But the *Finis Latinorum* that is augured by the prophet also
announces the beginning of a new age of intelligence and holiness, the
era of the Paraclete when saints would be theosophists and artists. This
is the gospel spread by Péladan's transfigured Magus: pride that dies in
order to be reborn as devotion, subordination of an exalted self to the
incommensurability of the divine, loss of the superior, lonely man in
the "*Infinitas Christi*."[130]

4
The Mystic

Eugène Vintras and the Order of Mercy

The history of fin-de-siècle mysticism

The historical backdrop against which Eugène Vintras's bizarre heretical cult made its first appearance in France in the 1840s was one marked by a forceful resurgence of secular rationalism. Opposing Auguste Comte's Positivist assertion of mankind's progress toward scientific enlightenment, the fin-de-siècle mystics who were influenced by Vintras vaunted a higher knowledge they claimed was obtainable only from divine sources, insights that were yielded only by non-rational intuition. Instead of a confident march toward technological mastery, Vintras's followers believed that time itself was ending, overturning governments, hurling a church corrupted by materialism into the abyss of fire that would open with the coming apocalypse.

At the turn of the century, when Vintras's teachings began to exercise their greatest power among Catholic artists and intellectuals, the rise of Republicanism and scientific reason produced a backlash that drew the disaffected to the heretical prophet's message. In the aftermath of the 1879 election, with the rise of Jules Grévy, the declining political influence of the Royalists was further sealed by the death of the Count of Chambord, definitively dashing Legitimist hopes for a re-accession of the king. Despite the persistence of factionalist conflict between Radicals and Moderates, the latter assumed continuity of power between 1879 and 1885 when, under the leadership of Jules Ferry, a series of liberal laws was enacted. During the time of the Third Republic, the influence of the aristocracy diminished significantly in a government administered by members of the middle class, "lawyers or physicians, teachers or journalists, industrialists or financiers – well-educated and comfortably well-to-do" – but having "no noblemen or clergy-men among them."[1]

Among the reform laws passed at this time, the ideal of democratic education endorsed by the state was countered by vigorous expressions of anti-intellectualism on the part of reactionary Catholic artists. Superior to the profane insights gained by analytical reason, they believed, were the inexpressible truths unearthed in dreams, glimpsed in ecstatic visions, or received directly from God. Republicanism, with its penchant toward hierarchical leveling, was rejected in favor of the re-establishment of a new elite comprised of prophets and Mages. Accompanying the decay of a hereditary aristocracy of breeding was the ascendancy of a plutocracy of Philistines, loutish bourgeois millionaires besotted by self-indulgence, unmindful of the beauties of the transcendental, ignorant of the true nobility of self-denial. Caricatures of these figures began to proliferate in the literature of the period, from Villiers de l'Isle-Adam's Tribulat Bonhomet to Octave Mirbeau's Isidore Lechat. In the minds of authors and zealots, charity and altruism, suffocated by an atrophy of the soul, were sacrificed as the price exacted by scientific progress. This new materialist ideology, as Carlton Hayes has noted, fostered "popular indifference to Christian [...] practices by concentrating attention upon the 'marvels' of human achievement, by exalting engineers over preachers or priests, and by stimulating a greater ambition for creature comforts than for personal holiness."[2]

In reacting against the laicizing influence of liberal democracy, the church during the pontificate of Pius IX (1846–78) began to warn of the dangers of modern civilization. In his 1864 encyclical *Quanta Cura* and the accompanying Syllabus of Errors, Pius condemned the enshrinement of individualism, intellectual independence unguided by church teachings. Inveighing against free-thinkers and agnostics, bemoaning the noxious diffusion of anti-clericalism, deploring the anarchic irreverence of Freemasons, who advocated a relativist view of religions – all seen as superfluous and interchangeable – Pius had called for a return to the ideal of a Christian state, one in which the authority of Catholic leaders was recognized as paramount. As a matter of dogma, Pius's position was not new, but it still reinforced popular perceptions of the Church's defensive inflexibility.

Perhaps the matter that most galvanized the antagonism of fin-de-siècle mystics toward the church and that drew the most vehement response from Vintras himself was Pius's promulgation of the doctrine of Papal infallibility. In the 1869 Vatican Council, Pius had advanced the claim that, when speaking *ex cathedra*, the Pope, "by virtue of his supreme apostolic authority," was possessed "of that infallibility with which the Divine Redeemer willed that his Church should be endowed for defining faith or morals."[3]

Excoriating the Pope for his hubris, Vintras responded by decrying the institutional arrogance of church leaders more intent, he alleged, on consolidating their authority than on articulating sound principle. Affirming the inherent doctrinal validity of the Immaculate Conception, Vintras denounced the Pope for refusing "the divine authority of a sacredly explicit resolution." Vintras questioned the need to invoke the Pope's apostolic authority in upholding dogma whose incontrovertibility seemed to require no church approval, assailing what he denounced as this "act of lèse-majesté against God."[4]

The Decadents who, in succeeding generations, adopted Vintras's views, would echo the prophet's hostility toward Rome, integrating it into their own notions of decentralized religion. Believing in the heightened spirituality of the exceptional individual whose wisdom had been tested by the fire of self-discipline, they championed the figure of the mystic, who might be obedient to the church but was also more enlightened than its leaders.

In his analysis of the origins of the Vintrasian cult, Richard Griffiths notes the Decadents' embrace of a new form of Gnosticism. Vatic precursors, Griffiths says, they believed themselves to be in possession of "higher knowledge [...] not attainable by ordinary intellectual processes but only by spiritual enlightenment." Rather than acknowledge the infallibility of the Pope – able to think for his flock, anxious to make decisions on matters of faith, insistent on prescribing an understanding of the divine that disallowed direct experience – Vintras and his followers invoked the gifts of the seer, asserting his direct access to the realm of the miraculous. This sense of "being a minority," Griffiths writes, "may have been one of the causes for the desire which we often find in them, a desire to be themselves the depositaries of a true knowledge unknown to others."[5]

It is ironic that Vintras should have deplored the presumptuousness of Papal inerrancy while proclaiming himself to be a manifestation of the prophet Elijah. Appointing himself as the founder of a new church, Vintras also claimed to disseminate divine truths received in dialogues with Christ. However, his disaffection for the Vatican left an indelible mark on his successors. Decadent mystics, influenced by the secret disclosed by the Virgin in an apparition to the shepherdess Melanie in La Salette, had cited her denunciation of a clergy tainted by materialism, pandering to the wealthy, the *prêtres propriétaires* (property-owning priests) against whom Léon Bloy would fulminate in *Le Sang du Pauvre* (*The Blood of the Poor*).

To the Decadents, the appeal of this once-unlettered vagrant is traceable to Vintras's promotion of a religion rooted in a personal apprehension of the divine, a controversial heterodoxy that glorified sacrifice and extolled the penitential suffering that distinguished an aristocracy of holiness from a bourgeoisie of hedonism. Disenchanted with Republicanism and the moderating influence of leaders like Ferry, exasperated by the waning influence of traditional Catholicism and by the liberalizing of laws on the press, the Decadents were strengthened in their Restorationist aspirations, their orientation toward a religion shaped by esotericism, their quest for secret knowledge divulged only to a privileged few. Like Vintras, the Decadents professed beliefs not sanctioned by the Pope, sought knowledge not mediated and approved by church fathers. Wishing to reformulate an Eternal Gospel delivered to them directly, they were resolved to heed, not the pronouncements of the Vatican, but the voice of Christ himself.

Despite their penchant toward intellectual elitism, what distinguished the thinking of the writers most profoundly influenced by Vintras was a redefinition of hierarchy that would henceforth be modeled on Christ's prophesied inversion of positions of power – when, in the end time, the first would be last and the last would be first. Appealing to aristocrats whose secular influence had been diminishing was the idea of a new hierarchy of genius, devotion, and service. Vintras had attacked the church as a sclerotic institution serving only the wealthy, seeking only to preserve its own power, neglecting the wretched whom Jesus had come to save. In the new hierarchy announced in his teachings, the traditionally downtrodden – women and the poor – would be accorded the status of a new elect. Even as their suffering and anonymity, their oppression and neglect continued unabated in this world, they would perform work that hastened the Messiah's return. To be sure, this new vision of an eschatological hierarchy was the mirror opposite of the social hierarchy discredited by this time. Yet it was an order that disempowered aristocrats and Catholic mystics admired, one whose institution they ratified, and whose benefits they reaped.

Eugène Vintras and the Order of Mercy

As for the prophet whose heretical teachings shaped the views of the Decadent mystics, history has it that on August 6, 1839, there appeared to this unprepossessing manager of a cardboard factory in the little town of Tilly a threadbare figure bearing a cryptic message. Invisible to outsiders, this unnamed old man came to Vintras in a series of ever more luminous visitations. Subsequently revealed as Michael, the archangel, the supernatural host warned of the impending world's end. Vintras went on to receive other oracular announcements, accusations impugning the legitimacy of the royal family, invocations of divine vengeance on *Ninevah, the Harlot* – Paris, the wanton Babylon of the corrupted fin de siècle – calls for the fiery destruction of the Church of Rome, perverter of sacred dogma, city of abomination. The tocsin sounds, as Vintras writes in his apocalyptic vision: paving stones rip loose, dungeon doors burst open, chains break, and palaces shake like the leaves of a white poplar, ciboria are overturned, sanctified Hosts fly away, chalices roll on flagstones, and altars sweat drops of blood and poison.

Born in Bayeux in 1807, Vintras, in his early life, led an unremarkable existence as a vagrant factotum, hawking lace and cotton print, selling stolen goods, serving brief prison sentences for various misdemeanors, relocating first to Paris, then to Caen. Maurice Garçon, in his biography of the prophet, sees little foreshadowing of Vintras's later notoriety: "No truly serious misdeeds can be imputed to him. Timid in his acts of larceny, he lived by doing whatever was expedient."[6] An unexpected awakening of Vintras's faith in 1838, followed by a pilgrimage to La Délivrande later in that year, augurs little of Vintras's later audiences with angels.

Vintras's acquaintance with a certain Ferdinard Geoffroi, a notary distinguished as much by fraudulent business dealings as by his legitimist leanings and messages from John the Baptist, began in Caen in 1837. Bringing to their association "his legal knowledge, his taste for adventure, certain singular relationships, and an invaluable erudition,"[7] Geoffroi impressed Vintras with his connection to various mystical societies and his commitment to the Naundorff cause. It was through his relationship with Geoffroi that the fin-de-siècle visionary first conceived of the establishment of the Order of Mercy, intuiting the glorious Parousia to come. Vintras's unusual spiritual temperament and political proclivities were already in place when, two years later in his home in Tilly, he received the first of the hagiophanic visions that would inform his later teachings.

Biographers like Garçon and historians of the era have had difficulty explaining the transformation of this unschooled character into the incarnation of the prophet Elijah, as Vintras professed himself to be. An often lyrically gifted visionary, Vintras evolved from his modest origins into a mystical heretic whose doctrine was fiercely denounced by the church and whose eschatological vaticinations exercised consider-able influence over important writers of the era. Casting himself as a successor to the second-century prophet Montanus, who also entered into a state of ecstasy in order to transmit pronouncements from the Holy Spirit, Vintras preached the dawning of the Third Age of the Paraclete, etymologically identified as the Comforter and Intercessor, whose coming would signal an end to the age of the salvatory Passion.

From being "the bastard child of a poor working girl,"[8] an often jobless transient, and occasional petty criminal, Vintras emerged as an electrifying orator and prodigious Biblical scholar, whose charisma and intellect enthralled his followers. Despite being dismissed by critics as a copycat and fraud, Vintras propounded an apocalyptic doctrine that exercised immense appeal. In proclaiming a non-rational apprehension of the divine, in replacing the obsolete hierarchy of an hereditary aristocracy with a spiritual hierarchy of martyrs and visionaries, he prophesied the end of a world in which his followers felt themselves strangers and the coming of a new age when their values would be vindicated.

Consistent with the behavior of cultists formalizing their rebirth and entry into a true church by abandoning an old identity and severing existing social ties, Vintras's disciples were re-christened with the name of an angel – a name, forgotten, he maintained, at the time of their spirit's descent and imprisonment in the flesh. Generalizing his own role as *the Organ*, adopting the name Sthrathanaël, Vintras assembled his core congregation in Tilly in 1839, where he installed a sanctuary upholstered in crimson velvet, dedicated an altar to the Sacred Heart of Jesus and another to the Virgin, and began disseminating the teachings that would revolutionize his countrymen. "The reign which is at hand is no longer the reign of fear and calculation. It depends entirely on Grace, but it offers men all the beauty, riches, and delights of heaven, as much as can be experienced by a creature exiled to the world of men. This kingdom is the kingdom of Love. The Holy Spirit will spread over a regenerated world the divine fires of an ardent charity, one awaited by all those inwardly lamenting the injustice, the selfishness, and the rapacity of the people of this unhappy century."[9]

As Vintras's colloquies with angels became more frequent and better publicized, he increasingly attracted the censure of the church. From the outset, Vintras had professed unwavering adherence to Catholic ortho-doxy. Of the prophet's vision of the glorious inauguration of the age of the Paraclete, Vintras's lieutenant had admonished followers: "Do not believe this future will bring any change to the church of Jesus Christ, to its dogmas, its sacraments, its moral philosophy, or its worship. It will not be a new religion but rather the triumph of the present one: Catholic and Apostolic."[10] However, Vintras's dialogues with saints, his manufacture of miraculous Hosts inscribed, he insisted, with letters written in Christ's blood, resulted first in his imprisonment for fraud in 1842 and then his excommunication and relocation to Belgium and later to London, where he maintained his church in exile.

In *L'Eternel Evangile* (*The Eternal Gospel*), Vintras begins by reinterpreting Biblical narrative, retelling the Genesis story, describing the revolt by Lucibel, Vintras's name for the Angel of Light, recounting the Fall and man's banishment from Paradise. Identifying himself as the last of the Old Testament prophets ("Behold, I will send before you Elijah the prophet before the great and terrible day of the Lord comes" *Malachi* 4.5), Vintras asserts the need for a new Gospel whereby evil will be struck down, the serpent crushed underfoot, and the messianic Eagle will be freed and given flight. The Seven Thunders of Truth, which an angel had ordered sealed, will be released, so that the scroll that Vintras reads will be terrible and solacing, "bitter to [the] stomach but sweet as honey in [the] mouth" (*Revelation* 10.8).

As the vessel in which Elijah manifests himself to man, Vintras foretells matter's rarefaction into light, the suffering body's volatilization, crucified flesh resurrected as *pneuma*, insufflating man's soul and buoying the wings of the Holy Spirit. "Elijah came in the alliance of the body-people, but he will return with the generation of the soul-people."[11]

In Vintras's oceanic, often unintelligible prose, he describes Elijah's understanding the generative principle of creation, his seeing material bodies turned into prayer, atoms of mud made pure like baptismal tears. Watching the fermenting acceleration of corporeal beings through the necessary changes of form, he observes bodies being rendered incorruptible, the beatified entering into the celestial spheres "without having to undergo first their soul's stagnation." The Elect, enjoying "the full leavening of the leaven,"[12] experience the combustion of the Just, becoming "the devout who rise in flames."[13]

Following the Dolorist era when an embodied God was conceived, was born, and died to redeem the world, the age of the Paraclete will witness a eugenic ennoblement of the chosen, an absolution of the sexual act which, having caused man's fall, will allow him to rise again. In the Third Age, only an aristocracy of pure souls will be fruitful. "The action of the Paraclete," says the astrologer, Gévingey, in Huysmans's *Là-bas*, "will extend to the generative principle; the divine life will sanctify those organs which will procreate only the elect, beings exempt of original sin and no longer needing to be tested in the furnace of humiliation. This is the doctrine of the prophet Vintras, that extraordinary illiterate who wrote so many solemn and ardent pages."[14]

Despite such presentiments, Huysmans's gloomy characters feel the time is far away when the Reign of Fire will succeed an era of mediocrity and greed, when Jesus will appear "in a whirlwind of glorious meteors."[15] The utopia Vintras foretells seems an impossible chimera in a fin de siècle hallowing the triumph of materialism, money worship condemning the wretched to be despoiled and mocked by rich bourgeois. Before the elevation of the *soul-people*, sin's scoria must be burned away, fired in the crucible of suffering, consumed in the furnace of humiliation.

The suffering woman

In his book *Holy Tears, Holy Blood*, Richard D. E. Burton remarks on a singular phenomenon occurring in France in the latter half of the nineteenth century. Believing it was their duty to carry on the work of the Passion, many French women had welcomed unspeakable torments, "not just for their own individual salvation, but more pertinently, for that of their nonbelieving fellow countrymen and women for whose sake they willingly assumed, and even actively sought out, pain [...] and ultimately death in order to redeem them – literally 'buy them back.'"[16] When Vintras promoted women to positions of importance in his church – when he assigned them the responsibility of undoing the original sin they had caused – he accorded them new influence while defining their role as expiatory victims whose suffering was uniquely efficacious. While, for Vintras and his followers, women were still seen as intellectually inferior, inarticulate beings governed by instinct, they were afforded an immediate apprehension of the divine that was denied men dominated by their analytical faculties. Compassionate and merciful, given to weeping and bleeding, women suffered in silence to redeem the sins of their children, yet they knew God in a way that was disallowed male priests.

Not surprisingly, among the tenets of Vintrasianism that most appealed to the mystic writers of the fin de siècle was the promotion of the Virgin Mary as merciful intercessor. Vintras's cult of Mary goes beyond familiar Catholic hyperdulia, in designating all women as mediators whose suffering brings pardon and delivers grace. As Richard Griffiths notes, Vintras associates Mary with the Gnostic conception of

Sophia, who, in her higher form, had remained above, "in the sphere of light," and who, in her lower form, had been trapped in the realm of darkness and corporeity. "Through this duality *Sophia* became the fallen divinity through whom the mingling of light and dark, of spirit and matter, in the world, had been achieved; she was also seen as the intermediary between the lower and higher worlds and an instrument of redemption."[17] Griffiths cites a passage from the text of the *Sacrifice Provictimal de Marie*, one of Vintrasism's central rites, to illustrate a woman's role in effecting man's spiritual elevation: "Oh, created Wisdom, you who have forever been the unchanging reflection of Wisdom Increate, it was thanks to your prayers and maternal mediation that the law of penitence allowed us to hope for our re-ascension, to hope that we will attain our supreme end by being created anew as angels."[18]

Vintras may rejoice in the consecration of *la Femme Assomptive* (the Assumptive Woman), who, in emulating Mary, catalyzes evil into forgiveness. But while men are purified as seraphs and fly into immateriality, woman's role is to remain below and bring forth sons condemned to die. Vintras anticipates the fin-de-siècle filiation of Eve and Mary, both afflicted with the pain of childbearing, giving birth to offspring they mourn forever.

In Vintras, man remakes himself in the image of his Creator, becoming spiritualized as a reflection of the Holy Spirit, a wing, a flame, a breath. "Despite all human defects, this Spirit-Man remains no less an Angel, and as a consequence, more justly and more perfectly similar to Jesus Christ. Without ceasing to be God, the Word was made flesh, and the Angel, without ceasing to be an Angel, was joined hypostatically with the flesh made man."[19] Women, on the other hand, eternally engender suffering bodies. So when, in Vintras's Gospel, Mary stands at the foot of Christ's gibbet, she says her eyes are opened, "and I saw that my maternity was not extinguished and that my unspeakable tortures were those of a new childbirth."[20]

Preceding the death of Decadence when flesh will be cast off, suffering intensifies so that the spirit is released. In *Là-bas*, Huysmans describes his admiration for the painter Matthias Grünewald, whose Crucifixion shows the transformation of man into divinity. Radiating out of the cloaca of the ignoble body churning with sanies, dissolving into sweat and serosity, is the miraculous charity that redeems. According to Huysmans, Grünewald's genius is to capture the moment when the Son gives way to the Spirit, and when corporeity turns into love. Apocalyptic visionaries like Vintras embrace this sense of salutary catastrophism, as humanity's rebirth comes only after the flesh is broken down. Sacrilege on a cosmic scales, horror, monstrousness, and perversion are harbingers of the decisive moment when the Messiah will return to expunge them. Decadent mystics like Huysmans seek to identify the point where the soul emerges from the tortured body, demonstrating pain's efficacy as an agent of penitential transmutation. In Vintras, it is the Mater Dolorosa who accomplishes this theogony. Having given Angels to the Heavens and a Redeemer to Mankind, she will deify Creation: "I will bring forth gods from God."[21]

While women were assigned a central place in Vintras's church and were admitted to the priesthood in the Ordre de la Miséricorde, their privileged role was to suffer in the body so that the body could be transcended. As Huysmans writes, before seekers could experience a mystic fusion with the Lord, acceding to the ineffability of *unitive life*, it was necessary to pass through "the twilight of purgative life."[22] "Saints have a noisier, more expansive role, crisscrossing the world, creating or reforming monastic orders, converting idolaters, acting with their eloquence from the pulpit, whereas women writhe in silence on their beds."[23]

Joseph Boullan, who succeeded Vintras as the leader of the Order of Mercy, was the first to suggest to Huysmans the occult significance of women's suffering. At the time of Huysmans's visit to Lourps in August 1885 – a sojourn fictionalized in his novel *En Rade* (1887) – Huysmans's long-time friend and mistress, Anna Meunier, had already begun exhibiting signs of deteriorating physical and mental health. Huysmans's helpless contemplation of Anna's agonizing decline, cul-minating in her death in the asylum of Sainte-Anne in 1895, focused the author on the mystery of the suffering of innocents. So when the novelist met Boullan for the first time in 1890, he was comforted by his theory of Mystic Substitution, the notion that "many Christians engaged in the work of expiation suffered from mysterious diseases, which were not to be confused with diabolical maladies and which no doctor should attempt to cure."[24] Having persuaded Huysmans that Anna's illness was possibly "of divine origin,"[25] Boullan impressed the author with the power and the purpose of redemptive suffering. These convictions remained with Huysmans through his life, allowing him to greet death with equanimity, enabling him to refuse treatment for the mouth cancer that would kill him in 1907. In a letter to Adolphe Retté, Huysmans describes suffering's redemptive virtue: "Remember the reply that Jesus made to Saint Teresa when, overwhelmed with tribulations, she could not help complaining to him of his severity: 'Daughter, that is how I treat those I love.'"[26] Never, as Huysmans believed, did God compromise the freedom of his children. Never did he impose his will on those too weak or too unwilling. "Always, throughout the ages, he found saints willing to pay sin's ransom with their suffering."[27]

Yet while Huysmans accepted the harrowing of the body, the humbling of the ego as an antidote to the tepid religiosity of his peers, it was his view that men were wordsmiths who wrote at desks or preached from pulpits, while women writhed in bed, undoing sin with their afflictions.

The most spectacular phenomenon associated with the heresy of Vintras reinforces the connection between God's will and human suffering, women's agony translated into men's visionary language. For the first time on June 24, 1840, Vintras's followers witnessed the inexplicable appearance of communion Hosts in the sanctuary of Tilly. Later that year, Vintras, in the company of two disciples, was in the midst of lifting from the tabernacle a cardboard folder containing the Eucharist when, upon opening it, he exclaimed that the Hosts were imprinted with a heart outlined in blood, vermilion and still fresh, as the prophet ascertained.

In succeeding months, similar events occurred with impressive regularity: empty chalices miraculously filled with ambrosial wine, celestial music, pleasing odors that seemed to emanate from nowhere. Yet no supernatural mystery was more dramatic than Vintras's bleeding Hosts. In 1841, on Christmas night, in a state of visionary ecstasy, Vintras received from God a communication that the image of the bleeding heart had come from heaven, and that if Christ had manifested himself to Vintras in that fashion, "it wasn't blood that fell; it wasn't an image that it revealed. It was Christ's living heart, living as it is in the Holy Eucharist."[28]

The identity of the species of the sacrament as substance and appearance – Christ as food and body – is reconfirmed in Vintras's Hosts, where the Crucifixion drama is re-enacted in the present. Tormented flesh, usually associated with the martyrdom of women, is indistinguishable from male language expressed in texts of blood. God, abstracted as the *Logos* or incarnated as his Son, shares male and female attributes as matter and as spirit. According to Brooke Hopkins, Christ is often conflated with his mother. A "maternal imago" representing "certain strikingly feminized qualities: patience, nurturance, the ability to love,"[29] Jesus, in the Eucharist, figures Mary as sacred aliment: "the infant's incorporation of the mother, her breast, the nourishment from her body."[30] As Vintras writes, there is no sorrow comparable to the Virgin Mother's, whose heart is pierced with swords and whose pain is written as forgiveness.

As Griffiths comments, Vintras's Sacrifice Provictimal de Marie is "a cleansing rite freeing man from the fetters of matter and bringing him nearer to the spiritual redemption which would announce the Third Reign."[31] With Huysmans's "propitiatory victims" and Vintras's Provictimal Sacrifice of Mary, there is an imprisonment in the body whose crucifixion frees the spirit, female martyrdom described in male texts that announce an end of corporeity, that efface the difference in status between genders. Eliphas Lévi, the thaumaturge and historian of magic, may dismiss Vintras as a madman, calling his sect "anarchic and absurd."[32] Yet he refrains from discrediting the supernatural authenticity of Vintras's bleeding Hosts. "Doctors have analyzed the vermilion fluid that issued from these Hosts and have concluded that it truly was human blood."[33] Despite Lévi's pronouncements, it matters less if Vintras's prophecies were the delirium of a madman, if his rapturous visions were hallucinations born of a disordered mind. Whether a mystic or a charlatan, Vintras's significance lies in his reflecting the mystical thinking of an era that sought to mark the moment that a tortured body turned into a liberated spirit.

Transcending the body

The function of women's bodies in facilitating escape from the world and accession to an ethereal realm is also illustrated in the Vintrasian practice of *ascensional redemption*, which Stanislas de Guaïta calls "the great Arcanum of the Carmel."[34] An idea whose inspiration is ascribed to Boullan, it was a ritual which, as Guaïta says, involved all manner of perversion yet was a central ceremony in the worship conducted in the Order of Mercy.

Having infiltrated the sect, Guaïta's Rosicrucian brother, Oswald Wirth, compiled correspondence which he believed provided conclusive proof of the pseudo-mystical debaucheries engaged in by Vintras's followers. Lévi, in a brief allusion to these sacrilegious rituals, describes participants gesticulating, weeping, "exclaiming 'Love! Love!'... you will permit us to omit the rest" as Lévi writes discreetly.[35]

While being colored by his antipathy for Vintrasianism and its adherents, Guaïta's account of the historical derivation of this rite and its symbolical significance confirms Vintras's view of the body as an instrument of its transcendence. As in Grünewald's painting where degradation of the flesh allowed a revelation of the soul, Vintras's ascensional redemption involves a carnality that purifies – indulgence in sexual excess in order to undo man's first transgression. The rite, as Guaïta argues, is modeled on a Talmudic allegory adopted from the *Zo'har*, in which "the bodily vitality of the first couple was infected in its very sources by the ferment of lust that mixed itself in."[36] In condemning Eve to endure the pain of childbearing, God inflicted a suitable punishment, centering it on the organs "*through which she sinned.*"[37] Women who had been agents of the Fall are enlisted by Vintras to undo the consequences of original sin.

According to Guaïta, Vintras – in spite of his modest education – had intuited the principle of a hierarchical ordering of beings, the phylogenetic interconnectedness of simple and complex life forms, "the innumerable links between mineral, vegetal, human, celestial, and spiritual existence,"[38] all structured, Guaïta says, by "the law of biological gradation." As sex was the act that caused the Fall, it was also the act that ensured redemption. Initiating movement up and down the moral, physical, and spiritual levels of being, Vintras's ritual allowed a sanctification of the generative organs, with copulation serving as an instrument of its own exoneration. Intercourse with higher entities resulted in the practitioners' *celestification*, while sex with animals or elementary beings ennobled or raised them up, so that the ritual's effect was "enable them to climb, rung by rung, the ascending ladder of life."[39]

Like other detractors of Vintras and his *lupanar sacré* (sacred brothel), Guaïta ends by enumerating the deplorable consequences of such exorbitancies: adultery, incest, bestiality, incubism, onanism – "established as acts of worship, both meritorious and sacramental."[40] Whether these accounts are accurate or exaggerated, the practice of ascensional redemption depended, as Guaïta argues, on the principle of *the body in glory*. The notion of flesh as a crucible of suffering or an agent of redemption was one that gained widespread acceptance among fin-de-siècle intellectuals. Vintras's bleeding Hosts return the risen Christ to the point of his departure, as body fluid that buys back sin, food shared among the consumers it elevates. In order to allow the ongoing ascension of men transformed into angels, Christ must continue to descend into the suffering sacrament.

The triumph of materialism

In *Le Glaive sur Rome*, Vintras describes being awakened in the night by a radiant celestial emissary. Escorted as in a nightmare through penitential zones of labyrinthine catacombs, Vintras sees souls engulfed in passion's flame, mired in the ordure of egotism, condemned to suffer in a prison-body never used to convey love. A sticky teratologic specimen, goat-footed, hydra-headed, shakes a cavern's walls with its blasphemous shrieks. It is, as one sufferer says, the horrible body of their appetites, "all the hideousness of our guilty satisfactions."[41]

Elsewhere, an impassive woman, with a star adorning her forehead, sits on a throne above a basin swarming with crablike creatures, their claws clamped on the flesh of others unprotected by a shell or carapace. In another maze strewn with sacred relics and torture instruments – iron collars, crucifixes, heated metal coffins in which victims are entombed alive – the suffering mingle with their priestly executioners. Pleas for mercy, cries of pain become bodies raining blood that inundates a ditch piled with "tonsured men wearing tiaras or mitres."[42] In Vintras's retributive metaphysic of mystical suffering, sounds of agony become the body of the punished tormentor: "the prayers and supplications issuing from this multitude of victims were transformed into pieces of flesh."[43] Re-enacting the horrifying mystery of the Incarnation, the lot of the damned is to be scourged as the embodied failure of their remorse. Those hoping to drink from the cup of forgiveness see their aspirations revert to an impulse to sin. Transubstantiation is rendered inoperative by the transgressor's guilt. Christ who absolves becomes a snake that ensnares, and the mouth that confesses becomes the mouth that eats sin. "At that moment, an enormous serpent darted forth at their tongue. It entered their throat and made them feel the pain of suffocation. It went down further and bit into their lungs, and swelling like barrels, it split open their chests. They gave off a roar loud enough to frighten hell itself."[44] First the Word that absolves turns into the unattainable Eucharist; then the devil chokes off contritional speech, becoming the blasphemous tongue that makes the penitent mute.

In a profanation of true faith symbolized by the immaculate Mother, the mystical Schekina, Vintras sees a golden idol concretizing all of man's transgressions: "their cupidity, their deceit, their hypocrisy, their fraud, their contrivances, their infernal trafficking, and their prostitution."[45] Like Huysmans, who also considered capitalism diabolical or sorcerous, the essence of a perverted wish for transcendence, Vintras's Idol is the Wanton of the Apocalypse, "The Great and Savage Apostasy."[46]

What Vintras sees in his vision is illustrative of a Decadent belief that evil identifies the physical body as *telos*, not as the site where suffering redeems the sins of the flesh. Writing in *Le Diable et l'Occultisme*, Papus argues: "God is the Spirit whose final antithesis is Matter. The devil is what gives matter pre-eminence over the spirit."[47] While refuting paranoid rumors of Luciferian cults spreading across the world,

Papus still locates evil in materialism as immanence. The devil works by frustrating the power of language to abstract objects into sacred meanings. Unenslaved by the iconolatry blighting misers, kings, and clerics stooped beneath the magnificent weight of their priestly raiments, the poor are purified by dispossession. Conversely, Papus writes in his pointedly anti-Positivist comment: "The true priest of the Adversary on earth is the materialist/atheist for whom all spiritual forces are the product of a cerebral weakness disposing them toward mysticism."[48]

In his eschatological dream, Vintras reaffirms the fin-de-siècle urge to check the incontinent sprawl of physical reality. Images of softness, viscosity, excrement, putrescence, and immoderation characterize his descriptions of hell that look forward to Sartre, while heaven is pictured as adamantine and clean: "a place of magnificent simplicity."[49] Decadent mysticism as a minimalist principle of distillation situates God in his name, matter in intelligence, diffuse ideation in prayerful attention.

As an agent of diabolical hygiene, money simplifies and concentrates, turning present objects into putative values. Money-adoration is also an expression of faith. But by hyper-cathecting things that money makes absent, the materialist represses the urge to take flight. The capitalist, chained to substances occulted as symbols of exchange, is earthbound while, in Vintras's vision, the pure are inspired by Adonai, who has flames shooting out from his soles.

Sacred sublimation

In Vintras's vision, the Jubilee is experienced as incandescence and perfume, clarion music, fire consuming matter into celebration. As light produces fire, as fire produces air, as air produces water, earth – "in each of its humid divisions" – produces bodies whose isolation is reabsorbed "into its principal center." Priests of the divine Word, through the performance of their sacrifice, lift the humble up from the elemental levels of their being: "from instinctivity, abstractivity, and specialty" until they re-experience "luminous unification."[50] In these synesthetic intuitions of ecstatic correspondence, fragrance, sound, and color – trinitarian constituents of Light – are like the justice, truth, and wisdom that man recomposes in the eternal Word.

In the Third Age, the officiants in Vintras's Church of Mercy will be *Eucharistic* and *Victimal Pontiffs*. Their rites will re-enact the transformation of suffering corporeity into nourishment that saves. A divine commensurability harmonizes thought and expression, and the priesthood operates as a brotherhood of artists: "their language will be purified like the inner sentiments of their soul; their words will be solemn and lofty like the truths they are charged with teaching."[51] As they poeticize virtue, they blast evil with thunder.

Like the prophets who preceded him, Vintras devotes most of his vituperative energies to denouncing his enemies' malfeasance. The clerics who persecuted him are taxed with vainglory and greed. Coveting power and prestige, they served themselves and not the Lord. But in excoriating the Church of Rome, Vintras does more than execute revenge on those who banished him as a heretic. Vintras adopts, modifies, and reformulates established dogma in unorthodox ways.

Having championed a belief in the Immaculate Conception, as Griffiths says, "years before the promulgation of the dogma,"[52] Vintras inveighs against the Vatican for advancing the same doctrine as an expression of Papal infallibility. Vintras's insistence on feeding the naked and giving drink to the thirsty refines traditional Christian exhortations to raise up the fallen and welcome the prodigal. Preaching and practicing mercy, Vintras's pontiffs are taught to emulate the Virgin Mother, who swayed God with her petitions. "She begged for forgiveness for her nation, and with a hand stretched out over her people, called for compassion and mercy."[53] Succoring the poor, his followers will hasten the coming of the Era of the Holy Spirit. "Since the kingdom of Jesus Christ witnessed only his humiliation, suffering, Passion, and death, the splendor and brilliance concealed by this merciful labor will appear to the eyes of the universe, bringing confusion and death to the selfish."[54]

As men are descendants of angels and again become souls disincarnate, they will celebrate the sacrament through the power of their sacrifice. New gods, the Elohim will be life-sustaining nourishment: "men, living as we have lived, will become generous Hosts. By joining their suffering to the suffering of their brothers, they will combine their debt and reduce it to flour, flour kneaded with the tears from their hearts. They will become the life, the strength, and the spiritual power of that Host by virtue of the love of Jesus Christ."[55]

In Vintras's production of Communion Hosts covered with Christ's blood, he goes beyond the Gnostic rejection of the scandal of the Incarnation, since flesh is sublimated and sanctified by pain.

Likely originating with Vintras and propounded by Boullan, the doctrine of Mystic Substitution is used in an economic model of Redemption as transaction: Christ as the creditor, mankind as the debt-holder, suffering as liquidation of one's own or others' trespasses. Willingly performed, sacrifice is currency that buys back. Those continuing the

Passion aim at balancing the ledger, achieving a zero sum where nothing more is owed – when guilt has been repaid and the suffering body becomes superfluous. Not standing in a position of subservience or need – the refractory child begging for forgiveness, the prodigal bankrupted by ruinous self-indulgence – man is no longer obligated, and owing nothing, is liberated.

The cult of the poor

But until that time, paupers, vagrants, mendicants, and pariahs are riches that the profligate both squander and despise. Applied to the poor, the psychoanalytic dictum that money is excrement reinforces the idea of the exchange-value of misery. As money substitutes for the commodities it abolishes, the unsightly poor suffer in place of the wealthy they redeem. Squalid, the poor are money stripped of its glitter and its sheen. While money may be odorless – *pecunia non olet* – the indigent are black, pestilential, and invaluable.

A squatting, golden idol symbolizing surplus, money opposes the vagabond as an embodiment of scarcity. The duality of the sacrament as the Philosopher's Stone of alchemy and as sustenance for the spirit is captured in the poor, who are food that consumers are ashamed to eat. As Bloy writes the blood of the poor is "the money one worships, the Eucharistic money one drinks and one eats."[56] The poor man, whose exploitation is both "money-gain" and "mouth-gain,"[57] becomes, in a soteriological economy, both worthless and priceless. Manure fertilizing regeneration, suffering plants in the corruptibility of the body what it harvests in the immortality of the soul.

When Vintras reiterates the Christian precept that "the poor are truly the living members of Jesus Christ,"[58] he does more than indict the church for its love of opulence and pomp, for money spent on altar dressing rather than on nourishment for the hungry. Members of Christ's body – Hosts kneaded with tears and blood – they are figures of the hypostatic identity of Christ's humanity and divinity.

Fraternalism

The prominence that Vintras accords to the misbegotten and ill-favored not only served as a reminder of the Christian virtue of humility. It also established Vintras's church as a model of the hierarchy of Christ's flock, in which the prostitute, the repentant sinner, the pauper, and the vagrant were lifted up while the rich and influential were cast down from their thrones of power. Vintras's followers, often members of a disenfranchised aristocracy, responded favorably to this idea of an institutional reordering, in which generosity and self-sacrifice replaced hereditary privilege. For them, an aristocracy of character could effectively be demonstrated by a willingness to use their talents in the service of humanity.

Consistently, in Vintras's teachings the most execrable of vices is the selfishness that locks the sinner in a prison-house of egotism, oblivious to the woes of others, unengaged in Christ's Passion. For the Catholic mystics whom Vintras influenced, the poor offered an escape from self-involvement, a release from the confines of solipsistic introspection. Charity brought a restoration of a lost sense of fraternalism, flight from "this great penitentiary that it changes into paradise."[59] Unlike the selfish person plunged in the immobilizing nirvana of his narcissism, the altruist is restless in the bestowal of the gift of himself. The apocalypse envisaged by the fin-de-siècle mystic marks an end to the self-sequestration of the Decadent recluse who, "out of aristocratic disdain, locks himself in his interior universe, away from the vulgar ambitions of others."[60]

The Thebaïd of the artist immured in the sanctuary of his cherished singularity is opened up, and the individual merges with a multitude of neighbors. While mystical experience is autistic and isolating, incommunicable to the profane from whom the ecstatic is cut off, the Decadent visionaries who follow in Vintras's footsteps still proselytize and preach in works intended for an audience.

The aftermath of Decadence, as Pierre Citti has remarked, saw a revalorizing of the idea of energy exchanges, a reinvigorated sense of nationalism and of political engagement. While Vintras's prophesied rebirth in the era of the Holy Spirit, his fin-de-siècle successors were affected by their contemporaries' ideology, by a sense of solidarity with a chosen brotherhood of the enlightened. The lifelessness of a church paralyzed by institutional rigidity is countered by what Vintras saw as his message of inclusion. The pageantry and splendor that seemed to mock the disinherited had reflected a Decadent aesthetic of elitism and claustration. Leaving behind a fallen world of loneliness and lovelessness meant renouncing the self-adoration that had truly been impoverishing. The loss of self in God, a relinquishment of materialism, sacrificial service in the interest of community all accompanied the Decadents' rediscovery of transcendence.

For Vintras and his disciples, the sterile *culte du moi* was superseded by a cult of Mary. As a condensation of the virtues of maternalism and clemency, the forgiving and forgiven woman is "a figure for a new humanity"[61] – "a great sinner who loved enough so that her sins were turned into a perfume of inestimable worth."[62] While Mary's lot is to bring forth a god who is destined to be crucified, she also announces an era of consummation and fulfillment: "she signifies also the slumber of a patient Mercy that one day will enable us to find the plenitude of our hope and achieve the dearest object of all our desires."[63]

Conclusion

Vintras himself did not live to witness the fruition of his visions. His most elaborate explanation of the Order of Mercy's charge, his articulation of the important role of women and the poor, came when the prophet was living in exile in London in the 1850s. After Vintras's release from prison in 1848 came the period of "the great revelations" as Garçon has described them. Persuaded of the need to reward his followers for their steadfastness, Vintras re-established his Church in Tilly, where he combatted accusations of apostasy and regaled disciples with further miraculous displays of bloody Hosts and wine-filled chalices. Having been cast out of the church, he invoked his role as the new prophet in order to lay claim to the sacerdotal prerogative to celebrate Communion: "wishing to renew his priesthood, God made his prophet the first pontiff and ordered him to consecrate a new apostolate."[64]

In May of 1848, Vintras beheld in a vision Jesus, accompanied by Adam and Melchizedek, his Genesis precursor, all bearing nacreous scepters, cups of blood, and swords of gold. Instructing Vintras in the details of the new liturgy, specifying the sacerdotal accoutrements he should use, Christ ordered that Vintras wear a chasuble embroidered with the image of an inverted Cross, symbolizing an end of the Reign of the Suffering Christ and the advent of the Reign of Christ in Glory.

Of course, the more flamboyant the accounts of Vintras's theophanic experiences, the more vitriolic was the church's condemnation. In February of 1851, Pope Pius IX issued a missive to the Bishop of Nancy, in which he denounced Vintras's claim to have founded a new apostolate consisting of laymen, his proclamation of the coming of the Third Age. Having resorted to these infernal machinations to subvert "the true doctrine of Jesus Christ," Vintras, as Pius fulminated, had set everything in motion "to turn the faithful from the truth of the Catholic faith and lead them into the danger of eternal damnation."[65]

With the church's increasingly strident attacks on Vintras's ministry, the time was also ripe for the explosion of a new scandal that would shake the prophet's movement. Accused by a disaffected disciple of fomenting orgiastic practices, engaging in sodomy, sanctioning licentious or unnatural acts, Vintras found himself characterized as a pervert and devil-worshipper, a reputation that has followed him to the present day. Leading fin-de-siècle occultists were among those who propagated this rumor: "Eliphas Lévi, Stanislas de Guaïta, Jules Bois credited it without hesitation," with the result that Vintras's name "is synonymous today with an immoral and shadowy priesthood."[66]

Threatened anew with arrest and incarceration, Vintras fled the country in 1852, setting up his church in exile in Belgium and then in London, returning only occasionally to visit various church centers in France, exercising his itinerant leadership of the Order of Mercy until he died in 1875 after a brief illness during a sojourn in Lyon.

Despite the sulfurous odor and fiery Satanic halo enveloping Vintras's ministry, it was his vision of the approaching end of the world that touched succeeding generations of philosophers and artists. In Vintras's teaching, the seemingly unbearable hardships visited on the faithful were not misfortunes to be endured but treasure that bought salvation. Appointed to positions of authority in Vintras's church, women were seen as doing what men could only talk of. By imitating Mary, they could stay God's vengeful hand. By consenting to the suffering that was designated as Eve's punishment, they could dedicate the pain of childbearing to bringing forth a race of angels. Parturition will end, Vintras believed, with the birth of a newly spiritualized humanity, when the need for suffering will pass away, when "death shall be no more," "when night will be no more", when man will "need no lamp or sun for the Lord God will be their light" (*Revelation* 24. 4, 5).

Among the artists and intellectuals of the fin-de-siècle generation, Vintras's doctrinal legacy was considerable and lasting. Preaching the gospel of an aristocracy of the dispossessed, he announced that, with the dawning of the Third Age, they would be the inheritors of Christ's kingdom.

In the apocalypticism of Ernest Hello – in the anguished sense of his unworthiness – one hears echoes of Vintras's advocacy of self-sacrifice and abnegation. In J.-K. Huysmans, whose characters praise Vintras in *Là-bas*, there is a millenarian hope in the eternal reward of the despised. The doctrine of Mystic Substitution that Huysmans would embrace has its theological roots in the teachings of Vintras. And Léon Bloy's martyred mistress, the visionary madwoman Anne-Marie Roulé, was surely conversant with Vintras's prophesies, as Richard Burton has alleged. "Like Vintras and his followers, Anne-Marie proclaimed the imminent arrival, after the reigns of God the Father and God the Son, of

God the Holy Spirit. She prophesied that Jesus was about to be released from the cross by Elias, and that a 'secret,' akin to the one given to Mélanie at La Salette, was about to be revealed, with her [...] as its prophet."[67]

What unifies these writers is their belief in an eschatological reversal – when the poor, Christ's wounded limbs, would be made whole and rehabilitated, when women, who, in accepting to be crucified with Christ, would effect the salvation of the sinner and take their rightful place in paradise. Artists and intellectuals, excluded from the redemptive work of sacrifice, would have as their charge to announce the Messiah's glorious return.

Indeed, for Vintras's Decadent descendants, the Dolorist exaltation of salvatory suffering became especially fervent when the expected child was the Paraclete. Similarly, at the end of days, when's flesh's harrowing was suspended – when the pleasures of the senses and gold's gleam transfixed no longer – the wealthy would be cast down and the disenfranchised lifted up. For Vintras, the Church of Rome, corrupted by its arrogance, would give way to a new religion that was truly universal, where Eucharistic Pontiffs were the hungry consecrating bread, and when Victimal Pontiffs were sanctified by pain endured for others. A willing sacrifice of the one meant the joyful rescue of the many. Vintras's message is thus an affirmation of fraternal generosity: As the Eternal tells the prophet in his initial apparition: "I will instruct you in the truth of charity and love. I will cultivate you in the way that humanity needs to be cultivated. I will fashion you so that, within you, you will feel the life of your brothers, so that you will know the glory that comes from living in them. You will suffer in them as you would in your own limbs, and you will come to think of yourself only by thinking of them. You will come to know the one true happiness described by the Apostle of the Gentle: you will find glory in the art of losing your soul in order that you may better seek the soul of your brothers. You will master the science of forgetting your Self in order to remember the legitimacy and greatness of Them."[68]

Ernest Hello: selected writings

Despite the Vatican's energetic condemnation of the Prophet of Tilly, Vintras's controversial doctrine, with its message of apocalypticism, resonated powerfully in the generation of Catholic mystic writers. While formally professing adherence to orthodox church teachings, authors like Ernest Hello, Léon Bloy, and J.-K. Huysmans aligned themselves with Vintras in insisting the end time was approaching. Typical was Hello's view expressed in a letter to Bloy, in which the writer conveys his impatient wait for the coming of the *Event*. For Hello, calamity and conflict were harbingers of the return of the Messiah: "The approaching war is probably the kind in which the Event will present itself. It must be different from ordinary wars. It must be the one that announces the Apocalypse."[69]

Signs of the world's end were found in the triumph of capitalism over faith, in the decay of morals, in the institutional corruption of the church. A priesthood seen as compromised by power-lust and simony, a people genuflecting before the idols of commerce and materialism, a nation put to shame by pursuing colonial adventurism appalled writers already disheartened by social decadence and secularism.

Yet there was danger in espousing openly the tenets of Vintrasianism, as Maurice Barrès shows in his novel *La Colline inspirée* (*The Sacred Hill* 1913). There the Baillard brothers, visionary dreamers serving God in their remote parish in the Lorraine, prove susceptible to Vintras's brand of fulgurating Messianism, his view of Christ's rehabilitation of the disinherited and the downtrodden, and his emphasis on redemptive suffering by which the forsaken are redeemed.

In the novel, Barrès introduces Vintras as a secondary character, paraphrases his ideas, and measures their impact on unsophisticated listeners. After visiting Vintras in his Carmel in Tilly, Léopold Baillard recounts to congregants his memorable audiences with the prophet. At that time Vintras had denounced a clergy estranged from God by scientific reason – for whom divine truth was not conveyed by revelation: "bishops have allowed religion to sink to the level of human nature; rationalism has corrupted them. And now a prophet has risen up."[70]

Incurred by sacrilegious overreaching by the Pope and church leaders, the forthcoming disasters predicted by Vintras confirmed existing views of a decadent society verging on collapse. Reading Vintras's maledictions on Pius and his henchmen along with newspaper accounts of worldwide calamity, Léopold is convinced of the imminent extinction of the race: "that year, Léopold was particularly well-served. In September, there were cases of cholera, in October, there was plague in the Persian Gulf. In November, there were livestock epidemics and great losses on the Stock Market."[71]

Barrès's novel makes the point that the maladjusted and disenfranchised find ready consolation in the promises of a salvatory eschatology. Responsive to the notion that Christ's return will bring a redistribution of wealth and power, Baillard expresses views voiced before by Ernest

Hello, a belief in a *reversal of values*: "the surfeit of the poor," "the final elevation of the humble."[72]

Like Vintras, who, in administering L'Ordre de la Miséricorde, had appointed women to positions of influence and power, Baillard promotes Soeur Thérèse as his liaison with the transcendental. Intuitive and sensitive – both a visionary and hysteric – Soeur Thérèse is assigned the role of prophetess and seer, Priscilla to Baillard's Montanus, male and female messengers of the divine. Like Vintras and the Decadent writers who were swayed by his predictions, Baillard adopts the Dolorist principle of participation in the Passion. The end of the Second Era of the Martyred Son can be hastened, as Vintras thinks, if the faithful climb the Cross and perform Christ's expiatory mission. In an ecstatic colloquy with God, Vintras had heard angels pronounce humanity's death sentence. Wishing to intercede, Vintras had pleaded for God's forbearance. *Too long*, as God had answered, *have I witnessed the celebration of the Roman Mass. Too long have I seen my Son put to death anew each day.* Explaining to Vintras that it was time to say *the new Mass*, God had told the Organ it was the faithful's turn to complete the work of the redemption: "It is now up to humanity to perform the act of divine sacrifice. It is up to men to become the victims, to offer themselves up entirely. Humanity will be the new Christ, and Jesus will finally enter into his repose."[73]

While in the novel, Vintras's followers agree to be crucified with Christ, their impracticality and zealotry cause their psychological decline. Victims of their gullibility, they are expelled from the church and their community.

Imbued with naturalist elements of medical determinism, Barrès diagnoses the Baillards' fanaticism as pathological. Yet the story of the ruthlessness of the Church's war against the renegade priests recalls the Pope's inexorable prosecution of his campaign against Vintras. In Barrès, the inchoateness of the Baillard brothers' sentimental mysticism is informed as much by the "inspirational quality of the landscape"[74] as by the persuasiveness of Vintras's precepts. For Barrès, cultivation of the *ego* was of paramount importance, and so a religion of spiritual self-annihilation, the dissolution of souls in God, was attributable to an anomalous interaction between a place and its inhabitants – the lonely Lorraine countryside, suffused with its ghostly pagan history, and the dreamy autochthons with their consoling visions of Jerusalem.

However much Barrès describes the Baillards' adoption of Vintrasianism as a product of spiritual geography, the novel's subject demonstrates the persistent influence of the heresy well into the early twentieth century. Richard Griffiths notes the interweaving of some of Vintras's central teachings with a fin-de-siècle worldview that shaped a literature of mysticism. Still, he concedes these authors rarely mention the prophet's name or published writing. "For the reason that Vintrasism reflects so accurately certain aspects of the religious beliefs of the nineteenth century, it is impossible to conclude, solely on the evidence of similarities of doctrine, that an author's work was necessarily influenced by Vintras."[75]

Against the historic and intellectual backdrop of a turn of the century dominated by religious moderation, laicization, republicanism, and scientific reasoning, the Catholic authors who arguably were affected by Vintras professed the same belief that divine truth was apprehended through revelation. They adopted the same anti-intellectualism, embraced suffering in a way that seemed masochistic to their practically-minded peers. Inhospitable to assertions that mankind was progressing toward enlightenment, they saw a race drowning in depravity and approaching its final hour.

Vintras's reverence for the suffering poor as members of Christ's body is elaborated in the Dolorism propounded by Vintras's successor, Joseph Boullan, and thereafter became a doctrine that found favor among the fin-de-siècle mystics. Vintras's opposition of the faithful's humility to the arrogance of the Pontiff evolved into an advocacy of self-abnegation that culminated in the mystic's ego death. Both Vintras's cult of Mary and the pro-feminist structure of his church led to the Decadents' consecration of women as conduits of the divine.

Ernest Hello, virtually a forgotten figure in the history of French letters – "posthumous before he died," as Léon Bloy writes acerbically[76] – warrants reappraisal for his influence on two major disciples of Vintras: Léon Bloy and J.-K. Huysmans, the most prominent of the mystically-oriented fin-de-siècle Catholic writers. One reason for Hello's disappearance into critical oblivion is the fact that his writing is unamenable to genre classification. Born in Lorient in 1828, educated in the law, Hello turned to writing in order plead "the special cause of Catholicism."[77] Married in 1857 to Zoé Berthier, an overprotective and controlling wife whose influence Bloy deplored, Hello spent his life in part in Paris and in part in Keroman, where he died on July 14, 1885.

Hello's only venture into fiction-writing, his *Contes extraordinaires* (1879), received mixed reviews from Barbey d'Aurevilly, who found many of his fantastic tales unworthy, and pitying disdain from Bloy, who deplores the collection's "inexpressible wretchedness."[78]

After the demise of *Le Croisé* (*The Crusader*), which he founded in 1858, Hello contributed to the publication *La Revue du Monde Catholique*

(*The Review of the Catholic World*), championing a view of the church "as hierarchical, centralized, and authoritarian."[79]

Hello's books include a polemic against Ernest Renan, biographies of Ruysbroeck and Angela of Foligno. Hello's mystical exaltation and patient study of Scriptural symbolism earned him recognition from a few of the fin de siècle more colorful figures, including Huysmans, Remy de Gourmont, and Robert de Montesquiou. However, during his own time, Hello's work was generally neglected. Jean-Claude Polet admits to understanding Hello's absence from literary histories if the definition of literature "is limited to fiction and ingenious techniques of expression."[80] However, Polet argues that Hello can be rescued from his taxonomic pigeonhole, as a writer of works expressing "superannuated devotion," if one assigns a central role to the sacred in human life – if "*mens divinior*" directs the thinking of an author.[81]

Because Hello regarded literature as a vehicle for illumining man's relationship with God, he dismissed what he regarded as fastidious analyses of psychology, fictional contrivances that glorified man's weaknesses and vices. For Hello, "who hated levity, caprice, and convention," "there was never more than one true art: that of the Holy-Spirit itself."[82]

Hello's use of literature as a forum for incriminating the vanity of literature is a trait that reappears in leading fin-de-siècle Catholic novelists – in Léon Bloy, whose only novels decry the insipidity of modern writing, in J.-K. Huysmans, whose post-conversion texts are leached of their earlier Decadent shimmer, and who acknowledged "that the demands of literature are incompatible with the demands of faith."[83] Huysmans's attempts at magnifying God, he feared, had diminished his expressive power, leaving him a monochromatic style, "gray and dull, without any great communicative force."[84]

In Hello and his successors, the praise of poverty as a virtue extended to a mortification of the author, whose linguistic cleverness is humbled. While no correlation establishes that if God is great, art must be small, these writers equated the death of self in God with an aesthetic of asceticism. Emancipation from the prison of terrestriality and pride meant, for Hello, a renunciation of comfort, wealth, and status, and as importantly, an acceptance of the poverty of the human word. By himself, a man is nothing. His work is nothing, if not doxological. "Creation is possible only if one creates in imitation of God, by affirming, in the way that God does, only the things that truly are."[85]

Two short texts By Hello ("Ludovic" in *Contes extraordinaires*, "Prière à sainte Catherine" ["Prayer to Saint Catherine"] in *Prières et méditations*) demonstrate his view of art as dispossession, as material divestment, a disciplining of the ego, self-abnegation enacted in man's soul and in his language. In "Ludovic," the most celebrated of Hello's *Contes extraordinaires*, the eponymous protagonist is a man of means and social standing, until, one day, inexplicably, he rejects his life of indolence and pleasure, afternoon outings in the woods, evening excursions to the theater.

According to Hello, the vacuity of life on earth divorced from God, the futility of wealth, achievement, and celebrity, entailed withdrawal of interest in mortal life and worldly things. For Hello, who once observed "I have a monopoly on infinite weakness,"[86] *le néant* [nothingness] was the term that best epitomized man's lot. The only avenue by which one nears an appreciation of the divine is by differentiating one's nullity, one's transience, and limitations from the incommensurability of God, defined as the negation of man's nothingness. What appears to the materialist as the totality of the real must be consigned to non-existence so that, by its absence, it reveals what is. "The person who shapes marbles cuts the block, sacrifices matter, and frees the form: that is the natural operation," as Hello writes in "Les Ténèbres ["The Shadows"]." "The person who forms a statue into the divinity cuts away nothingness, sacrifices form, and disengages fire: that is the supernatural operation."[87]

The descent of Hello's Ludovic into the obsessiveness of avarice begins with a similar disentanglement of essence from superfluity. Like the mystic who frees himself from his fascination with glittering objects, undoing the bewitchment of desires that shackle him to bodies, Ludovic applies the Midas touch that turns possessions into gold – gold that, in its deadness, should inspire revulsion and disdain.

The tragedy of Ludovic is like the purification of the saint, as both accept privation ensuring greater intimacy with their god. Hello illustrates how Dolorism applies to the practice of the miser: "the will to suffer and make others suffer for the thing that one adores."[88] Ludovic exhibits the abstractive vision of the Kabbalist, condensing the body of the real into sums and calculations, and of the paranoiac, for whom the haphazardness of events is a harbinger of doom. The self-immolation of the martyr, tortured as a sign of privilege and election, is displayed by Ludovic, who wishes to open himself up, mingling the essence of himself with the distillate of riches, mixing gold, the blood of substances, with blood, the gold of life. The subject's mystic fusion with a transcendental entity is enacted as the cutting of the miser's hand that grasps his money: "One day, he had bruised his hands by convulsively squeezing the worshipped object. Ludovic was pleased to see the drop of blood that had appeared on his bruised finger. The blood had touched the gold, and the gold had touched the blood."[89]

Hello establishes a parallel between the miser's relinquishment of pleasure and the ascetic's flight from the illusion of bodily life apart from God. Both exchange the dynamism of desire and satisfaction for the stasis of equilibrium that Freud associates with the death drive – the tendency of living things to seek a state of rest, a recovery of inorganicism and entropic immobility. Since *le néant* seeks to counterfeit itself as energy and life, money-worship, in abolishing the object it replaces, institutes a nihilism to the second power, the negation of what is nothing.

Thus, Hello shows the connection between avarice and religion, between gold as sacred fetish and the privileged knowledge of the holy. Manipulating symbols allows access to the sacred, where material reality has been sublimated into value. A chicken as a food source becomes useless as its payment, yet saving money and going hungry afford a spurious purity and detachment. As Brown writes, "the value conferred on the useless object, and the prestige conferred on the owner, is magical, mystical, and religious, and comes from the domain of the sacred."[90] Hello contrasts the power of Eros, the vital energy of the world, with money as the Thanatotic restoration of anhedonia and lifelessness. Gold is the symbol of the divorce of misers from their libidinal satisfactions. It is what cuts them off from others objects, strands them in the timelessness of anti-physis. As Ludovic amasses money, "the domain of the unnatural approaches. The monstrous begins to growl in the vicinity."[91]

Immanent in words is the desire to turn back into referents, as cash desires its re-materialization as the commodities it eliminates. Similarly, the *conte extraordinaire* should end with God's extraordinary reappearance, but the avarice of Ludovic brings no miraculous theophany. "The nature of things wants money to turn back into substance. The five-franc coin can become a chicken or a book. It can nourish the mind or body, can create healthy blood or robust ideas. In the house of Ludovic, the opposite occurred. Natural things turned into money, not to become natural things again. They did not return to the game of life but remained metal forever."[92]

Hello's meditation on money-adoration as idolatry anticipates Huysmans comments on the Satanic origins of capitalism and underlies the fin-de-siècle sanctification of poverty. Instead of following psychoanalysis in linking religiosity and avarice – the timeless gleam of gold and the immaculacy of the disembodied soul – Hello opposes money's power to destroy to God's power to create. In Hello's story, both are abstract principles generating absence. Both cancel the value of books and chickens as nourishment for souls and bodies. But the deathliness of money, hyper-symbolized by the coffin of Ludovic's cashbox, contrasts with God's inexhaustible capacity to fill nothingness with being.

When Ludovic encloses in the strongbox the gold in which material objects have been entombed, he houses emptiness in a tabernacle and makes his cellar into a shrine. Since sacredness increases as a function of inaccessibility, Ludovic fetishes the container, the inviolability of its locks, spending money on the safe that prevents him from handling his money. Converting material to metal, he gives up the life of symbols' bodies. Once his fortune is made untouchable, its value becomes indestructible and infinite: "The object was taken out of circulation, shed its perishable form, and entered into its immortality."[93]

Hello's association of God and Gold, Mammon and Jehovah, is made explicit by the word Ludovic chooses for his combination lock. Four tumblers with four numbers, represented by four letters, together form a word which, when composed, unlocks the safe. "What word should be chosen?" Hello writes, interrogating the Gematria of the miserly. "The word itself would become sacred by being identified with gold."[94]

Ludovic's deification of money, his choice of *God* or *Dieu* as password, suggests that, more than hidden gold, it is the magic word that acquires holiness. The apophatic statement, the unsaid title, the sacred shibboleth endow an onomantic power in God concentrated as his Name. Locked away in esotericism, knowledge grows greater by being hidden. The *Tetragrammaton*, the four letters that constitute God's Name, are the strongbox of the word whose meaning is unknowable and therefore priceless.

When Ludovic forgets the word and cannot retrieve his treasure, his adoration of the symbol and desecration of its meaning incur punishment for perverting a religion that spiritualizes by annihilating. In Hello's *mise en abîme*, he shows containers that nest inside containers, each concealing the contents they are entrusted with protecting. Like alchemy, enclosing wisdom in arcane symbolic boxes – behind images of the phoenix, the caduceus, the dragon – avarice is shown to be a profane hermeticism. If money is seen as excrement and if what money buys is excrementalized, only the impregnable container, the forgotten key are given value, in an occult system where secret knowledge is its status as occult.

For Ludovic, as Hello writes, gold had first devoured the thing, the strongbox had devoured gold, and God had been devoured in his soul by the hyper-symbolic nothingness of gold that was worshipped in God's place. The sacred thing is therefore equated with the means of its recovery: utterance of the word *Dieu*, the Alpha and Omega that Ludovic forgets. "God was the point of departure and the point of arrival," Hello says of a religion predicated on the nothingness of bodies. "GOD"S NAME WAS AVENGING GOD."[95]

The ransom for corporeal beings is a religion that redeems, poverty that absolves, suffering that buys back. The talismanic value of the icon, coin, or fetish is its etymological value as the *telesma* that acts as payment.

For Hello, avarice is a disorder, a blasphemy, a transgression since it substitutes a false system of obliterative symbols for a faith whereby Christ redeems man's nothingness with his death. When five francs occult a chicken, money assumes a sacred value. When literature pretends to beauty, it not only eliminates the thing it represents; it also dethrones religion and replaces it with aestheticism, proclaiming the heretical doctrine of *art for art's sake*.

It is unsurprising that Hello showed little interest in fiction, a demiurgic exercise performed by the lowly god-impersonator. Rather than tales or novels, Hello turned to a literature of petition, writing sacred history, hagiographies, *prières et méditations*. In subordinating the divine as content to art's ornamentality as container, Hello felt that literature had lost its relationship with God: "art has fallen; the place of beauty is henceforth closed to art."[96]

Doxological expression, originating in the nothingness of the supplicant, rises up as song toward the perfection of the eternal. As Hello comments on the flower: "The blossoming rose offers the sun the spectacle of combat between manure and the light."[97] Thus, in Hello, art-as-worship conveys the modesty of the speaker. Rooted in the manure of humility, adoration blooms as beauty.

Hello who, in a prayer to the infant Jesus, had asked to learn the joy of small things – to love the peace, the calm, and the childhood of Nazareth – requests, in an address to Saint Catherine, to experience the pure negation of self. "What must I do to lose myself? How must I proceed? Teach me to forget myself in sleep, my Lord, until you eclipse me for eternity in your glorious awakening."[98]

Unlike the nothingness of money – infertile and inert – the *néant* of the believer is unfathomable like God. In his analysis of Hello, Jean-Claude Polet remarks on the homology of art, its attempt to utter the unutterable, and art's subject, divine grandeur, beyond language and beyond compass. Art's objective, Polet writes, is to "move in the opposite sense of God's revelation and creation, rising up again from the object to the principle, dying to the part of the self that resists the desire for the infinite: the visible, material, corporeal part of a being whose weight prevents him from re-ascending the ladder of paradise."[99]

In Hello's recourse to a rhetoric of inadequacy and surrender, apophatic approaches to being are a denial of nothing. Thus, he refers to his writing as performing its immolation: "In order to speak of the infinite, we must take the word *finite* and offer it as a sacrifice. Is there not a relationship between this operation of human language and the act of the flame which, in wishing to speak of the infinite in its way, seeks a victim for it to burn?"[100]

Staged on the level of language, the mystical desire to be consumed in fire motivates Hello's stammering use of prefixes of negation: *infinity*, *immensity*: *without end, without measure*. Unlike the name of God, uncircumscribable in its abundance and charity, property is "the impersonal name of unhappiness. Its proper name is the self."[101]

For Hello, the inversion of apophasis is *epectasis*: an ascension toward perfection that can never be completed, "unending progress in faith toward a beatitude that is perfect."[102] In Saint Gregory's use of the word, it is an eternal, rising journey, acquisition of knowledge that is boundless and self-multiplying. Epectasis is the opposite of Ludovic's locked cashbox, without stasis or limitation, exclusive of "the idea of completion."[103]

To Saint Catherine Hello prays that his heart be dilated, that his insignificance be magnified, that God's majesty be magnified, "according to my misery and your mercy" (suivant mes misères et vos miséricordes).[104] The more bottomless the petitioner's abjection – the more inexhaustible God's riches – the more generous the gift.

What, in Huysmans, will be the bodily martyrdom of Saint Lydwine, what, in Bloy, will be the combustion that burns his heroine's worldly ties, is performed in Hello as a ceremonial holocaust of language. For Hello, style in art is the personal name of his unhappiness.

For the miser who forfeits pleasure, poverty is misery self-inflicted: delight in objects and other people locked in a strongbox of abstention. The egotist governed by "self-will and self-love"[105] is a closed container inside of which nothingness conjugates with itself. Self-interest, self-possession only create a greater emptiness, so Hello asks to be turned outward, granted the blessing of self-forgetfulness: "Until now, I have known myself in me. Grant that I may know myself in you."[106]

Mysticism which, for Hello, is self-effacement in the word, guides him away from the declarative voice, too prideful, too assertive, and toward the optative mood, by which the writer consents and acquiesces. *Que votre volonté soit faite.* May thy work be my work. May I break free, altogether and wholly living from myself, and rise up in the prayerful incense of my offering. "May I be animated by you, filled with joy by you, glorified by you."[107] May it be so. *Amen. amen.*

J.-K. Huysmans: *Sainte Lydwine de Schiedam* (1901)

Although the flamboyant prophet Vintras had been one of the most controversial religious figures of the era – excommunicated from the church, driven into exile, deemed a Satanist, characterized as an incarnation of the heretic Montanus – he aroused less vehement condemnation than his successor, Joseph-Antoine Boullan. After Vintras's death in Lyon in 1885, Boullan had already positioned himself to assume leadership of the sect. No less endowed than his predecessor with a flair for the dramatic, Boullan had taken the title of Pontiff of the Divine Melchizedean Chrism. In imitation of Vintras, who had claimed to be the new Elijah, Boullan had professed to be the re-embodiment of John the Baptist. And "since Vintras had proudly displayed a mark in the shape of a dove in the center of his forehead," Boullan "had a cabbalistic pentagram tattooed in the corner of his left eye."[108]

While Boullan provoked the censure of leading fin-de-siècle occultists, who denounced the orgiastic practices the Pontiff allegedly had sponsored, he also gained the admiration of the era's foremost chronicler of the supernatural, becoming the mentor to J.-K. Huysmans in matters of the occult. In disseminating Vintras's teachings, Boullan further popularized the idea that, following the appearance of the Anti-Christ would come a final, cleansing cataclysm, wiping away a society corrupted by "the Stock Market, gambling, and horseracing."[109] Such notions were appealing to reactionary Catholics like Huysmans, already disgusted with a world tainted by cupidity and materialism. Like many of his right-wing brethren, Huysmans had felt alienated from the church, disillusioned by the progressivism of Pope Leo, who, to Huysmans, had responded weakly to the growing trend toward laicization. For Huysmans and Léon Bloy, the priesthood had become beholden to the rich, abjuring mystical asceticism in favor of comfort and modernism.

In *Là-bas*, the astrologer Gévingey had railed bitterly against the ecclesia, whose liberalism seemed to signal a triumph of the devil: "Look at that timorous, skeptical Pope we have and his impotent schemes; look at our episcopate of Simonists and cowards; our flabby, good-humored clergy."[110] This conversation among occultists marking the conclusion of *Là-bas* is interrupted by exultant cries arising from the street, heralding the January 1889 election of General Georges Boulanger. A Franco-Prussian War hero and staunch detractor of monarchism, Boulanger was seen as threatening to dissolve the Republic and make himself a dictator. Despite the brevity of Boulanger's triumph and his suicide in Belgium in 1891, his ascendancy was viewed by Huysmans as a sign of dismal things to come. Contemplating the immediate future, Huysmans – like his character Durtal – saw only the "whirlwinds of ordure appearing on the horizon."[111]

The eschatological gloom with which Huysmans viewed the fin de siècle came from a sense of cultural decay and entropic devitalization, as a cadre of "dysenteric souls" reigned over a cold, exhausted planet. Yet Huysmans's anticipation of the apocalypse had been, paradoxically, a cause for optimism since only disaster would allow for cosmic renewal to ensue. As Jean-Marie Seillan remarks, Huysmans shared the anarchist's conviction that political disintegration was a necessary precondition for rebirth. Sickened by the laicizing policies of the State, he shared with other counter-revolutionary Catholics "a desire to see the modern world vanish into a cloud of blood in order that it might re-emerge, once it was purified of its vileness."[112]

Yet Huysmans's eagerness to see the world end made him feel no less an exile in his era, and, like Durtal, he sought refuge in historic recreations of the Middle Ages. Those centuries, to Huysmans, had been a time when evil was majestic, when the people had been on fire with religious zeal. At the century's end, there had been no heroic figure capable of inspiring the faithful: "where have they gone, those saints who will save them?" as Durtal's comrade wonders.[113]

In 1898, Huysmans had finally retired, after almost thirty years of peaceful toil, from his position at the Interior Ministry. Wishing to find a nurturing spiritual environment where Christian writers and authors could benefit from association with a religious order, he had prepared to become an oblate at the Benedictine abbey in Ligugé, moving into a house built the following year adjacent to the monastery. There after meditating on a project he had been long been planning, he began writing a biography of the saint, born in 1380, in the author's own ancestral homeland.

In Huysmans's withdrawal into fifteenth-century hagiography, he illustrates the relevance of Vintras's teaching on the apocalypse and the central role of women in hastening the coming era of the Paraclete. At the same time, he acknowledges the limited role assigned male authors, who are relegated to acting as chroniclers and record-keepers, witnessing a redemptive act but unable to take part in it. For Huysmans, there are no nineteenth-century saints who work to welcome the Messiah, and miracles are regarded as purely historical phenomena. Less effective than Vintras's priesthood, the Catholic historian delivers inspirational messages intended to uplift his audience. Huysmans assumes a more important role as a prophet than as a historian, but whereas in bygone eras, the martyr's suffering repaid the debt of mankind's sin, the author suffers in his powerlessness to do more than transcribe and remember. In *Lydwine*, the sacrificial act to which Huysmans acquiesces is to subordinate the artist's role to the redemptive power of his subject.

Liquidating the debt of history

It is therefore unsurprising that writers associated with the Catholic revival followed Huysmans in exploring mysticism through a study of religious history. Like his predecessor, Ernest Hello, Huysmans had turned to hagiography. And when Huysmans looked for living applications of Vintras and Boullan's teaching – a longing for the apocalypse, a belief in the inspirational role of women, respect for the sanctity of the poor through whom Christ's Passion was re-enacted – he could find no better illustration than the religious records of the Middle Ages. Unlike his contemporaries who wished to experience only full bellies and empty minds, Huysmans sought to understand the religious fervor enflaming Catholics of bygone centuries. Hoping to grasp the experience of unitive ecstasy bestowed upon the visionary, Huysmans identified with the martyr whose life he reconstructed. Indeed, his research showed that the saints whose celestial transports were most shattering had also lived in times when the world was convulsed by calamity and war. Like other Decadent hagiographers convinced that "history is repetition,"[114] he sought a religious avenue for escaping from time as futility and entrapment.

Huysmans's biography of the life of the Blessed Lydwine of Schiedam, a fifteenth-century practitioner of Mystic Substitution, was motivated by a need to explain the mystery of suffering and to discover how participating in the Passion brought an experience of resurrection that marked the dénouement of history and the beginning of the Messiah's reign on earth. It was Boullan who first taught Huysmans the principles of reparative Dolorism, explaining that the disease that was gradually consuming Anna Meunier might be a sign of her election, her role in paying the price of others' sins. To Huysmans, Anna's involvement in the practice of Mystic Substitution could be projected on a cosmic scale as the martyrdom of Saint Lydwine.

The opening chapter of Huysmans's book describes the torments of Europe's body as a macrocosmic image of the harrowing of Lydwine. As Elizabeth Emery writes in an insightful analysis of Huysmans's text, the end of the fourteenth century proleptically announces the fin de siècle – presented as an eschatological crisis, not a discrete moment in history. Medieval kings and queens embroiled in sanguinary intrigue were supernatural embodiments of wickedness and chaos. Pestilence and slaughter, raised to paroxysmal levels, seemed to augur the world's end that Huysmans's readers knew had not occurred. The tableau or *panorama* that Huysmans paints of Lydwine's era explains the author's comment on the point of his martyrologic undertaking: "I am not writing her life from an historical standpoint but from the point of view of a mystic," as he writes in a letter to Arij Prince.[115]

The backdrop of Huysmans's life of the unspeakably tortured visionary, a propitiatory victim who expiates the sins of others, is not so much an historical document produced by archival research as a Biblical picture symbolizing the tumult of the end of time. As Emery writes: "Despite his wish to summarize the history of fourteenth-century Europe, Huysmans surrenders to his imagination, reproducing stereotypical images of the end of the world: battles, famine, plague, wild animals. His unbridled imagination finally carries him away, and he abandons historical exactness in order to develop his moral and symbolic vision of an era in which every event makes reference to a divine order."[116]

While Huysmans's writing may mitigate the penance of his audience – historical consciousness experienced as repetition and frustration – his paradoxical evocation of the apocalypse as recurrence shows that Lydwine and her epigones had not freed man from time as malediction. Huysmans's strategy may be to hide the specificity of history behind the timelessness of the struggle between the light of Good and Evil's shadow. He may ignore the problems and issues that particularize his time: "tuberculosis, syphilis, the development of industry," in order to dramatize concerns more relevant to religion: "the lack of religious fervor, Satanism that was raging."[117] Yet in the nineteenth century, what Seillan calls "the politics of martyrdom"[118] also required suffering to offset specific national disgraces, liked the Dreyfus affair, a French officer's alleged act of treason, evil-doing linked by Huysmans to the spreading plague of Jewish influence. However, in Huysmans's biography, the Dolorist identification of Europe and the saint's body suggests a model of the Crucifixion as an eternally re-staged pageant whose completion allows the martyr to free her beneficiaries from time's Purgatory.

Huysmans's lifelong meditation on the mystery of suffering had afforded him an insight into time and guilt and punishment whose interconnectedness has been the object of psychoanalytic study. As a man of faith anxious for fulfillment of the Messianic promise, Huysmans awaited an apocalypse that would bring an end to history. To Huysmans, "it might be necessary to aggravate the plight of victims since it was only from a catastrophe that a potential benefit might arise."[119] As sin creates the past, necessitating the work of expiation, "only the abolition of guilt," as Norman O. Brown remarks, is able to "abolish time."[120]

The psychoanalytic axiom that instinctual repression begets neurosis, producing time as a measurement of alienation from the body, also suggests that an Edenic past is recoverable as eternity reached when sin has been forgiven. As the locus of transgression, the body is a medium of redemptive suffering, so when sinners repay the debt of guilt, they move from corporeity into heaven. Accompanying birth, original sin entails a fall into separateness, whence the mystic's longing for lost unity, for fusion with the Lord.

Suffering and the end of time

In writing *Sainte Lydwine de Schiedam*, Huysmans solves the mystery that had perplexed him, discovering the utility of suffering that is visited on the innocent. Rather than a trial to be endured, it is a privilege conferred by God, catapulting martyred subjects from a quotidian hell of unawareness into the incommensurability of pain and joy that, as extremes, become identical. By identifying with his heroine, Huysmans is able to "subdue his suffering, converting it into inner joy, into expiatory prayer, into a permanent hallelujah."[121]

In his previous novels, Huysmans's protagonists had lived time as the ticking of a clock, its hands moving in endless, pointless circles. Man's existence was not driven by the engine of God's plan. It did not culminate in a decisive moment of salvation or damnation but ebbed away *downstream* across a landscape of desolation, of failed relationships, insipid dinners, thwarted flights into transcendence. "Schopenhauer is right," as Jean Folantin concluded: "'man's life swings like a pendulum between sorrow and boredom. There is no point in trying to speed up or slow down the movement of the clock. All one can do is fold his arms and then do his best to sleep."[122]

Through the maturation of his faith, Huysmans had outgrown a view of suffering as an inverted image of ennui, had stopped believing that the only way to escape the misery of life was to administer the anesthetic of automatism or sleep. By 1903, when he published his autobiographical novel on monasticism (*L'Oblat* [*The Oblate*]), Huysmans may have abandoned his belief that monks performed the expiatory work of others – that the cloister served as an "instrument of Providence which refined evil in the crucible of voluntary suffering, thereby protecting the world and ensuring its survival."[123] Following the 1901 passage of the Law of Associations, prohibiting the formation of new monastic orders within France, Huysmans had faulted Pope Leo for not vigorously responding, blaming the Pontiff for his sympathy to Republican ideas. The Vatican was thus complicit in the weakening of monasticism, whose charge was to offset the cumulative evils of human history. The problem of suffering was redefined as abstract and atemporal, undertaken in all eras by martyrs succeeding one another through the centuries.

In *L'Oblat*, Huysmans pictures Suffering as the faithful lover of the Savior, her loyalty inspiring martyrs to become the betrothed of Christ themselves. Suffering in *L'Oblat* is the structuring principle of history, a consequence of birth, a recompense for the Fall, a dependable companion whose presence lasts until the end of time: "She was the first-born of the work of man, and she has pursued him since then on earth, following him beyond the grave and to the threshold of Paradise."[124] Beside Christ in Golgotha, she is a fiancée and partner, the female counterpart of the *Beneficent Torturer*, whose cruelty is a blessing. The Crucifixion celebrates the nuptial union of flesh and pain, a marriage consummated as the end of separateness and time.

Huysmans's epithalamium is permeated with mystical eroticism, with the death of Suffering shown as simultaneous with the death of Christ. *La Douleur*, as Huysmans writes, fits a ruby crown around Christ's head, which, like the diadem of thorns, is "an emblem of royalty." Having verified the scourge, the heaviness of the hammers – having assured herself of the bitter gall and the sharpness of the lances – she climbs up on the gibbet where the marriage is consecrated, the union "of these two reprobates of the earth." Deliverance and accomplishment show that time has been abolished since Pain is widowed "at the very moment she was loved."[125]

It was by meditating on the example of the life of Blessed Lydwine that Huysmans intuited the meaning of being crucified with Christ. As the believer is enjoined to love his neighbor as himself, he must also welcome suffering, "loving it in memory and in imitation of Christ's Passion."[126] When Huysmans was diagnosed with mouth cancer in 1906, he refused treatment, rejected morphine injections, insisting he did not seek a cure, expressing a hope that, in his death agony, he might emulate Sainte Lydwine.

Huysmans's biography of Lydwine is meant to be instructive in picturing the future saint as an unexceptional young woman – pious and obedient yet reluctant to accept her mission to liquidate the guilt begetting history. One of the lessons that Christ imparts to Lydwine is that the opposite of agony is not the transports of the soul, out-of-body flights to Paradise. It is the torpor and insentience of daily life cut off from God – oblivious to sin, untormented by remorse, unaware that history is the dead time of selfish apathy. Only the Blessed experience the pain and rapture that enable them to come alive.

Jean Pot, Lydwine's confessor, describes anguish and ecstasy as overlapping and interchangeable: "In a way, God reconciles the two extremes of agony and bliss [...] and the soul would burst if martyrdom of the body did not let it catch its breath and afford it more delight. It is by completing the journey of suffering that one ascends into joy."[127]

Huysmans's text incriminates a religion of prudence and moderation, in which an undemanding God asks no sacrifice of his children. The convulsive life of martyrs transports them from the Dark Night of the Soul to an absorption in the generative center of creation. Once enlightened, Lydwine experiences time as neither biological nor historic. Stricken by insomnia, denied the narcissism of unconsciousness, she is constantly responsive to God's voice. Subsisting on the Eucharist, she orders time, not by meals and appetites. At first, the liturgical calendar structures her awareness of human action, but when she flies with angels, Lydwine is lifted out of history.

The martyr of time

Huysmans begins his book by indicating that the point of Lydwine's suffering is to balance the scales of good and evil, pay off the deficit of history, re-establish an equilibrium in a metaphysical economy: "God never seemed more attentive in monitoring the balance between vices and virtues, piling up, when the scales of iniquity descended, the agonies of saints that served as a counterweight."[128]

Huysmans frames the looming conflict as a military Armageddon, with the leaders of France and Flanders, Italy and England described as reprobates and usurers, lunatics and weaklings laying waste to an entire continent already devastated by disease: On the one side, Satan mobilized his legions, emptying the precincts of hell. On the other side, the cloistered nuns, the hermit saints, and mystic visionaries seem to constitute a paltry force to combat the accursed army: Saint Catherine of Siena, Saint Françoise of Rome, Saint Lydwine, Saint Colette armed only with "the indulgences of the Paraclete."[129] Huysmans's image of a cosmic clash of Manichean enemies sets the narrative of Lydwine in an extra-temporal dimension. But while agreeing to substitute herself in order to undergo the punishment for humanity's crimes, Lydwine is anchored in her time and is still provincial in her outlook. She devotes her suffering to save the souls of errant priests and repentant drunks, autochthons unimplicated in the struggle to forestall the apocalypse.

Huysmans persistently cites his sources – Johannes Brugman, Thomas à Kempis, Jan Gerlac – to fix his subject as an ordinary and simple young Dutch girl: solitary, blond, contemplative, and cheerful, responsible in performing her duties as a housekeeper, devoted to the Virgin, with whom she shares a prefigurative sense of intimacy. Particularized by her time and role, Lydwine still performs the same redemptive mission as the few monks who, in 1902, continued to liquidate the debt of human sin, within cloisters seen by Huysmans as "again besieged by diabolical forces."[130]

Throughout Huysmans's compendium of nosological monstrosities, he shows Lydwine as incapable of thinking outside the historic framework of her era. Her plunge into the reparative agonies she endures for mankind's benefit starts with an ice-skating accident that occurs on an outing with her friends. Lydwine looks like her countrymen, practices her faith the way that they do. Even the miraculous decomposition of her suppurating flesh, its mystical distillation into an odor of sanctity, brings its conversion into a substance that is particular to her homeland: "the peculiarly Dutch fragrance of cinnamon."[131]

Even when Lydwine is accorded remission from her torments, escaping from her bed and body on trips to Paradise or Purgatory, she is imprisoned in the conceptual box of the history of her epoch, seeing higher and lower worlds as imaged in medieval iconography. Huysmans's comments on the solipsism of the fifteenth-century imagination reflect on him as well, since his landscapes of the afterlife are constructs of the sensibilities of the fin-de-siècle artist. "God almost always adapts his visions to the imagination of those receiving them."[132]

Taking account of the mystic's temperament, cultural origins, and habits, God adjusts the spectacle to the spectator while augmenting its intensity, haloing it in a "glorious atmosphere inexpressible in words."

There is a disabling of the saint and author, who in their attempt to convey the vision, have to re-materialize the ineffable "in human language accessible to the crowd."[133]

By assimilating Lydwine's glimpse of Heaven, Hell, and Purgatory to canvases by her contemporaries, like the German Stephan Lochner – by reproducing images of burning dungeons with barred windows, the clanking of iron chains, the shackled damned impaled on pitchforks – Huysmans shows himself, more than his heroine, confined to the pictorial history of museums. Lydwine is allowed by God to see things with a clarity "disallowed the feeble senses," and so can rise above the representational conventions and limited lexicon of her time. But Huysmans – unblessed with the gift of atemporality and omnipresence – has only recourse to his memories of the infernos of Bosch and Breughel, the paradisiacal gardens in the paintings of Van Eyck. The mystic can go to places that her biographer cannot, and while the martyr is liberated from language and personality, the historian is constrained by scholarship and history.

Dispossession and eternal life

From his acquaintance with Abbé Boullan, Huysmans had learned the principles of reparative Dolorism, a validation of suffering as more than gratuitous existential accident. In *Lydwine*, Huysmans's analysis of the mystic's path to unitive experience explains his emphasis on the saint's acceptance of pain and dispossession. As Eugène Vintras had extolled the poor as members of Christ's body, Huysmans also links the literal dismemberment of the saint to her loss of friends and comforts, the erasure of body boundaries, a suppression of individual will that comes with being crucified with Christ. Unable to escape repression which condemns him to live in time, the Christian imagines acceding to eternity by dying and being born again in a mystic union with the Savior. Mnemonic traces of guilt and anger, neurotic symptoms trap the body in a past where suffering does not forgive.

In the economy of mysticism, Christ as "the greatest Mendicant"[134] asks the faithful for generosity, the surrender of material goods, a relinquishment of anxiety, the repurchasing of innocence through a forfeiture of everything. The poor, who are Christ's children, can enter eternal life because they have nothing, no attachments, because they are dispossessed of objects which, as Brown says, "have to be seen as crystallized time in order to be possessed as property."[135]

Lydwine's purgative life begins with an apprenticeship in asceticism, which is signaled by her willingness to be unencumbered of relationships. Feeling obliged "to pledge her virginity to Christ," she prays to be afflicted with an illness that disfigures, and when her wishes are fulfilled, her martyrdom begins. Social suicide is a first step toward reconciliation with *the Bridegroom*, since human love, "in excluding God, is only a parody of genuine love," "a form of selfishness between two people."[136]

Bodily life, like time in Purgatory, can be more speedily concluded when suffering hastens the blessed death that finally sets one free. Guiltlessness is paid for by the torments of the saint, enabling a return to the eternity of childhood. Thus, the church treasures the innocent who are persecuted, realizing: "the tears of its martyrs are the waters of its Fountain of Youth."[137]

However, Lydwine is slow to accept the reparative task that is assigned her and, at first, her pain is exacerbated by the spectacle of others' happiness. Only with the intercession of Jean Pot, Lydwine's parish vicar, is she able to perform the mission she is delegated. Jean Pot is the first to explain that the martyrs whom Christ has chosen are "counterparts of the Son," who, in continuing the Passion, afford him "the possibility to continue suffering for us."[138]

Jean Pot confides to Lydwine that the self who dies with Christ is the perpetrator of original sin, the old Adam, the fallen being who is subsequently resurrected in righteousness and purity. Humanity, as he elaborates, is governed by two laws: "the law of solidarity in Evil and reversibility in God, solidarity in Adam, reversibility in Our Lord."[139] As Huysmans would later learn through the evolution of his faith, the greatest sacrifice is also an act of violence against the self, the killing of the corrupted being identified as *le vieil homme*. Through writing *Lydwine*, Huysmans learns that the martyrdom endured by women extends to all those who accept self-mortification in the name of a holy cause. The old Adam – the prideful stylist – consents to being sacrificed in order to be reborn as an artist glorifying God and not himself.

Crucified with Christ

Dan Merkur, in a study of medieval mysticism, argues that, in the middle of the fourteenth century, contemporaneous with the life of Lydwine, religious seekers were told to meditate on the experience of the Passion – not from the viewpoint of a witness, but from the perspective of Christ himself. Beginning with Bernard de Clairvaux (1090–1153) and continuing in Henry Suso, this practice was meant to guide the visionary through a shared experience of Christ's agony and end with a rebirth to serenity and wisdom. What Jean Pot describes to Lydwine as Mystic Substitution – the voluntary expiation of the evil done by others – also suggests the martyr's substitution for Jesus on the Cross.

Quoting from the thirteenth-century Cistercian abbot Stephen of Sawley, Merkur shows how, in prayer, the subject was to undergo the Crucifixion personally: "See how dearly [Christ] purchased your love, how willingly he gave himself for you; there the weakness of the hanging [...] will be yours, the pallor of shaking limbs yours, the shedding of blood yours, and the last breath of the crucified yours."[140]

Instead of consciously guided imagery or hypnagogic reverie, Lydwine's experience of the Crucifixion is physically enacted. Through her endurance of the myriad ills with which she is afflicted, through the sense of spiritual dereliction that repeats the Dark Night of the Soul, her martyrdom is not an act of surrogacy but an experience of completion. As Jean Pot advises her: "Say to Jesus: I want to place myself on your Cross. I want you to hammer in the nails. He will accept this role as executioner, and his angels will assist him."[141]

As Lydwine plays the part of victim and Christ the executioner, the reversal allows the process of expiation to be finished. Christ assumes the role of Father who permits the suffering of his Son, while Lydwine is the child whose innocence is the holocaustic offering. With the attainment of self-forgiveness come the death of the old Adam and the rebirth of a self freed of resentment, guilt, and terror. Whereas, in *L'Oblat*, Suffering is the Fiancée who tests the nails and mounts the Cross, in *Lydwine*, it is Christ who brings the thorns and rope and gall, and who, in the final moment takes down the body of the Saint, lays it on his knees, so that Mary can embrace her, "happily, like a big sister."[142]

The regimen Jean Pot prescribes for Lydwine's meditative exercises exactly matches the contemplative practices endorsed by Saint Francis and Saint Bonaventure. At the end of both, there occurs a mystic death of the *old man*, who is resurrected as a new being, transformed and joined with Jesus.

Accompanying phenomena: incineration in the furnace of the divine, the manifestation of Christ's sweetness as perfume emanating from rotting tissue, appear in Huysmans's text and in the writings of medieval saints. The punishing flames of hell, the cleansing fires of Purgatory become the ecstatic conflagration of a self reborn, phoenix-like, in Christ. In order to find salvation, as Saint Bonaventure writes in *Itinerarium Mentis ad Deum*, "ask desire not understanding, [..] darkness not clarity, not light but the fire that totally inflames and carries us into God by ecstatic unctions and burning affections. This fire is God, and *his*

furnace is in Jerusalem; and Christ enkindles it in the heat of his burning
passion which only he truly perceives who says: *My soul chooses hanging
and my bones death.*"[143]

The homology of suffering and rapture as transfigurative *Passion* is
expressed in the mystical language that Huysmans attributes here to
Lydwine. Thus, she imagines being possessed by Christ, liquefied "in
the forge of Love," entering into a state of fusion, and being poured "in
the nuptial form of his Cross."[144] This death and resurrection sequence
is the transmutation of the body's substance, vaporization of gangrened
flesh into a scent of flowers that is everywhere. Thus, the Bride can say of
Christ: "A bundle of myrrh is my beloved to me; he will linger between
my breasts."[145]

Jean Pot's admonishment to Lydwine about her ordeal and its
promised outcome illuminates the Saint: "The scales fell from Lydwine's
eyes."[146] But completion of the phase of purgative suffering and illumi-
native prayer is still far from completion in the perfective experience of
beatitude.

Loss and recovery

Jean Pot compares Lydwine's experience of temporality to Christ's
panoramic apprehension of mankind's past and future vices. As a propitiatory victim, Lydwine is a prisoner of others' history, the deposit of
their guilt and the precipitate of their sin. But as Jean Pot reminds her,
Lydwine is no different from her predecessors, other martyrs boiled in
oil, cooked on grills, broken on wheels, sawed in half, or shredded to
pieces with iron combs. Whereas Lydwine and her sisters see only the
evils of the past – "idolatry, incest, sacrilege, and murder" – horrible
iniquities filing by across the centuries, Christ, who is endowed with
the prescience of a divinity, sees the future as the endless procession of
mankind's trespasses – the coming men who continue to steal and crucify their Savior, "in order to satisfy their lust and passion for lucre."[147]
Omniscience confers on Christ the capacity for prospection, making the
future ineluctable, adding it to the deficit of history, causing him to need
the help of handmaidens willing to climb the Cross themselves.

Yet Pot advises Lydwine that physical suffering is always compensated
and that the torments of the body are redeemed by spiritual delights.
Suffering for others, she disintegrates into pieces, her body broken up
and shared among the lost souls that she helps, becoming like the
Eucharist distributed among communicants.

Lydwine's lesson in asceticism begins with an alienation from her
body, no longer the cutaneous container of her organs and identity.

Lesions, abscesses, open wounds, and oozing sores: Lydwine becomes the spectacle of her physical porosity. After undergoing the loss of bodily integrity, she experiences what Huysmans calls "the abandonment of things."[148] Not an elimination of her capacity to derive enjoyment from reality, this disconnection is experienced as the inhospitality of an environment no longer domesticated by familiarity, no longer pacified by anthropomorphism. It is what Camus refers to as "the primitive hostility of the world"[149] – estrangement from the things that formerly gave pleasure: crackling embers in the fireplace, the sight of scudding clouds outside the window – "these miserable, little nothings that occupy an invalid were denied her."[150]

Interpersonal attachments, the love of family members are construed as excluding God, whom Lydwine had betrayed. So when Lydwine mourns the death of her beloved niece, Petronille, Christ is jealous and abandons her to her lonely martyrdom. Like Jesus, who himself had felt forsaken on the Cross, Lydwine lives the Crucifixion as a banishment to solitude, as hopelessness, desiccation, a crushing nihilism of the soul.

Lydwine's journey ends with her participation in the Crucifixion of the Savior, but before that, she experiences an environmental death, a decathexis of treasured objects, the emotional inhumation of longtime friends, the stilling of her heart and of the voices of the world. But as she loses her capacity to receive nourishment and love, she grows in her ability to give nourishment to others. By vacating herself, she learns the joy of multiplicity, living through the sinners whose penance she alleviates.

Once Lydwine is able to eat nothing but the Eucharist, she lives on nourishment as holiness, "for eating well means eating goodness. It mean eating God," as Marc Smeets writes.[151] As selfishness is the sin that turns the subject away from God – a refusal of alterity, an autophagia of affect – Lydwine undergoes the Passion in order to be reborn as *compassion*, her body a salvatory image of Europe's ravaged body. Like nineteenth-century France, corrupted by Republicans and Dreyfusards, the deterioration of the Holland of Lydwine augured a jubilant rebirth. After Lydwine's mystic death and reunion with the Savior, she is freed from time as the ensnaring residue of humanity's collective guilt. Accompanied by her guardian angel, she experiences the gift of bilocation, an ability to move about in time and visit more than one place simultaneously. Yet this migratory freedom only adumbrates the blessings still to come, when her physical death delivers her into ubiquity and eternity.

In her out-of-body flights to Paradise, Lydwine sees heaven, according to her history and temperament, as relief from a life of scarcity and hunger: "as a vision of a magnificently vaulted banquet hall, where meats were served on silverware placed on tablecloths of green silk and wine was poured in cups of crystal and gold."[152] Through her sharing in the Passion, she comes to see divine rewards as banquets served on linen or as wine in crystal goblets. Reborn in Christ, she undergoes a transubstantiative operation and is dispersed as sacramental food into the people whom she succors. First as the smell of clove and cinnamon, then as violets and lilies, "symbols of humility and chastity,"[153] Lydwine evaporates in death into a scent that is unrecognizable, "an unanalyzable scent, so restorative and fortifying" that the people gathered around her "needed neither sleep nor nutriment for two days and three nights."[154]

Rebirth in others

As with her martyred sisters, Lydwine's purpose is to redeem others with her agonies. But after death, she is transformed, both as essence and as species, into the food of life assimilated by the sinners whose guilt she expiates. Eaten and inhaled, as nourishment and perfume, she enters into others, is pluralized and dissipated, joining with the fortunate for whom she is annihilated as herself. Indeed, Huysmans imagines a similar fate awaiting the male author, transposed as the text that is distributed to the public. Publication of his work becomes a Eucharistic feast whereby a writer dies yet lives again in the readers who consume him.

When the debt of guilt is settled, history ceases to imprison. Having bound man to the objects that he mistakenly had coveted, enslaving time makes way for mobility and freedom, and for Lydwine, everlasting life brings dissemination into those she saves. Purgatory as the *topos* of a confining temporality is thrown open so that tortured souls escape into a heaven that is everywhere.

Unpardoned, Lydwine was at first the child who is chastened by the Father, but having died with Christ, she moves beyond the Passion to compassion, her suffering universalized as identification with the world. When he is no longer a merciless executioner, an introjected God is not experienced as guilt incurring self-arraignment and self-punishment. Once she is crucified with Christ, the martyred mystic feels no more rage; she ceases "to have unconscious cause to fear retaliation." As Merkur adds, "self-forgiveness constitute[s] permission to experience the euphoric ecstasy of a clear conscience," and with the recovery of innocence, "resurrection follow[s]."[155]

Since only the Father can act as judge, inexorable and retributive, only the child can deserve his disapproval and his sanction. Thus, Lydwine's absolution entails an alteration in her status, so when she is brought down from the Cross, Mary embraces her "like a sister."

In a strikingly rich theophany, Christ manifests himself to Lydwine, both as the infant and as the adult Son with bleeding nail holes in his hands. In another vision, Lydwine takes her place in "in a cloud of virgins dressed in white,"[156] spotless women assisting in the nativity of the Newborn. Rewarded for having joined Christ and for assisting in his death throes, she is rewarded by helping Mary in the celebration of his birth. Seraphs, as Huysmans writes, pick pearls of sound from harps of fire. Others weave swaddling clothes from the blue smoke of burning incense.

Again apologizing for the descriptive inadequacy of his writing, Huysmans pictures Lydwine reciting the liturgical phrases she learned in childhood, performing "the ceremonial practices she was familiar with here below."[157] Constrained by the rote doxological formulations she had memorized, Lydwine underscores the inexpressible magnificence of her vision with the simple language of God's praise, the poverty of Huysmans's prose.

However, the beauty of the scene lies in the resurrection of Lydwine's innocence and the nativity of a self who is both a child and the child's mother. The people saved by Christ and his handmaidens are strewn as myriads of lights across the galaxy, as "an immense trajectory of milk illumined from behind by a thousand stars."[158] The miraculous lactation that Lydwine experiences marks her transformation from guilty child to providential mother, as the elixir of life changes from martyr's blood to mother's milk. As Jerôme Solal remarks, this substitution of liquid elements denotes the passage from self to others, from singularity to multiplicity, from Lydwine's confinement in her bed and body to her dilation into those consuming her: "milk, that wonderfully sensual substance that expresses *being with*, a mother's gift that brings satiety."[159]

Having died with Christ and lain beside Christ's corpse on Mary's knees, she participates with the Madonna in the experience of Christmas. What Vintras had said of Mary is also true of Lydwine: "She spoke little, and yet how powerfully she drew Brides to the Bridegroom's sacred sanctuary. The odor of her sanctity transported men and ravished angels. She was the incense that cherubs bore to the feet of the Eternal

Master's throne. She died of love, but she fought death with the power of her love."[160]

After her death and rebirth in Paradise, Lydwine's good offices continue – in the posthumous performance of the statutory three miracles: an invalid child from Delft, bedridden for eight years, who invokes the Saint and finds that, all at once, she has been healed; a crippled nun from Gouda to whom Lydwine manifests herself and who enlists the other monachals to recite five Our Fathers and Five Hail Mary's and then sees that her leg is straight and that she is able to walk again; another nun from Leyden who, having prayed by Lydwine's tomb, finds a cancerous tumor on her neck had disappeared while she was sleeping.

From Eve to Mary

Huysmans's hagiography may draw on the archival sources he identifies, but his picture of the Blessed Lydwine is a product of the fin-de-siècle imagination. From Vintras, Huysmans derives his sense of the perpetual apocalypse, his gender classification of men as prophets, priests, and artists, and of women as the fortunate who can see God face to face. Huysmans propagates the fin-de-siècle ideal of holy dispossession, material scarcity compensated by the abundance of the soul's joys. In *Lydwine*, suffering frees a self encased in comfortable indifference, scattering it in the multitudes saved by her sacrificial fervor. The era of the Paraclete, which Vintras had predicted, brings a deliverance from history, the Second Age of the Suffering Son, and an accession to eternity as a renaissance of innocence.

Furthermore, in *Lydwine*, Huysmans sketches the new role of the writer, one in which he is no longer marginalized by being unfit as a martyr, no longer disqualified by his intellect and language. Like Vintras and Boullan, professing to be descended from the prophets, Huysmans reaffirms the importance of the vaticinator and his message. Suffering because his gender leaves him ill-equipped to suffer, he still announces the apocalypse prepared by the torments of Eve's daughters.

Huysmans's text continues after Vintras's Cult of Mary and his ritual of ascensional redemption, where Eve was rehabilitated by repeating the sin that earned her punishment. The teleological purpose of the banishment from Eden comes with the death of the old Adam and the birth of the Messiah. The woman who is driven out for eating from the Tree of Forbidden Fruit becomes Eucharistic nourishment that gives satisfaction without end. Once her punishment is welcomed and her suffering embraced, Huysmans shows an Eve re-virginized and sanctified by the dedication of her penance. To the woman, God had said: "I will greatly multiply your pain in childbearing" (*Genesis* 3.8), but in her willingness to die with Christ for the children she brings forth, woman is made immaculate, her integrity restored by pain. Dolorism, in consecrating the agony of childbearing, shows its culmination in the joy of engendering new life: souls liberated from a Purgatory of self-incrimination, a self that is reborn in munificence and charity. Ceasing to be the temptress, Eve finds the purpose of her suffering when, in redeeming her unforgiven child, she fulfills her destiny as God's mother.

Léon Bloy: *La Femme Pauvre* (*The Woman Who was Poor* 1897)

While Léon Bloy may have been only indirectly influenced by the millenarian doctrine of Eugène Vintras, it was from the Prophet of Tilly that Bloy derived his impatient hope in the world's end. Bloy shared Vintras's outrage at the institution of Catholicism, which he denounced as venal, spiritually tepid, guided solely by material concerns. It was Vintras's praise of the suffering poor that Bloy carried to fanatical extremes, Vintras's belief in the sanctity of women as martyrs that directed Bloy in the creation of his fictional heroines. Richard D. E. Burton maintains that Bloy's visionary mistress, Anne-Marie Roulé, had been conversant with the principal tenets of Vintrasianism, sharing them with the writer, convincing him that the age of the Crucified Son was nearing its conclusion and that it would soon be followed by a glorious sunrise accompanying the Reign of the Holy Spirit.

It was from Bloy's relationship with Anne-Marie, and later with Berthe Dumont that he drew his portrait of the Dolorist saint, not a woman living in a romanticized medieval setting, but one struggling to survive in contemporary Paris, where her torments and ecstasies inspired artists modeled on Bloy himself.

Born in Périgueux in 1846, Bloy was first exposed by his devout mother, Anne-Marie Carreau, to the strain of Christian mysticism that would seethe in his later writing. After relocating to Paris in 1863, Bloy met and came under the influence of Barbey d'Aurevilley, whose reactionary Catholicism further propelled Bloy to abjure his earlier atheism and declare his conversion to the church in 1870.

Like Huysmans, whom over time he identified as his nemesis and enemy, Bloy based his faith on a view of male artists as evangelist/transcribers who recorded the rapturous visions of inarticulate female saints. However, Bloy's central contribution to the martyrology of the fin de siècle – his refinement of the mystic thought that was becoming prevalent in the era – came from showing how Dolorist self-abnegation could be practiced in the modern world. Bloy takes the oceanic, often barely intelligible prophetic admonitions of Vintras and applies them, not as Huysmans does, to a distant historical figure from medieval Holland, but to a few desperate, yet fervently confident religious seekers living in the heart of nineteenth-century Paris.

In Huysmans's biography of Lydwine, the saint's visions of Paradise and Purgatory had been conditioned, the author argues, by the iconography of her era. When Lydwine had flown with her guardian angel to different areas of the afterlife, what she had seen had been divinely adapted to her cultural conditions. Since Huysmans's experience of hell and heaven came through identification with his subject, Lydwine's mystical raptures – and Huysmans's appreciation of them – were products of a particular historical consciousness. On the other hand, in Bloy's fiction, the experience of ecstatic transcendence is shown as being accessible to characters resembling his own contemporaries.

While Bloy shared Huysmans's disaffection for the commercial vulgarity of modern society, his relationships with Anne-Marie Roulé and Berthe Dumont had afforded him a glimpse into the lives of martyrs living in the muddy streets and squalid neighborhoods of nineteenth-century Paris. It is as an *épisode contemporain* (a contemporary episode) that Bloy's heroine takes part in the Passion of Christ, undergoing an annihilation of self in the divine. It is there that she experiences death as an emancipation from material comforts and from the people she loves. The sacred poverty that Vintras had extolled is embraced and lived by Bloy's heroines, whose sainthood disengages them from history and who approach beatification in the era they live in. When Clotilde Chapuis in *La Femme pauvre* is unburdened of possessions, freed from the love of her husband and son, she stands on the threshold of a personal apocalypse translating her from exile into eternity.

When Bloy first met Berthe Dumont, beggar-woman and morphine-addict, in the streets of Paris in January 1884, offering shelter to the vagrant and her mother in his home on the Pavillon d'Asnières, he seemed to be re-enacting the same ambiguously predatory and charitable impulse that had caused him to give sanctuary to prostitute Anne-Marie Roulé seven years before. With each woman, Bloy witnessed the initial conflagration of his mistress's faith, then stood helplessly by while both women were swept into a gyre of madness or disease. While the martyrdom of Anne-Marie had begun with her prophetic illuminations and then had degenerated into the insanity that caused her internment in the asylum of Saint-Anne in 1882, Berthe had contracted tetanus suddenly in 1885, driving her penurious benefactor out into the streets, in a fruitless search for money and assistance.

Yet Bloy's participation in the sacred mystery of the Passion of these martyred saints only exacerbated his alienation from a world he already regarded as indifferent to suffering and devoid of spirituality, As was the case with Huysmans, Bloy's faith, in its evolution, was inextricably interwoven with his disgust at the deplorable state of French art and letters at the century's end. Porte-parole for the author, Bloy's male protagonist is a Catholic writer incensed at the pleasure-loving, pain-avoiding mediocrity of his co-religionists, enraged by the vapidity of his more successful fellow-artists. Bloy's unenviable reputation among critics who bemoan his "singularly uncharitable Christian polemic,"[161] emanates from his vindictive lamentations over the plight of fin-de-siècle literature and faith. Digressive tirades against bumptious editors and talentless scribblers, turgid invective against flaccid clerics and avaricious Jews form a picture of nineteenth-century society as Purgatory, in which the intervention of a saint becomes a matter of ever more pressing urgency.

The eagerness with which Bloy awaited the end of time arises from his sense of estrangement from a world shown as hostile and hellish. Yet to his credit, Bloy uses his fiction as more than a forum for self-pitying vengeance. Bloy's feelings of literal and spiritual dereliction in a society ruled by Philistines led to an apprehension of the function of mystical suffering as a way to hasten the apocalypse. Taken from his harrowing experiences with Anne-Marie and Berthe, Bloy creates his image of a martyred heroine haloed against a dark backdrop of poisonous literary banquets, sordid urban slums, bitter exclusion, heartlessness, and desolation, showing how she burns with a despair that is finally purified into ecstasy.

The apparition at La Salette

In flight from the faith-shriveling inhospitality of the capital, both Huysmans and Bloy had found a springboard for their faith at the pilgrimage site of La Salette. A barren and remote mountain village near Grenoble, La Salette was prized by both Huysmans and Bloy for "its physical inaccessibility – proof of La Salette's superiority over its 'democratic' counterpart Lourdes."[162] The importance of La Salette in Bloy's personal theology, its privileged place in the spiritual geography of fin-de-siècle Catholics, Bloy's association of the Weeping Virgin who appeared on the mountain with the Dolorist martyrs illumining his fiction explain the significance of the location in turn-of-the-century French mysticism.

In his 1908 commentary on the Apparition, *Celle qui pleure* (*The One Who Weeps*), Bloy recounts the miracle of La Salette and explains its eschatological implications. In 1846, a generation before the flourishing of the fin-de-siècle Catholic revival, the Virgin Mary is said to have appeared to two cowherds – Mélanie Calvat and Maximin Giraud – in a pasture on Mont Planeau overlooking La Salette. Scintillating in a golden gown woven with flame, wreathed in flowers of unearthly beauty, she had uncovered her face, Bloy writes, only to reveal it "streaming with tears."[163] Inviting the children to approach her, she had instructed them to warn of disasters to come: famine, war, crop failure, the decline of a moribund church, all presaging the coming of the Anti-Christ, who would usher in a time of upheaval and tribulation climaxed by a fiery apocalypse.

Bolstering convictions that the end time was nearing, the secrets confided to Mélanie and Maximin had left a profound impression on Huysmans, who underwent his own conversion on a pilgrimage to La Salette. Even greater was the influence on Bloy, who devoted much of his writing to chronicling the life of Mélanie, producing meticulous exegetical commentary on the address from Mary, and examining the relationship between nineteenth-century Catholics and Our Lady of Sorrows, whom Bloy would refer to as *The One Who Weeps*.

As for the secret – having cast the clergy in an unflattering light – Mélanie's admonition first met with incredulity and suspicion. But after an 1847 investigation and extensive questioning of the guileless young witnesses, an official report authenticating the miracle was submitted to Pope Pius IX, and its conclusion was ratified by the Holy See in August 1848.

Notwithstanding church verification of Mary's message, neither sacerdotal reform nor a collective recommitment to the principles of sacrifice and austerity ensued. In Bloy's opinion, the Virgin, who had told of restraining God's wrath, would soon no longer be able to continue protecting her children. "If my people will not submit," she cautioned, "I will be forced to let my Son's arm go. It is so heavy that soon I will not be able to restrain it any longer."[164]

Much of Bloy's writing seems fueled by anticipation that the extinction of zeal among his Catholic brethren would ignite God's anger and trigger universal destruction. Part of Bloy wanted Mary's compassion to fail so that Christ's punishing arm would come down on humanity.

On the other hand, the Messianic promise, unfulfilled for almost 2,000 years, struck Bloy as a violation of the covenant made with those who suffered with Christ. An abrogated pledge, the postponed apocalypse constituted an embarrassment to a God who had abdicated his role. For Bloy, as Albert Béguin writes: "History has not yet become the history of the definitive Kingdom. From century to century, it has pursued its frightful course, requiring all the attention of a prayerful spirit, all the difficult humility of a humble heart to accept the scandal of these infinite delays. It is not easy to forgive God for abandoning his children, more cruelly orphaned since God's Son died for them, more unable to understand why Satan has so much power over their obscure destiny."[165]

Embittered and impatient with the Messiah who did not come, Bloy expressed his frustrated apocalypticism as a sense of exile on the earth, as a feeling of dereliction in a world where holiness and self-denial were despised. Bloy himself had visited La Salette in 1879, accompanied by his spiritual mentor, Abbé Tardif de Moidrey, who had echoed the Virgin's condemnation of a clergy guilty of pandering to the wealthy, worldly priests stigmatized by Mary as "cesspools of impurity." According to Bloy, the nineteenth-century priesthood, defiled after authorizing a religion of luxury and self-indulgence, had come to regard its mission as amassing money "by all means compatible or incompatible with the dignity of their cassock."[166] For them, the wretched who re-enacted Christ's Passion were dismissed as mere disturbances of the rich man's peace of mind. Occasionally benefitting from others' eleemosynary impulses, the poor were advised to remain concealed in the dark corners of sanctuaries. No less grave than the moderation of Catholic faith was the profanation of the Sabbath, a tendency to treat the day as an occasion for money-making commerce.

However, Tardif, who had died during the pilgrimage to La Salette, had been most influential in shaping Bloy's metaphysic, imbuing him with a belief in the secret meaning of Creation. Practitioner of a comprehensive system of Scriptural interpretation, Tardif had convinced Bloy of the Bible's occult symbolism. Arguing that every Biblical passage was "to be taken as referring to the Holy Trinity,"[167] Tardif had bequeathed to his disciple a "mystical approach to history."[168] From Tardif, Bloy had concluded that all events were eschatological portents requiring urgent deciphering, the world a "cryptogram" to which a universal algebra could be applied. For the enlightened exegete, "the word *Chance* was an intolerable blasphemy."[169]

The author in exile

Bloy's conception of the universe as an unriddled system of explanatory symbols underpins the design of his own fictional world, structured by classifications of martyrs and evildoers, artists of the profane and artist of the sublime. Similarly – as in his contemporaries' works – Bloy's characters are grouped by a typology of gender, in which men are artists producing images whose purpose is to illumine the human condition as exile, and women, who, because they are unseparated from the divinity by language, experience the transfigurative pain that returns them from banishment to Paradise. In Bloy's most famous novel, *La Femme pauvre* (1897), a woman's mystical experience is not situated in the remoteness of medieval history, but in being written as an episode in the life of a fin-de-siècle *Parisienne*, presents the issue of religious ecstasy as one having immediacy and relevance.

Yet it was only later in his career that Bloy concentrated on women's spiritual prerogatives, as his inaugural novel, *Le Désespéré* (*The Hopeless* 1886), charts the religious itinerary of his hero, Caïn Marchenoir. Bloy's alter ego, Marchenoir is another Catholic fanatic, the mouthpiece through which the author airs his unorthodox beliefs, vents his professional grudges, and expresses his apocalyptic longings. Consigned to the novel's background, Marchenoir's mistress, Véronique, is an *illuminée* and martyr, but her status as a visionary is compromised by her decline into despair and paranoia.

Rather than focusing on woman, Bloy begins by describing his hero's invocation of the hieratic privilege of the vaticinator/poet, whose nominative authority confers supremacy over all beings. In Eden, as Marchenoir explains in a gloss of Tardif's cosmology, God bestowed on man the authority to name all other creatures. A secondary power or coefficient of the *Logos*, the transitive act of naming conferred mastery of the world. To name as object, for Marchenoir, may not be the same as to create it, but by infusing it with meaning and identifying its relationship to man, Adam took possession of the things he subjugated through understanding. Like man, who as the catechism teaches, was fashioned in God's likeness, animals were made by Adam, "created in the image of his reason."[170] As Marchenoir elaborates: "When our first ancestor named the animals, he made them his. He not only subjugated them as an emperor would. His essence penetrated them. He fixed them, joined them to himself forever, mixing them into his destiny."[171]

Yet as an emperor is irremediably cut off from his subjects, whose subservience, otherness, and suffering are unfathomable, so man is alienated from the creatures over which he has dominion. Names are an anthropocentric optic that muddies and distorts: "we perceive beings only in relation to other beings, never at their heart, never in their essence," as Marchenoir summarizes.[172]

Despite his grandiloquence and obscurantism, Marchenoir – as a God-inspired poet – is still disjoined from the world that is illuminated by his genius. Self-exaltingly described by Bloy as a modern judge of Israel, an evangelical ravisher whom the celestial legions cannot resist, Marchenoir still does not know the sufferings of the tigers he watches in a cage. His language is a darkening glass through which imperfect knowledge passes. The name that man attaches is the garment covering an object, a veil at once concealing and beautifying the body of the real.

When Marchenoir speaks, his words measure their distance from their referents, compelling him to re-enact the experience of the Fall. Consistent with Vintrasianism, Bloy equates woman with Truth, "*Sophia*, or Wisdom (a divine principle which had fallen from the realm of light into the realm of matter)."[173] Denied access to the Truth except through Analogic poetry, men are "sleepers" condemned to operate in a shadow-land of images, approximations of what will be revealed "when all things hidden are revealed,"[174] when *the perfect comes*, enabling us to see things "face to face" (*Corinthians* I. 13.2).

In Bloy's principal works of fiction, he marks his writing's evolution from author-centered stories to mystical attempts at capturing woman's apprehension of the divine. In his meditations on Mélanie and the miraculous apparition at La Salette, he had refined his appreciation of the Virgin Mary as the new Eve, so that, in *La Femme pauvre*, he achieves a final synthesis of the mystic's thematic interests in suffering woman and salvation. Through Bloy's vicarious participation in the tribulations of his anguished mistresses – first Anne-Marie Roulé and later Berthe Dumont – he was able to move from a fiction of vituperative retribution to a visionary literature of spiritual transcendence. In personalizing Vintras's teachings on poverty and suffering, Bloy identifies with his female characters and then accompanies them on their journey, which he believes will end with a liberation from a fallen world of materialism and irreligion. From his sainted heroines, Bloy finds the way from Purgatory back to Eden. In following Tardif's global system of symbolic correlations, Bloy learns that woman is both Eve, the earthly Eden, and Mary, the celestial Paradise: "the Immaculate Conception, [...] the sublime Garden found again."[175]

In *La Femme Pauvre*, Caïn Marchenoir describes arriving in La Salette, already broken and cast down after the recent death of his infant son.

Bloy's angry protagonists often rage against an unresponsive God whose justice they see as doubtful and obscure. In an era of insolently triumphant materialism and faltering devotion, Bloy's characters are not far from embracing the devil of miscreants and pariahs portrayed by Jules Bois: "the Satan of the disinherited and the poor, ruler of the sorcerer, the bandit, the irredeemable traitor, the miserable outlaw, and the rebel."[176] Nor are they unlike Huysmans's Canon Docre who, while officiating at a Black Mass in fin-de-siècle Paris, inveighs against Christ as the Champion of the Rich, "Beloved Vassal of the Banks," "God of business."[177] In an era rotten with hedonism and sacrilege, Bloy's faith is sustained only by the sanctification of suffering.

For Bloy, a woman's participation in the Passion is marked by the supersession of Mary's tears for Christ's blood. When, in a provocative comment, Bloy writes that "the Blood of the Poor is money,"[178] he both incriminates the wealthy whose comforts are ransomed by the wretched, and sacramentalizes the poor man's blood as a viaticum that redeems.

The prototype of Marchenoir is a pilgrim he meets at La Salette, a man unable to forgive himself for killing another in a duel. He teaches Marchenoir about the holiness and innocence of animals, recommending the unawareness that likens them to man before the Fall. Wishing to emulate Saint Francis in cultivating a fraternal bond with all living things, he had sought to learn the forgotten language of animals and stones. Like Marchenoir, he regards Creation as a universal hieroglyph, beginning with the Lamb and Calf as symbols of the Son, then continuing with other elements in a theriographic mystery. These animals are "the alphabetical signs of Ecstasy," he says, keys to the "everlasting history of the Trinity."[179]

From his encounter with a grief-disabled sojourner in La Salette, Marchenoir had evolved his own idea of a universal hermeneutic, whereby the misery of man's condition during his passage on the earth could be deciphered "in the Kabbalah of dates," "in the most deeply hidden Arcanum of facts."[180]

However, for Bloy and for Marchenoir, the Book of Explanations had remained unwritten. Fueled by Mélanie's predictions, expectations of the apocalypse seemed to be borne out by world events: the Franco-Prussian War, then the ascendancy of *la Culture allemande* (German Culture) in 1913, which, according to Bloy, prefigured "the final extinction of people's souls."[181]

Like Bloy, Marchenoir devoted his talents as a writer to truculent denunciations of the affluent bourgeoisie, lamentations of their indulgence in selfish otiosity. An unattractive trait shared by author and protagonist is their use of literature as a forum for settling scores and scourging enemies, complaining about the unenthusiastic reception of their books. However, in moving beyond his feelings of personal persecution, extensively documented in the volumes of his journal, Bloy stands out among the other fin-de-siècle mystic writers by describing how the practice of Dolorism might afford an actual deliverance from a fallen world.

As is indicated by the title of Bloy's first autobiographical novel, man's lot is to narrate his earthly destiny as *un désespéré*. A concomitant of Bloy's magnification of the victim and the martyr is his attack on those identified as oppressors and executioners. Bloy's fictional writings are used as campaigns of revenge, *livres à clef* replete with arraignments of his confrères, whose success he deplores as "the Divine right of absolute Mediocrity."[182] Paul Bourget, Guy de Maupassant, Jean Richepin, Alphonse Daudet are among those splashed with Marchenoir's stercoraceous vituperation. J.-K. Huysmans, whose views on suffering were similar to Bloy's, is the target of especially corrosive execration.

While Bloy's analyses of the mystical ecstasies of women are pleasing in their simplicity, his social criticism is swollen with obscure phrases, clouded with neologisms. Unusual rhetorical effects, threatening annihilation or conveying sarcasm, make his texts a place of exile for his readers as was the world for his characters. Cataplexis promises eschatological doom for fools and Philistines. Deinosis invites audience scorn for writers who prostitute their talent. Cacemphaton heaps the mud of scurrilous ridicule on those who mock Christ with their *bégeulisme cafard* (hypocritical prudery) and emasculate religion with false piety. Covering his contemporaries with "scatological reprobation," Marchenoir "saw the modern world, with its institutions and ideas, foundering in an ocean of mud. It was an Atlantis submerged in a sump."[183]

Inspiring antipathy and dread with his scathing diatribes, Marchenoir, at one point, is invited to a literary banquet hosted by impresario and editor Abraham-Properce Beauvivier (Catulle Mendès). But after listening to hours of persiflage and self-anointment – "prehistoric witticisms and tertiary puns"[184] – Marchenoir erupts in insults he hurls at the other guests. Having ensured his place is lost in the community of writers, he is relegated to the loneliness of his apartment in the city and dies there without receiving the consolation of the last rites.

In *Le Désespéré*, Bloy writes his *Purgatorio*, a penitential narrative telling of children who die, lovers who are lost, friends who, when summoned, arrive too late. In a novel without solace, Bloy's world is a small, self-centered place, where sorrow comes from being unappreciated and unread. Bloy's hero, like the Jews that Bloy tirelessly castigates, is misunderstood, itinerant, homeless, and despised. After the death of his father in the novel's first section, Marchenoir makes a winter retreat at La Grande Chartreuse. There, under a frigid canopy, in a landscape of snowy desolation, he meditates on seclusion and sainthood, reflecting on what Huysmans calls man's solidarity in Adam and reversibility in Christ, "that transcendent law of supernatural balance condemning the innocent to pay the ransom of the guilty."[185] Coveting the ascetic simplicity of conventual reclusion, he inquires about the possibility of joining the order. But one of the Carthusians, recognizing in Marchenoir a man of language as engagement, persuades him that he is unfit to take a vow of silence. Like Marchenoir, Bloy had himself considered the possibility of a monastic vocation and, in 1877, had spent a ten-day retreat at La Grande Trappe at Soligny. However, like his character, Bloy discovered he was unsuited for monastic life, and so, estranged from society, both the author and his hero reassume their desolate status as vagrants on the earth. As a writer contemptuous of the public whose attention he solicits, a believer infuriated with the God whose deliverance does not come, Marchenoir, like Bloy, is a stranger in society, a trespasser in God's kingdom and so inhabits an intermediate zone between higher and lower realms. Despite the stridence of his misanthropy, he treasures the loyalty of friends, the devotion of his mistress, and sees suffering, not as a crucible where sinners are purified by fire, but as a sacrificial duty that connects him to his brothers. A generous impulse expressed in action is an anonymous text that binds its author to an audience raised up by an unseen benefactor: "All of Christian philosophy lies in the importance of acts of free will and in the notion of all-enveloping and indestructible solidarity with one's brother."[186]

Already in *Le Désespéré*, Bloy's protagonist intuits that the writer's task is not to fill 400 pages with jeremiads, but to mute his voice in order to amplify the eloquence of God. On the level of writing, the ego death fusing the worshipper with Christ requires a deletion of the message, a humbling of the author. As Jean-Claude Polet writes, this discipline "proceeds through negation, with the intention of establishing the super-eminent qualities of the divinity, saying that God is unknowable, infinite, and incorruptible."[187] Moving from the nullity of self to the totality of God, Bloy sees a religion of suffering that obliterates the artist, creating emptiness that only the sacred can complete. This is the trajectory described by Bloy's novels: from self-pity and resentment, from vengeance and paranoia, to mystic self-effacement that brings a promise of release. Herein lies the paradox of Bloy's long and bitter novels: the use of language as an instrument of self-invalidation, his discovery of the uselessness of expressions of ire. After the glorifying picture of the genius Caïn Marchenoir – after Bloy's recourse to literature to denounce the vapidity of literature – there is a gradual eclipsing of Bloy's novelistic alter ego. His sole remaining role is celebrating inarticulate female martyrs, saying what women communicate in mystic ecstasy or tearful silence.

Martyrdom and ecstasy: Bloy's holy women

Just as Véronique Cheminot, the Dolorist sibyl in *Le Désespéré*, is the fictional precursor of Clotilde Chapuis in *La Femme pauvre*, the madwoman Anne-Marie Roulé, whom Bloy had met in 1877, is the forerunner of Berthe Dumont, the morphine-addicted prostitute who is transposed as the saint in Bloy's second novel.

Bloy's inferential view of mysticism – observed by men and lived by women – can be seen in his affiliation of woman and suffering. Eve, who mourned for centuries for the children she bore in pain, is completed and redeemed by Mary, who weeps forever at La Salette. The tears of Mary, "which the Flood can only inadequately represent."[188] are a spectacle compelling the Redeemer to return. Mary's sorrow for humanity, reflected in Christ's compassion for his mother, suggests the vale of tears whose baptismal water washes away original sin. For Bloy, the Virgin's weeping is a cause for humanity's rejoicing, just as suffering is a blessing that ensures the penitent's absolution: "Rolling down from Calvary, Our Lady's tears fall in cataracts on the living. All are drowned in them, and the most fortunate among are submerged at incommensurable depths."[189]

In *Le Désespéré*, Marchenoir lives with his mistress, Véronique, a reformed prostitute with fiery hair whom he had saved from a life of ignominious vagrancy. More than a literary work, the soteriological rescue of Véronique is a masterpiece of efficient grace which Marchenoir is grateful to have authored: "He was as proud of his Véronique as he would have been of a beautiful book."[190]

In her previous life of sexual depradation, Véronique had been given the admiring soubriquet *la Ventouse* (the Sucker). Even in her street name, Bloy's heroine is linked to her role as one who dispossesses, assisting in a hygienic regimen that restore her lovers to humility and nothingness.

Following Marchenoir's retreat at La Grand Chartreuse, his return to a life of literary vexation begins what John Coombes calls "a disconnected episodic series:" tirades against the artistic mediocrity of his era, the poverty and hardship he endures with Véronique, "their shared religious fanaticism, leading to her madness and incarceration," and finally to his death "and a kind of murky apotheosis."[191]

Aware that her protector still finds her sexually attractive, Véronique undergoes voluntary self-mutilation when she has her teeth pulled out in order to inspire less temptation in her lover.

Marchenoir, condemned to die alone in his miserable apartment, unconsoled by Extreme Unction, unattended by his friend, makes a cameo appearance in Bloy's next novel, *La Femme pauvre*, his celebrated treatise on a woman's path to sainthood. Marginalized, male artists and illuminators of sacred manuscripts initiate the heroine into the world of complex symbols. Bloy, devoting more time to exploring the mystery of woman as Sophia, ceases to catalog the image-veils with which her worshippers enshroud her. While Jean-Claude Polet describes the characters' passage through an expiatory interlude, seeing in the novel "a map of their destinies across the invisible realities of Purgatory,"[192] Bloy's book, in charting the evolution of Clotilde Chapuis from Eve to Mary, takes as its setting the postlapsarian world of banishment and wandering. Instead of in a garden of earthly pleasures, Bloy's Eve lives in her parent's foul repair, with its stinking mattresses, dirty walls, and cheap religious knickknacks. Unsuffused by innocence, it is a place where a young girl's naïve faith offends her stepfather's nostrils: "It stinks of the good Lord in here," he exclaims.[193]

Paralleling the Genesis account of shamed expatriation, the novel starts with Clotilde's assignment to pose naked as an artist's model. Nudity as self-awareness, punishing the Fall into duality, expels woman from childhood into the mortification of maturity. Since Bloy had followed Tardif in equating a symbol and its meaning, he saw Eve, not just as the occupant, but as the personification of the Garden. Rosemary Rodwell describes Bloy's adoption of the sensuality of the Song of Songs, affirming that "when [he] spoke of the Earthly Paradise as a symbol of woman, it was [...] her *body* to which he was referring."[194]

Subordinating a woman's unclothed flesh to its representation in painting is, for Bloy, evidence of sinful pride, iconolatry, and sacrilege, a profanation of art's purpose as doxological expression: "A purportedly religious art work that in no way inspires prayer is as monstrous as a beautiful woman who is unable to arouse anyone."[195]

Clotilde's encounter with a series of tutelary intercessors suggests Bloy's wish to set the novel, not in the hell of the Chapuis household, but in an intermediate zone of purgative redemption. That Clotilde escapes a Gehenna of abuse and degradation and is not exiled from an asylum of safety and unknowing confirms Bloy's view of the child/woman who inherits the sins of the father.

The caricaturist Gacougnol, the first of Clotilde's benefactors, uses art to show the modern world as a grotesque deformation of Creation. Bloy's own stylistic blending of exaggeration and buffoonery groups his contemporaries in a bestiary of *hippopotamuses* and *crocodiles*. Indeed, the path that takes Clotilde from the earthly garden to its celestial counterpart begins when Gacougnol escorts her to the Jardin des Plantes, a fin-de-siècle version of Eden in Paris. Having escaped the jackals of the Chapuis family, she is instructed by her mentors in the mystery, stoicism, and nobility of tigers.

The chronological overlap of *Le Désespéré* and *La Femme pauvre* enables Marchenoir to return and act as Clotilde's second teacher. Still eulogized by Bloy as an evangelist and orator, Marchenoir acknowledges the infirmity of human art, which shows its subject refracted through the lens of anthropocentrism. Marchenoir laments the plight of artists toiling after the Fall: "I await the clairvoyant poet who will write the 'Paradise Lost' of our aesthetic innocence."[196]

Similar comments deprecating the utility of Bloy's own calling, subordinating men's sophistication to the simplicity of women, proliferate in the novel's second section, where male artists begin to vanish. First Gacougnol, targeted by Clotilde's stepfather and mother, is found knifed in the chest and dies days later in the hospital. Marchenoir's death agonies alone in his apartment reprise the conclusion of the preceding novel. And Clotilde's husband, Léopold, the illuminator aged by sadness and misfortune, finds that his eyesight has dimmed so that he must abandon his profession. After Clotilde is educated in medieval history and art, her teachers become superfluous and make way for the heroine, as the novel begins to focus on her developing relationship with Christ.

Like Léopold's conversion, Clotilde's evolving spirituality is a matter that Bloy concedes his novel cannot convey: "Art has nothing more to say once God manifests himself."[197]

As a refugee from her childhood home and an exile from the garden, Clotilde cannot become like Eve and re-enter the innocence of Eden. Lacking fluency in the language of animals and stones, she can only guess at the secret thoughts of the tigers at the zoo. Yet as a foreigner in the modern world, she is always oriented backward – toward the first mother, toward a time of simplicity and faith. Encouraged by a missionary she had encountered once in church, she prays to Eve whom she remembers having guided her in dreams – to *an adorable country* where lions and nightingales had swooned with melancholy. She is told by Gacougnol of her affinity with the Middle Ages, a time of zealotry and mysticism, "ten centuries of ecstasy," a fortress of prayer built on the ruins of innocence: "an immense church of the kind one will see no more until God returns to earth."[198] Yet the poverty that is Clotilde's birthright as Eve's daughter must be exchanged for the poverty that qualifies her for the beatitude of sainthood.

Deliverance from time

Like medieval man, Bloy's characters live in the hope of an apocalypse – not the joyful consummation that Vintras had predicted, nor the recurrent cataclysm described by Huysmans in *Sainte Lydwine*, but humanity's imminent extinction, of which Bloy discovered portents everywhere. After the Deluge of guilt and remorseful sorrow – after the lachrymal baptism that engulfed the world – they await the baptism of flame allowing them to be reborn in paradise. Following the apparition of *Celle qui pleure* came Mélanie's vision of *La Dame en Feu* (the Lady of Fire). And following the punishment for eating the fruit of the Tree of Knowledge comes the thirst that binds the sinner to Jesus on the Cross. The Thirst for God is unlike "the desires of the mouth that cost man everything. On the Tree of Calvary, which is at once the new Tree of Life and Knowledge, there hangs a fruit a thousand times more beautiful and delicious than the one that Eve desired."[199] Eve, who had been banished for violating the taboo on *consumption*, is redeemed by Mary, whose suffering ends with its accomplishment, the *consummation*.

In Bloy's book, Clotilde is redeemed by exchanging suffering endured for poverty embraced, when pain is not a curse visited on the self but a blessing conferring grace that can be bestowed on another. With Marchenoir's death, Bloy loses his pretext for indulging in chapter-long digressive indictments of his coevals' irreligion and literary mediocrity. Increasingly unconcerned for the society in which his characters have no home, he turns the narrative toward religious allegory, oneirical prefigurations of the coming stages of a soul journey.

The epigraphic subtitle accompanying the opening of the novel, *épisode contemporain*, ceases to refer to the historical specificity of the final decades of the nineteenth century and, as Polet says, signifies "the potential simultaneity of the episode with every moment in time."[200] This is a cyclical, recurrent, liturgical present, "the time of penitence and purgation, a duration through which the Christian seeks to pass from the world of death to the world of eternal life."[201] An indefinite period of expiatory suffering, the story unfolds in the time that is needed, the time that ends in the experience of deliverance. As the story ceases to be a tale of personal affront, becoming universalized as a chronicle of man's Fall and possible redemption, Bloy situates mystical experience on a level beyond time, where contemporaneity is equated with eternity.

Bloy, at one point, injects his own voice into the narrative, congratulating himself on abandoning the conceit of naturalist verisimilitude: "plausible stories," he writes, "are unworthy of being told."[202] Filled with annuciatory dreams, symbolic adumbrations, episodes of mystical clairvoyance, the temporal frame of Bloy's novel becomes increasingly elastic, telescoping the past as promise into a future of fulfillment.

Clotilde's migration from a water-world to the realm of fire is signaled by the comments made by the missionary who once addresses her in church. Describing her as a descendant of Eve, Mother of the Living, he admonishes Clotilde to remember him *"when you are in the flames."*[203] It is only in the final pages that the patriarch's prediction comes true, when Clotilde has finished the purgative cleansing of her life, having transformed herself from the child of Eve to the epigone of Mary.

Bloy describes Clotilde returning one night from a banquet of literary luminaries, an agape attended by the kinds of artists Bloy never tired of excoriating: Huysmans, pseudonymously represented as Folantin from his novella *A Vau-l'eau*, Bohémond de l'Isle de-France representing Villiers de l'Isle-Adam. With her head throbbing in the aftermath "of that singular, intolerable evening," Clotilde falls asleep, whereupon phantoms begin to file by, "before the open eyes of her soul."[204] In her dream, against a backdrop of sunlessness, pitch, and compaction, she sees Gacougnol stabbed, Marchenoir stooped under an unbearable weight, Léopold standing in an inferno, hair ablaze, arms crossed impassively.

Filled with anticipatory signs, Bloy's book incorporates the theme of poverty as its dearth of narrative surprise. In Tardif's cryptogram of the eternal text of Creation, every event is predetermined, every conclusion written in advance.

The suffering of the subject and the "Pleasures of the Lord"

Yet despite Bloy's claim to have rid his novel of naturalist verisimilitude – uncovering under its apparent adventitiousness the text of a divine teleology – his narrative follows the characters' passage through the reality of their worsening misery. Paralleling Bloy and Anne-Marie's progression along Way of the Cross, through dismal Parisian neighborhoods, Clotilde and her husband first occupy a cramped tenement whose walls are permeated with soul-blighting effluvia, "something between the stench of a corpse-filled ditch and the alkaline suffocation of a cesspool."[205] Thereafter, the couple finds even greater hardship when they move to a suburb where they are tormented by scandal-mongering neighbors.

Loss and despoliation, experienced on an interpersonal level, explain the theme of poverty as the deprivation of love, the severing of ties to the world. The death of Clotilde's infant son, Lazare, poisoned by the stinking toxins that fill their apartment, re-establishes her link to Mary, "the spotless Mother of thousands of millions of children destined to die the most infamous death, soiled by the most indescribable filth."[206] So great are man's suffering and penury that, at times, Bloy feels his writing's purpose is disqualified: "In the Presence of the death of a child, Art and Poetry are truly pitiful things."[207]

Clotilde's first loss comes as a child, when, having inherited her parents' guilt, she is dispossessed of innocence as a condition of her birth. Further impoverished by the carelessness with which she loses her virginity, Clotilde is water whose pollution her tears cannot clean: "my spring is dried up," she thinks, "my limpid water has turned to mud."[208]

Mother of a son who dies, Clotilde experiences Eve's pain of child-bearing, then suffers again when she sees him depart the world. Human beings who cannot remember God's face see in their children a reflection of a forgotten divinity. Uncorrupted, inchoate, they are purity uncompromised: "their children, for them, are a Paradise of Delight."[209] Parents left to contemplate their coffins relive expulsion from a garden guarded by an angel with a sword of fire.

Separated from her teachers, bereft of her baby, Clotilde comes to know a poverty different from a scarcity of material comfort. Bloy who, in *Le Sang du Pauvre* (*The Blood of the Poor*), denounces those too miserly to give alms, women whose diamonds are bought with the death of colonized Africans, shows Clotilde having a dream on the relation of debtors and creditors. A homiletic parable, it features Christ as *Proprietor*, an owner demanding a settling of accounts with heartless landlords who drive out their tenants. Christ, whose family was denied sanctuary and was made to sleep in a stable, is asked by the poor, "the members of his body," when there will come an end to their suffering: "What time is it on the clock of your interminable Passion?" – Time to pay your rent," he answers the wealthy, "or to go into the street and die with the children of dogs."[210]

Following Clotilde's dream, the novel concludes by showing Léopold and Clotilde completing their experience of transience, as unsheltered, ephemeral beings who pass on the earth. In harmony with Bloy's conception of the dispossession that sanctifies, he defines poverty, as Ernest Hello had done, not as a matter of proprietorship, but as one of ontology – not as the *nothing* that one has, but as the *nothingness* that one is.

Henceforth, the couple's home is a paupers' graveyard in Paris where they gather with family and friends at their tombs. In Bloy, the cemetery is a place where murder is forgotten, a necropolis of infanticides carried out long ago, children slaughtered "in abattoirs of misery"[211] and who now sleep under crosses carrying no name. Pulverized bodies dispersed in the soil contradict the idea of a place of rest for the dead. Often Clotilde feels Lazare's presence, can hear him speaking in her ear, saying that everywhere is the dead child's home, "because souls have no place."[212] Blessed are they who mourn, Christ says, for they shall be comforted.

No longer suffocating in a room smelling of charnel houses, Lazare lives "in the Light, in Beauty, in Love, in Joy without limit." As remission from suffering is found in the telluric womb of the mother, "Paradise lost is the cemetery," Marchenoir says.[213]

"For Bloy," as Roswell comments, "the holy nature of all women stemmed from the fact that one woman's body had been chosen to contain the Saviour of the world. In medieval symbolism, the garden was a figure for the virginal matrix in which the Saviour was conceived as well as being the Paradise into which he drew the soul."[214] The earthly diaspora through which Bloy's heroine wanders gives way to the home of her physical person. According to Marchenoir, Christ's birth had been celebrated by angels proclaiming "Glory to God" and Peace to men, both *in* and on earth. Among the time-eroded, rain-obliterated inscriptions on infants' graves, Bloy writes the end of his narrative of their inconsolable parents.

While Bloy's biography might have lacking in drama and dynamism – while his personal life was spent uneventfully "in the drab landscapes of the Paris suburbs," remaining, until the end, as John Coombes writes, "unutterably unattractive, friendless, and joyless,"[215] the spiritual itinerary mapped out in his fiction ends in a quiet transfiguration.

Conclusion

On the night of May 25, 1887, a date whose specificity blends into an aorist eternity, Clotilde is alone in the house, her husband having left several hours ago. "The book that they made together had finally been finished."[216]

The final scene of the novel restores the thematic unity of water and fire, sorrow and its mitigation, movement and rest, grief and rejoicing. After reading the Office of Mary, Clotilde listens to Baudelaire's hymn to appeasement: *Sois sage, ô ma Douleur* [Be still, my sorrow], the poet encourages his Sister. Hear, he writes, "la douce nuit qui marche" [the soft night that walks].[217]

At nine o'clock, while Léopold is on the other side of Paris saving strangers from the conflagration at the Opéra-Comique, Clotilde has a premonition of the momentousness of the hour. After rescuing adulterous lawyers, provincial notaries, maidens whose virginity is certified by salesmen, Léopold had re-entered the inferno and, in fulfillment of the missionary's prediction, had stood immobile in a whirlwind, burning alive, "*with his arms folded.*"[218]

The final purgative destitution on her path to the perfection of poverty, Léopold's incineration frees Clotilde of her last attachment to the world. Her preparation ends with a final pillaging of the sanctuary, as her soul is scoured of the clutter of its treasure: the mosaics of feelings, the gemstones of thoughts, the enamels of old regrets, all thrown into the pit of an "infinite obsecration."[219] Experienced as percussion and effulgence, the fire that consumes Clotilde can catch when she alone supplies the fuel.

Immediately preceding the scene where Clotilde blazes with *the Pleasure of the Lord*, Bloy includes a Latin text from the *Celestial Revelations* of Saint Birgitta. There a soul that has been judged completes its incendiary changes: flames shoot from pores, teeth, studding the mouth like iron nails, pierce the palate, the tongue, pulled back through the nostrils, hangs over swollen lips, and skin, like that on bodies, covers the soul with its cold, dirty linen. This is the calamity awaiting the one not purified by sorrow's water: "cum lacrymis totis viribis suis."[220]

It is from this that Clotilde escapes as a holocaust and bridesmaid. It begins with a feeling of peace and lightness: "the quick, the ag-ile, Ag-nis, ig-nis."[221] Sparks swirl, flames, wrapping around her legs like undulating snakes, rise to her breast that melts like wax. A burnt offering and celebrant, a worshipper and shrine, Bloy's heroine is topologized as the place where she turns into herself. The theme of itineracy that is developed through *La Femme pauvre* concludes when Clotilde finds the place she belongs: "She sees herself in a cathedral of fire. It is the house that she had asked for."[222]

What had begun in La Salette with the vision of the inconsolable Virgin is finished with the bride's betrothal in fire. Neither the courage of twenty lions, Bloy writes, nor the strength of eagles' wings can stop the soul from being consumed in the furnace of the divine. For a moment, Clotilde experiences the end of separateness, as *Celle qui Pleure* is married to "Celui qui brûle" [the One who burns]."[223]

Widow of Léopold, Clotilde becomes nothingness complemented by Plenitude. Having glimpsed him as the "fire that walks before his face," Clotilde sees her reflection in God, discovering the utility of poverty as what empties vessels, making room for the reality that fills. For Bloy, Polet writes, "the definition of God as a Poor Man aptly translates the apophatic sense of his lofty theological concepts," identifying him as "pure Alterity, the Wholly Other, Absence, the Increate, the Absolute Lack of everything belonging to Being."[224]

In Clotilde's rapture, she experiences the impossible momentariness of eternity, fire that does not eradicate but that cleanses and rebirths – fire which, while expressing the desire to "bring all life to its conclusion, to its hereafter,"[225] changes extinction into universality and speed into timelessness.

Having burned with *la Volupté du Seigneur*, Clotilde is not gone. Instead, she is described surviving as weightless debris left from the ecstatic inferno, pale traces of her vanishing mortality: white hair, self-lessness, ubiquity, and silence "like the spaces of the sky."[226] Still caught for a while in the world below, she has escaped the enslaving periodicity of desire and possession, attachment and loss. "One enters Paradise, not tomorrow, not the day after tomorrow, not in ten years. On enters *today* if one is crucified and poor."[227]

After she sells her remaining possessions and gives her money to the needy, she makes her home in the falling rain. Colorless, tireless, she disperses herself in gifts and motion, enjoying the grace accorded her "never to have need of rest."[228]

There is a pleonastic transparency in Bloy's ideal of *la femme pauvre* – no woman is rich in the world's meretricious treasure. For her, friend-ship, food, and home are lures that beckon and deceive. The healthy and beloved are not eligible for Christ's selection. Only the beggar-woman

serves as an instrument of the apocalypse. At the end, Clotilde under-
stands that "a Woman truly exists only if she is without bread, without
shelter, without friends, without a husband or children. Only then can
she force her Savior to come down again."[229]

Rather than inhabiting the fire of a present that is forever, Clotilde
returns to the asylum of her solitude, in streets full of people, resigned to
live in time as the consciousness of imperfection. Rather than experiencing eternity, she knows only the patience of *not yet*. Unlike Huysmans's
Blessed Lydwine, seated at the celestial banquet in Van Eyck, Clotilde is
still alive, and Bloy's work is still unfinished. Driven out of Eden, they
toil and bear children. There is another diatribe against the rich to write,
another denunciation of hacks and hypocrites. There are more material
goods to give away. There is another day to spend in Paradise, where
"everything that happens is adorable," as Clotilde says.[230]

"The only sadness is not to be a SAINT."[231]

5
The Miracle-Worker

Huysmans's *Les Foules de Lourdes*

Following Huysmans's scholarly venture into fifteenth-century hagiography, he had hardly sought to sequester himself in solitary mystical contemplation. Like his fellow visionaries, Ernest Hello and Léon Bloy, Huysmans impatiently awaited the apocalypse but did not believe that millenarianism was incompatible with participation in worldly affairs. Indeed, as Jean-Marie Seillan remarks, it was during the time of Huysmans's service as an oblate at Ligugé – a period transparently reproduced in his volume of fictional autobiography *L'Oblat* [*The Oblate*], 1903)– that he became ever more passionately involved in the political controversies engulfing France and threatening to set at odds the interest of the church and nation.

Huysmans had seen his monastic dream of reconciling a love of reclusion and community withstand a mortal blow when, in 1901, the then French Prime Minister, Waldeck-Rousseau, had passed the Contract of Associations, a law requiring every congregation to apply for reauthorization by the state or run the risk of dissolution. The tepid church response to this institutional danger had sharpened Huysmans's disaffection for Pope Leo XIII, whose modernist disposition and Republican sympathies he had long found disappointing.

At the dawning of the new century, Huysmans's political beliefs remained colored by the conspiratorial notions that had shaped his thinking a decade earlier. The occultist ideas and worries about Satanism that were evident in *Là-bas* reappeared in Huysmans's comments about the Vatican's response to the new law. Presumably sponsored by the Jews and promoted by "Masonic mobs," the Contract, according to Huysmans, had not elicited a strong enough reaction by the Pope, thereby proving the writer's view that the pontiff had been corrupted by the "satanic sect" of Republicanism and that, in submitting to the growing forces of secularism, had entered into a "pact with the demon."[1]

Huysmans's deepening conviction in the dovetailing of national and church history prompted a wish to try to reconcile his religious ideals and political sympathies. If God's work was no longer reliably carried out by leaders of the church, if an experience of the divine could not be achieved through private prayer, the spiritual aristocrat had to become a champion of the people. Temperamentally, Huysmans was ill-suited to enter the realm of political action; his outrage was strictly personal, as Seillan has affirmed. "Not based on any partisan engagement, not rooted in collective struggle," Huysmans's "combativeness was only verbal."[2] Thus, it was by returning to literature that he could best describe the mystical experience afforded by social action.

What, for Huysmans, were complementary interests in supernaturalism and social justice appear together in *Les Foules de Lourdes*, where he equates the "evangelical ideal of the *Poor*, as representing Christ,"[3] and the socially marginalized toward whom the author's political compassion was extending.

Les Foules de Lourdes, the last book completed in Huysmans's life, marks a completion of the final stage in his evolution as a supernaturalist at the same time it signals a return to his methodological origins as a naturalist. As with many of his contemporaries examined in this volume, the maturation of Huysmans's views and the development of his faith show the adjustment of his political conservatism, his elitism as an artist, with an emerging wish to use his work in the service of the people. Belonging to an aristocracy of aesthetes, professing reactionary principles, Huysmans displays a solidarity with those whose suffering he strove to mitigate.

The arc of Huysmans's writing follows that of other fin-de-siècle occultists, moving from the isolated grandeur of the Magus/intellectual toward a re-establishment of fraternal ties with people benefiting from his knowledge. From superiority to sacrifice – from megalomania to self-forgetfulness – the spiritual seeker re-descends into the world of other people. No longer boasting, like the thaumaturge, of feats of occult virtuosity, he sees the mysterious hand of God at work in miracles of everyday generosity.

In *Les Foules de Lourdes* (1906), Huysmans begins by resuming the naturalist work of observation and recording. Undertaken after a 1903 visit to the pilgrimage site, Huysmans's book illustrates the convert's abnegation of self and the magnification of God through an acceptance of the humility of his art. Corresponding to the mysterious enormity of the miracles worked in Lourdes is the diminishment of their transcriber, as the author grows smaller, his contributions less obtrusive, and his text becomes the site where he experiences "the benefit of personal omission."[4]

In Huysmans's final novel, naturalism – as diagnostic methodology – is turned against itself in order to prove the operation of a supernatural agency. Identified by fin-de-siècle occultists as the most serious of threats, science is used by Huysmans to define the limits of empiricism, as naturalism marks the end point where it is succeeded by an art of the transcendental.

After acceding to the invitation of long-time friends Léon and Marguerite Leclaire to visit them in Lourdes and compile material for a book, Huysmans had arrived on March 5, 1903, and had found himself impressed, not by manifestations of divine mercy, but by the otherworldly tastelessness of Lourdes's religious architecture. "Roused," as Robert Baldick says, "to a fury of invective and abuse remarkable even for such a past master in the art of vituperation,"[5] Huysmans had raged against the hideousness of the Basilica, the Rosary, the Esplanade, profanations of art so hyperbolic they could have been inspired only by the Evil One. Unchanged through his career, Huysmans still considered art's perversion as unmistakable evidence of Satan's handiwork.

The limits of science and art

Yet apart from giving vent to his indignation at contemporary religious art, Huysmans entertained a far more important purpose in the execution of his project. Having come to Lourdes to exalt the Creator and humble himself as his creature, he had at first adopted a naturalist practice in order to refute Zola's naturalist allegations – that the miraculous healings effected by the Virgin were produced by auto-suggestion, by an abatement of nervous disorders, or by what Charcot had called *the faith that heals* (*La Foi qui guérit, 1893*). As Huysmans reasons, diseased tissue cannot regenerate instantaneously. "Nature cannot close a wound in a second; flesh cannot restore itself in a minute, but Zola refuses to recognize these spontaneous cures which he witnessed nonetheless."[6]

Indeed, the mortification of Huysmans as a writer begins with his following Zola's method. As an artist whose career had taken him from realist objectivity to the shadowy world of devil worship and the realm of necromantic warfare, Huysmans returns to the work of naturalism, as he observes and emulates the doctor – guided by science, chastened by skepticism, doubtful that the unexplainable phenomena occurring in Lourdes were genuine. In his visits to the clinic of Doctor Boissarie, the physician entrusted with documenting the authenticity of cures, Huysmans adopts the physician's practice of endlessly invalidating his discipline, using medicine to identify the limitations of medicine, verifying in naturalist language supernatural events whose significance transcended language. Huysmans's theory of the miraculous is conveyed by his new conception of literature, as the magnitude, the sacredness, and the mystery of his subject are measured by the modesty and smallness of their expression.

As Huysmans's own style had once conveyed the artist's individuality, his immersion in the crowds of Lourdes marks the final stage of his surrender of authorial pride. No longer immured in the splendid isolation of a library, in the tower of the Magus, in the fortress safety of the monastery, Huysmans disintegrates into the anonymity of everyone, his voice lost in the prayerful polyglottism of invalids from all over the world. Marking the final stage in the evolution of fin-de-siècle supernaturalism, Huysmans's writing abandons the exceptional self in favor of the anonymous community.

However, in the beginning of the book, Huysmans expresses his ambivalence toward Lourdes, linking his reservations to a revulsion for the throngs his title mentions. "To begin with, I dislike processioning crowds that go about bellowing hymns,"[7] writes an author insistent on respecting corporeal and linguistic boundaries.

In Huysmans's opening chapter, he highlights the opposition between his text's purpose as documentation and its value as an artwork. If, on the level of content, *Les Foules de Lourdes* addresses the authenticity of miracles, on the level of personal expression, it conveys the quiet spiritual development of the author. On virtually every page, Huysmans explores the phenomenon of immersion and dissolution: dirty baths in which suppurating invalids and menstruating women plunge their bodies, small candles lit by the poor that melt into a towering, amorphous wax offering illumined by many. The loss of self in the multitudes, the drowning of Huysmans's distinctive voice in the plurivocality of the chanting masses is transposed as the breaching of epidermal walls, the constant evocation of bodies that leak and ooze in images of hemorrhage, seepage, abscess, and gangrene. In the tradition of mystic writers inspired by Vintras's teachings on Dolorism, Huysmans identifies the body in pain as the locus of the miraculous.

For Huysmans himself, it is style that is the site of his mortification. Unlike art that exalts difference, liturgy requires standardization. The prideful author who had spoken in words unmistakably his own joins with pilgrims directing their supplications to the Virgin in ceremonies conducted collectively.

Crowds and coalescence

Believing the more discrete his authorial utterance, the more indisputable God's response, Huysmans mingles with the crowd, agreeing to pray as they do. Huysmans's willingness to coalesce with others marks a drastic alteration of long-held views on style and self, a violation of the boundaries of his identity and his books. Huysmans's dissolution in collectivity of anonymous, desperate worshippers involves an act of self-renunciation, a transient ego death recalling the mystic's experience as chronicled in *Lydwine*. The author who had defended the fortress of his identity, fiercely insisting on the inviolability of self as sanctuary, goes out among the people in order to champion their concerns.

Formerly, as Jean Borie has written, the Huysmansian body had not been "a point of contact and exchange with the outside," but "a citadel" within which the hero had barricaded himself, "directing his senses toward the external world in fear of a possible invasion [...] while everything inside him pleaded: "please, do not touch me'."[8]

Describing a night spent in a sleeping car on a train from Paris to Cologne (*De Tout*, 1902) Huysmans had expressed a horror of the discomfort, promiscuity, and exposure that are the least of the concerns of train travelers to Lourdes. Private space as impregnable enclosure, the stylistically inaccessible book, the art-upholstered Thebaïd: these had once been topological expressions of walls that regulated intercourse with a reading public. But during peak season, when Lourdes is overrun with dazed pilgrims quartered in hangars, sleeping on straw mats, housed under eaves, and garrisoned in dormitories, Huysmans endures the penance of contact with raw humanity's physical presence.

Returning from style to substance, from art to its material, Huysmans submits to *un bain de multitude* (a bath in the multitudes) – not Baudelaire's transient occupation of a passer-by glimpsed on the sidewalk – but a liquefaction of identity in the clamorous *turbus* whose numbers overwhelm their differences in language, dress, and custom. Huysmans often notes that the visitors who most willingly accept a disaffiliation from nation, class, and language are those most likely to benefit from the miracle of grace as cure. They are unlike the Belgians who refuse to join in communal prayer, establish separate outposts of comfort, and who, "after obtaining, at the time of their first pilgrimages, a number of striking miracles, experienced far fewer thereafter."⁹ As Huysmans observes, those most willing to abandon the precincts of convenience are the ones who are most blessed, those who do not turn Christ away but vacate the self in order to accommodate the divine. Huysmans realizes that extraordinary things happen when habits are relinquished and that miracles occur in places that are emptied of routine. No longer sequestered, like the Magus, in the austere privacy of his study, the author creates his text as agora like Lourdes's sacred sites that throng with visitors.

A countervailing tendency evident in the production of Huysmans's work is his corroborating the exceptional by testing it against the ordinary. In the account of his conversion, Huysmans consistently downplayed the momentousness of God's intervention. Related in *En Route* as "something like the digestion of a stomach at work,"¹⁰ the tale of Huysmans's encounter with the supernatural is further evidence of his equating faith with an act of artistic asceticism. Always fastidious in the maintenance of his person, jealous of the hidden recesses of his private subjectivity, Huysmans finally mixes with the crowds, agreeing to his incorporation in Lourdes's belly, where his spiritual growth depends on a digestion assimilating him to everyone.

Unlike Lourdes, indiscriminately invaded by diffident invalids and pious exhibitionists, Huysmans's books had not always been characterized as points of confluence for all comers. Formerly troubled by his writing's accessibility "to the dirty curiosity of crowds,"¹¹ Huysmans had guarded the privacy of his consciousness as an unpublished text, defining it as a meeting place for the man who prays and the God to which he prays. Distinguishing autobiography from personal disclosure, he had forbidden entry to those desiring details of his stay at Notre-Dame-de-l'Atre. Unlike the novel where readers come together, Huysmans's *pauvre être* is declared off-limits, his private thoughts no one's affair. Thus, Huysmans declines to speak to "simply curious people wishing to meddle in my private business, desiring to walk around in my soul as if it were a public place."¹²

Part of the miracle of Huysmans's acquiescence to literary humility is a democratized style that offers hospitality to everyone. Textual pilgrims welcomed in *Les Foules de Lourdes* include the faithful, the skeptics who still remain open-minded, historians interested in the account of Bernadette's vision, archeologists and scholars of comparative religion who learn of the Satanic ceremonies once conducted on the site, the raising of dolmens, the performance of blood sacrifices as part of the cult of Venus Astarte. Along with researchers and believers, Huysmans's book is open to teratology dilettantes, practitioners of the kind of pathology tourism that draws curiosity seekers looking for freakish entertainment.

The monstrous and miraculous

In *Les Foules de Lourdes*, Huysmans's prose grows plainer as the phantasmagoria of disease becomes more cacophonous and nightmarish. Different from Huysmans's Decadent masterpiece, *A rebours*, which had compensated for a spare plot with a lushly overdeveloped style, *Les Foules de Lourdes* replaces monstrous language with an experience of monsters, as life supersedes art and exceptional events plead for ordinary description.

At the end of his story, Huysmans succumbs to deformity fatigue while still declaring his predilection for "extraordinary cases, figures of nightmare," eyes attached to heads with tentacles and faces ravaged by leprosy. All that is left, as he complains, "are invalids without the luxury of a particularly horrible affliction."[13]

Yet what is conveyed in Huysmans's prose is a recognition that the purpose of a miracle as theatrical extravaganza is a restoration of the banality of health. Disgust, pathos, outrage, and shock are cured and returned to a state of oblivious indifference. With their ostentatious effects, miracles nullify their causes, unwriting narrative tragedy, reinstating the platitude of healed organs, mended limbs, unscarred skin, and regular features.

In the same way that naturalism had adopted the methodology of Claude Bernard, the miraculous in Lourdes acts as supernatural medicine, aiming at an elimination of the pretext for its occurrence. Naturalist fiction, as Pierre Citti observes, pits "a tyrannical milieu" against "a case of morbid individualism."[14] As God, in his mysterious workings, inflicts an ailment on his creature then inexplicably alleviates it, the naturalist author invests his hero with a rare trait or exceptional feature, then cures him of his singularity by assimilating him into society. As the miracle works to restore the ordinariness of health, it works in the opposite sense of the spectacular deeds performed by the Magus and the Satanist. The exceptionality of the thaumaturge is likened to a malady that God and those who serve him strive together to remove.

Huysmans rightly intuits art's homology with disease and difference, suffering and guilt, all straining for their cancellation and remission, all seeking a return to the inexpressiveness of health. Contrasting the discreetness of his conversion experience at La Salette with the clamorousness of the miracles he witnesses in Lourdes, Huysmans longs for absolution from the sin of creation. As *Là-haut* had concluded with a theophany unrelated in the narrative, Huysmans equates the expression of God's grace with a discontinuation of his writing. The angry desperation of Léon Bloy, the prayerful anticipation of Ernest Hello are expressions of impatience that the apocalypse takes too long in coming. While Huysmans, during his stay in Lourdes, sees no sign of the world ending, God's daily intervention in the lives of suffering pilgrims makes the need for art as supplication seem less urgent. Manifestations of the divine, miracles as quiet acts of altruism, enable the artist to define his role more modestly, as *Les Foules de Lourdes* suggests. When God speaks, as Huysmans says, the writer should fall silent.

As a stage set, La Salette had impressed the author as barren and denuded, empty of the dramatic terrain and theatrical appurtenances of Lourdes: "a place without trees or birds or flowers."[15] Conversely, Lourdes' topography is as colorful as its miracles, with its funicular traversing vertiginous mountain chasms over "a cheerful landscape from a comic opera."[16] Gaudily dressed crowds from exotic locales, conflagrations of wax and fire, fantasy terrain, supernatural phenomena, grotesqueries on parade: Lourdes as setting and narrative premise is as rich as its description is poor.

The miracle democratized

Characterized by absence and anticipation, La Salette had been an uncluttered version of the Huysmansian sanctuary. There, Huysmans writes, "one lives withdrawn into oneself."[17] In Lourdes, however, the miracle Huysmans undergoes is to be cured of reflexivity: "one feels opened out in Lourdes."[18] When Huysmans writes that "infinite Beauty is identical to God himself,"[19] he equates holiness-as-art, not with the gorgeous phraseology he confects, but with the beauty of the selfless acts that his fellow man performs. As both the principle of Dolorist reparation and an expression of Huysmans's masochist aesthetic, his initial belief was that visitors to Lourdes could help God in his work by consenting to their trials, thereby imitating Christ's Passion: "before the grotto, one should not pray that his ills be cured but instead that they be increased. One should give himself as a holocaustic offering, in expiation for the sins of the world."[20]

But then he comes to see that the practice of Mystic Substitution is just another way to position a noisy self on center stage. Not an act of self-omission, it was a petition for attention, casting a uniquely tormented subject as the leading character in his drama. In subordinating his narrative to its content – in becoming only one of nameless thousands – Huysmans is healed by what Zola called "the crowds' healing breath."[21] Where once the writer had been crucified by the ugliness of the world, posing as the hero in the story of its embellishment, he is now eclipsed by people who create beauty through their generosity – the caretakers, stretcher-bearers, nurses, and attendants who, through forgetfulness of self, invite the Virgin's intercession.

To Huysmans, it is this compassionate activity that best bears witness to God's presence, since the miracles seen in Lourdes are often sporadic and unjustified. Indeed, proof of the miraculous, as Huysmans comes to realize, is not always found in the spectacular suddenness of cures. Sometimes the most deserving are sent home still unhealed. Sometimes a child, blessed with a disappearance of paralysis, mysteriously relapses and his suffering resumes.

Huysmans's sense of justice is offended by these occurrences, and he argues that, if the divinity is equivalent to beauty made infinite, God should not seek his reflection in his creatures' disfigurement. Having been cast in the Creator's likeness, the monster is an outrage and a sacrilege, an insult to God's majesty as reflected in the mirror of human faces. Thus, the plea for compassion that Huysmans addresses to the Lord is an appeal that He protect the integrity of his image: "Remember the image of your Holy Face; it was anguished, bloody, but not repulsive. Save the dignity of your image, with a miracle, and clean this unclean face."[22]

As such, Lourdes's miracles are not a disruption of the natural order but a re-establishment of the harmony between the celestial and human orders, restoration of the harmony between God's goodness and its expression. Twisted limbs and leprous figures are texts enshrining aberrancy, which God, as the first author, can expunge and wipe away. The written record of a miracle is evidence of its effacement: dried sores, faint scars, new, pink skin. Like sojourners in a naturalist novel, the lucky visitors to Lourdes receive God's grace and then depart, healed of the affliction of their difference.

It is by being inscribed in the realm of interpersonal relations that miracles recover their dramatic power, in the community where diverse classes and different countries coalesce. In Lourdes, the supernatural manifests itself by eliminating separateness, as the blessed are those who work together and desire to resemble everyone. Not celebrated by a prelate stressing his sacerdotal privilege, Lourdes's Masses are performed collectively by priests from Portugal and Macao: "'We are going to give Holy Communion'" as one of them proclaims, to which Huysmans adds his comment: "the word *we* was an entire world."[23]

Huysmans's Dolorist belief in the redemptive benefit of pain is confirmed by Lourdes' turning into an ideal Christian microcosm. No stylistically tormented curiosity, Lourdes is a living work of art told in a lingua franca: "It is a profession of faith by an entire world emerging from the confusion of languages in order to express itself in the idiom of the liturgy. It is a concentration of all the individual petitions of the day that are then gathered in a sheaf of common prayer."[24]

Overshadowing the aesthetic blight on Lourdes caused by the Basilica and Rosary, exorbitancies that outrage public taste with their immodesty, is the humble work that people do to bring relief to others. While deploring the commercial exploitation of visitors by Lourdes' businesses – profiteering by trinket-merchants and hawkers of religious paraphernalia – Huysmans sees the city as an ideal society founded on the principle of charity.

Shaken out of their cocoon of habit by the ubiquity of suffering, Lourdes's helpers are moved by the sight of monsters to view complacency as monstrous. As Pierre Jourde writes, the presence of these specimens undermines the stability of the viewer's autonomy: "What happens in a helpless body? In blind flesh? At the bottom of the most extreme suffering? It seems that everything there is different, unheard of. Even more, the monster's dismembered, infirm body issues a challenge to us. It is an unimaginable world that takes us inside it because we can share the same space – because we can touch it."[25]

Unlike the structural ugliness of buildings immuring Huysmans in disgust, the hideousness of the deformed invites attempts to heal and mitigate. Walls of skin, of national provenance, of class affiliation are broken down, enabling people to come together. As Huysmans writes of Lourdes, "it is here that utopia begins."[26]

In Huysmans's book, health, like indifference, is an expression of narcissism enclosing a subject in self-sufficiency and well-being. Motivated to try to ease a victim's discomfort, helpers also violate their self-interested independence, making both pain and care monstrous and miraculous. Operating in the same way as medicine, naturalist texts like Zola's work to demystify the wonders of Lourdes, intending a transformation of incredible events into the nothingness of their explanation. Endeavoring to disprove miracles, diagnosing the pathology of generosity, Zola's version of naturalism seeks to cure difference and controvert the sacred inspiration of concern for one's brother. But like Doctor Boissarie in his clinic in Lourdes, patiently investigating the authenticity of miracles, Huysmans remains skeptical in order to believe and be believable.

Huysmans acknowledges the heterology of God's plan and man's books, realizing that while a writer creates a conflict that his dénouement resolves, the miracles seen in Lourdes correspond to no plot necessity, occur in response to no character development. As a narrative, Lourdes's miracles are illogical and unsatisfying, and in Huysmans's story, God remains an enigmatic hero.

The alchemy of suffering

In the opening chapter of *Là-bas*, Huysmans's protagonist, Durtal, had argued for the need to free naturalism from its rut, propelling it out of its fixation on adultery and madness. Rather than dealing with bodies racked by lust and disease, the novel had to complement its physiology-based themes with a parallel study of the state of man's spirit: "it was also necessary to plumb the soul, no longer try to explain life's mystery in terms of the sicknesses of the senses."[27]

The model for what Durtal had called *spiritual naturalism* is Matthias Grünewald's Crucixion canvas, where the painter had captured the ignoble flesh of the man and the supernatural charity of the incarnated God. According to Durtal, Grünewald had effected a synthesis of body and soul and permitted a refinement of naturalism into spiritual beauty. Going at once to "the two extremes, he had extracted from the most triumphant squalor the essence of charity, the finest distillate of despair."[28]

Moving from painting to social action, spiritual naturalism is evident in the selfless communalism of Lourdes. Emerging from the open wounds, the pain-furrowed faces, and the contorted limbs of the pilgrims to Lourdes is miraculous evidence of spiritual life, a soul appearing in the caregiver's attentions. As the Virgin had wept beside the crucified Christ, she is present at the spectacle of suffering's redemption of indifference.

After citing Grünewald's realization of the ideal of spiritual naturalism, Huysmans modifies his definition of this new form of art. Rather than tracing the development of man's spiritual being along "a parallel route" above his bodily existence, he describes a moment when tormented flesh turns into compassionate spirit.

In *Sainte Lydwine de Schiedam* (1902), Huysmans calls pain the Philosopher's Stone, an alchemical agent transmuting suffering into love. "The formula for this divine Alchemy which is suffering," as Huysmans writes, "is self-abnegation and self-sacrifice. After the necessary period of incubation, the Great Work is accomplished. Out of the crucible of the soul, the gold of Love emerges, which does away with all dejection and dries up all tears."[29]

Spiritual naturalism identifies a point of convergence where this transmutation takes place: cancer and charity, deformity and altruism, when bodily sickness becomes an impulse to alleviate it. This is the direction toward which Huysmans's later novels move, as he carries "spiritual naturalism, as he had discovered it in Grünewald, to its final extreme, examining the aesthetics of representing the disfigured body from the perspective of an imminent manifestation of the spirit."[30]

As Huysmans had interpreted the candle as a symbol – the wax as the white flesh of Jesus, the wick as his immaculate soul, the flame as "the emblem of his divinity"[31] – one might say that a body supported by love is consumed by pain's fire and then sent skyward as spirit. On the level of literature, a reverse alchemy occurs, as Huysmans, the self-centered stylist, sacrifices the treasure of language so that his work might be reborn as testimony to God's majesty.

In *Les Foules de Lourdes*, Huysmans illustrates the transformation of monsters into miracles, showing literature's transition from post-naturalist exhaustion to a revitalized art that manifests the divine. As Sylvie Duran comments, Huysmans's "craving for the monstrous" conveys a "need for marvels,"[32] for phenomena unshackling literature from its enslavement to empiricism.

In Lourdes, the monsters Huysmans encounters are not those featured in Vladimir Jankélévitch's nosology of fin-de-siècle anomalies: the self-admiring sophistication of the Satanist aesthete, the hypertrophic subjectivity of the rarefied Magus. These had been "narcissistic monsters" engrossed in abyssal self-study, oblivious to the world and the people inhabiting it, incapable of arresting "consciousness from lapsing into morbid self-scrutiny and self-analysis."[33] Previously, the fin-de-siècle thaumaturge had taken himself as his own object, disdaining the poverty of quotidian reality, isolating himself from others, locking himself in self-examination. Huysmans's pre-conversion fiction had foregrounded this involuted character, whose self had expanded to fill up the text, crowding out the possibility of plot and event. Inflation of this exalted subject had brought an emptying of the fictional world, congealing intrigue in stagnation, expelling others judged undeserving of attention: "a consciousness fascinated by its navel, anxious and diffuse, languishing from its love of subtlety, introspection, and tautology. It is a volatile thought, a hint of a thought, the scent of a hint. It is no longer anything."[34]

Conclusion

For the fin-de-siècle Satanist and xenophobe, the other had been considered a monster: terrifying, unintelligible, repellent, unfathomable. For the Magus, the plight of suffering humanity had been abstracted into theory. Those languishing on the sublunary plane had been refined into occult symbols. But by the end of the century, the esotericist's orientation inward had been replaced by social action, as artists made common cause with the people. Convulsive political events made aesthetic self-isolation increasing difficult; leading symbolist writers professed solidarity with the growing anarchist movement and voiced outrage at the repressive *lois scélérates* passed in 1893. In response to Zola's denunciation of the guilty verdict rendered on Alfred Dreyfus in *J'accuse* (January 1898), the artist community was further polarized, and political turmoil became more prevalent. In aesthetics, a return to nature and a rejection of the cult of artificiality accompanied the spread of nationalism and a reimmersion in the issues of the day. No longer able to stay sequestered in the gorgeous sanctuary of their intelligence, the occultist and Magus often renounced their escapist indulgence in hermeticism. "With the simultaneous return to nature, life, social action, and political engagement, it seemed that the entire vision of the world on which Decadent aesthetics had been based was quickly crumbling away."[35]

However, in *Les Foules de Lourdes*, Huysmans illustrates the reconciliation of supernaturalism and social action. In the aftermath of his meditation on spiritual naturalism, Huysmans had come to see the reality of the body of a suffering brother as more than a literary question. Whereas, the hyperacuity of subjective consciousness had been the pathology of the Decadent, the Catholic activist becomes aware of others' actual afflictions. By repositioning teratology outside the voracious subject, Huysmans restores the possibility of dynamic interaction: between God and his creature, between sufferer and nurse, between an unhappy world and those who strive to improve it. The lupus-ravaged face, the muscle twitching from chorea are the interface where spiritualism and naturalism come together. In Lourdes, the monster's body is where God is revealed as miracles and where miracles appear as the charity Christ prescribes.

First, naturalism cured the individual by making him indistinguishable from everyone; then esotericism neutralized the threat of others by elevating and insulating a quarantine self. After that, Huysmans introduces a literature of the miraculous that changes one into many, takes the privileged hero and merges him with the crowd, restoring the possibility of action, exchanging hopelessness for salvation. On the Cross, flesh dies before the spirit is reborn. In Lourdes, there arises from "triumphal squalor" "the purest essence of charity."

Les Foules de Lourdes marks Huysmans's abandonment of traditional forms of naturalism, a normalizing ideology ratifying the tyranny of the crowd. Yet it also signals a repudiation of occultism with its emphasis on concealment, on esotericism with its suggestion of inwardness and self-direction. Redefining the relation between man and God, between a human and his neighbor, the novel shows that the mystery of man's spiritual being is solved by returning to "the sicknesses of the senses."

No longer transfixed by self-reflection, Huysmans's narrator turns outward, in a movement etymologically suggested by the link between mirror and miracle – from self-contemplation to wonderment at God's works. No longer is the abnormal specimen a slave of fascinated introspection. Rather than constituting reality by training his gaze inward, he reveals the truth to others: "he displays it [il la *monstre*], so to speak."[36]

The freak – no longer recognizable by his tentacle-like eye, by the world-destroying absorption of his consciousness in itself – becomes the monstrous site where suffering is turned into solicitude. He is the place where one sees enacted the Christian principle of *agape*, the requirement that one's brother be loved as oneself. The monster is the point where plot stasis ends and where literature becomes an instrument of social reparation. Toward the body of the sick, Huysmans redirects his look: toward the point where art and human kindness manifest God's love as miracles.

Conclusion

In Jean Lorrain's "Lanterne magique" ("Magic Lantern," *Histoires de masques* [*Stories of Masks*] 1900), two blasé theatergoers are overheard discussing the aesthetics of supernaturalism during an intermission of Berlioz's *Sommeil de Faust* (*Faust's Sleep*). One character, proclaiming himself a partisan of atmospheric Gothicism, deplores rationalism's murder of sorceresses and fairies. Fantasy has been inhumed, he says, by clinicians and psychiatrists. Sylphs and dryads have given way to wax automata from Hoffmann. Gone are tenebrous witches' Sabbaths in the cypress groves of cemeteries, replaced by the electrified rooms and whitewashed corridors of hospitals. The wild-haired, undressed hysterics on display at the Salpêtrière may be picturesque in their somnambulistic fixity, but Lorrain's character admits to longing for "victims of demonic possession, the nuns of Loudon, the convulsionaries of Saint-Médard." Even the final bastion of romanticized insanity had been invaded by physicians who had localized and cured madness – "and with what methods," he exclaims, "with electricity and therapeutics!"[1]

Conversations like these were commonplace in turn-of-the-century France as a struggle played out between medicine and miracles – between the majesty of the unexplainable and the reductive clarity of diagnostics. For Decadents and Symbolists, for artists and believers, the discoveries of science did not map out a brighter future but only shrank the world's beauty to the cranial dimensions of the doctor.

At first, this conflict between and reason and supernaturalism played out in the domain of aesthetics, expressing "a reaction against the tendency of science to rob the world of poetry."[2] According to the Positivist worldview advanced by Auguste Comte (1798–1857), humanity had passed though the theological and metaphysical phases in its intellectual development and then had reached maturity in the positive phase when it had abandoned religion entirely. No longer crediting a supernatural agency for the phenomena he witnessed, man had ceased to look for causes and had limited himself to registering "observable facts."

Reacting against the aridity of this scientific vision, many fin-de-siècle artists sought to escape a reality they saw as impoverished by the disappearance of religion. Rejecting art robbed of Catholic pageantry, they wished to restore to their works the sublimity of the transcendental. Yet science had done its damage, eliminating the simplicity of earlier beliefs. And so where there had once been belief, there was now just regret: "in the face of the disappearance of religious faith, the only feeling that survived was nostalgia."[3] As a result, *Mysticism* became a shibboleth for artists unhappy with materialism, and many literary characters, after the fashion of Huysmans's des Esseintes, furnished their quarters with sacred bric-a-brac, ciboria, ostensories, ornamental bibelots disconnected from any religious application. It was not devotional asceticism that fueled this orgy of iconographic piety, but what Huysmans refers to as "diminished sensuality."

Religious themes were also popular in the artwork of the era. As Camille Mauclair comments: "The Salons were overflowing with Holy Women at the Tomb, with Calvaries, apparitions, and benedictions. It was a frightful consumption of missals and chasubles. Everywhere there were signs of faith, and the only thing missing was faith itself."[4] Satanism, likewise, afforded a frisson of the supernatural, and the Decadent devil Huysmans celebrated in his encomium to Félicien Rops conveyed an interest in evoking evil as titillating or dramatic.

Yet while science was condemned for impoverishing art, it was praised by fin-de-siècle occultists for allowing glimpses into extra-sensory realities. The research on magnetism done by Charcot and his disciples at La Salpêtrière lent scientific credibility to the seers who conducted séances to contact the dead. Relying on scientific authorities like British scholar William Crookes, occultists denied the dualism of soul and body, positing a radiant state of matter perceivable on the astral plane to which the medium and the somnambulist enjoyed access. It was navigating this boundary between the natural and supernatural that became the objective of the hierophants, magicians, and hermeticists who proliferated in the final turbulent decades of the century. Insisting on the empirical legitimacy of his studies, the fin-de-siècle Magus stressed his kinship with the scientist, as both were said to circulate from the phenomenal world of the senses, to the intellectual realm of thought, and into the divine sphere of final causes. As Guaïta writes, the same law that governs the attraction between the sexes determines the gravitation of the suns.

The same principle according to which the mollusk secretes nacre also explains how the human heart produces love. "Established sciences and occult sciences: their hieratic synthesis will gather in a single embrace all the branches of universal knowledge."[5]

Occultists like Papus and Guaïta took pains to show that esotericism was more than showmanship and charlatanism. While a stage magician like Robert Houdin could be dismissed as an illusionist or prestidigitator, whose power, as Houdin himself confessed, extended only to the tips of his fingers (*The Secrets of Stage Conjuring* 1858), genuine Magi like Guaïta saw themselves as descendants of Trismegistus, keepers of arcane wisdom from alchemy and the Kabbalah, secrets handed down from respected predecessors like Eliphas Lévi. Thus, in Guaïta's opening chapter in his exposition of occult doctrine, he had sketched out a history of esotericism dating back to India and the cycle of Rama. His priestly lineage positioned Guaïta in an unbroken chain of adepts, from Moses to Raymond Lulle, from Zoroaster to Fabre d'Olivet. Wishing to distinguish himself from vaudevillians who preyed upon the gullible, he deflected accusations that the Magus was a covert Satanist or necromancer. As Guaïta says, his goal is to rehabilitate "the noble Science that has been cursed and misunderstood since the treasonous acts committed by dissident Gnostics, that has been confused in the terrified imagination of the masses with impure Goetia, that has been decried by spurious scholars, whose empty dreams and delirious scholasticism it undermines, that has been anathematized by a priesthood fallen into disrepute since the time of its initiation."[6]

According his research an aura of seriousness and sobriety, the Magus worked in a private territory reserved for an aristocracy of knowledge-seekers. Thus, Guaïta comments on the fate reserved for dabblers and dilettantes, heedless tourists in the shadow realms of forbidden occult secrets. There was an astrologer who killed himself to confirm the accuracy of a horoscope, a spiritualist who went mad and died in suspicious circumstances, Eliphas Lévi swept into a gyre of near-suicidal melancholy.

In nineteenth-century France, interest in the occult had flourished in the poetry of Baudelaire and the fiction of Balzac, in novels like *Louis Lambert* and *Séraphita*, whose intrigues had been structured by the mysticism of Swedenborg. By the end of the century, research in the domain of psychiatry had lent an air of legitimacy to investigations into paranormal phenomena. Psychoanalysis, which would become so unreceptive to theories of the occult, was intimately associated with magic as early as 1885, when Freud studied hypnosis under the auspices of Charcot. At that time, "Freud's interest in the subject reflected the widespread public fascination with mysterious states of mind, including somnambulism, catalepsy, nervous illness and the fragmentation of personality."[7] Only later, at the time of Freud's falling out with Jung, did he abandon his interest in magic and embrace "a material, mechanistic theory of scientific rationalism."[8]

In the 1880s, when interest in supernaturalism began to flourish, there was an attempt to establish a distinctive brand of magic different from theosophy as it had been popularized by Madame Blavatsky in England. While putatively syncretistic, theosophy had drawn on Buddhist and Hindu teachings, defining humanity's evolutionary path toward universal brotherhood. Recurrent occult principles found in theosophic doctrine included the spiritualization of material bodies ordered by Septenaries or multiples of seven; rejection of the dualism of body/mind and matter/spirit; a belief that even the simplest physical entities were endowed with rudimentary consciousness moving them irreversibly toward the absolute finality of enlightenment.

Distinct from theosophy with its conspicuous Eastern influence, French occultism had been rooted in traditional Jewish mysticism and privileged the hidden meaning of letter and number combinations. Such rearrangements of elements, as Papus writes in citing Eliphas Lévi, revealed the etymological link between *Tarot* and *Torah*. In Papus's *Le Tarot des Bohémiens*, he had glossed over the visual symbolism of the Arcana and, citing his predecessors, Saint-Martin, Court de Gébelin, and Guillaume Postel, had connected the 24 letters of the Hebrew alphabet to the major cards in the Tarot, claiming that the Tetragrammaton, the four letters in the sacred name of God, were the key to unlocking all occult secrets. It was this word, *iod-hé-vau-hé*, that was imprinted on the apex of official buildings, "that radiated out from the center of the flamboyant triangle at the 33rd degree of the Masonic Scotch Rite, and that was displayed above the portals of our oldest cathedrals."[9]

While all initiatic practices frustrated the casual seeker, the numerology of Papus – like the clavicles in Guaïta – had been so freighted with abstraction that transmission of knowledge was subordinated to opacity. Magic which, for the stage magician, had provided entertainment and illusion, was arrayed by Papus in robes of secrecy, adorned with Rosicrucian symbolism, discouraging the importunate inquiries of the dilettante. Fin-de-siècle thaumaturgy, operating on two opposing planes, amused the gullible and edified the adept. The "Bohémiens" to whom the Tarot's wisdom was imparted possessed a bible containing the most precious wisdom of antiquity, yet it also gave them a livelihood since it was used in fortune-telling: "this Bible is an occasion of perpetual distraction, for it allows them to play."[10]

It was only in later years that the fin-de-siècle tradition of occult teaching expanded beyond the sacerdotal caste of hierophants and sages in order to embrace the principle of universal brotherhood that had been advocated by theosophists. As the century approached its end, the Decadents' emphasis on elitist isolation gave way to an emerging sense of political engagement. This was manifested in the supernatural realm as service to one's brother, an abandonment of the exclusivity of esotericism and the inexpressibility of mystic visions. Thus, in Villiers de l'Isle-Adam's *Axël* (1885–6), the title character spurned magic as emotionless, inhuman, uncomforting, and cold. In Jules Bois, the Magus was pictured as impassive and self-involved. Alone in his white vestments, amidst his alembics and retorts, he had stood before an altar with a skull bearing the inscription *Eris sicut Deus*.[11]

It was in the fiction of Joséphin Péladan that one saw a re-humanization of the occultist, who changed from an impenetrable sage to a teacher and mentor. Seeking a re-consecration of Catholic dogma, disdaining the superciliousness of the master, Péladan's characters had exalted the sovereignty of God over the grandeur of the initiate.

The imaginary Rosicrucian brotherhood that was assembled in Péladan's fiction, the Société de la Rose+Croix that he established in real life sought the reformation of a church whose leadership structure had become ossified, dissemination of a higher art redeemed of its secular vulgarity, edification of humanity by works of inspirational genius. Certainly, Péladan never lost his air of superiority and hauteur, never gave up his eccentric dress or his ornate, bombastic style. But while the *aristes* whom Péladan cultivated were, etymologically, *the best*, their task was to lift up humanity through the nobility of their example.

Péladan's hero, the Magus Mérodack, deplored the modern conceit of progress: "*Mediocre* is the word for our time and our race. For Western man, an electric doorbell constitutes a new stage of civilization, and the availability of hot water heat creates a hierarchy among peoples."[12]

Of course, there was a reactionary quality to Péladan's misoneist technophobia: his hatred for democracy, his contempt for faddishness and gadgetry. But even in Mérodack's effort to re-construct the Albigensian Abbey of Montségur – a Gnostic institution ruled by mystic asceticism – he had acknowledged the contribution of the spiritually enlightened and had defined their task as using magic on behalf of humanity. Péladan's conception of latria combined the idea of service and worship, so while still boasting of his Chaldean ancestry and artistic pedigree, he came down from the mountain on which his fortress was built in order to pass among the people with whom his wisdom would be shared. As Mérodack had said to his Rosicrucian brethren: "We love God; we believe in salvation; we bear witness to the light; in us, concern for our neighbor alternates with a cult of the abstract."[13]

In the domain of magic, the governing principle had been the exclusivity of the discipline, the exceptional wisdom of the initiate urged to be inimitable and sublime. Exceptionality is the sovereign good, as Péladan had written of the Magus: "the more one is solitary, the more he is himself, *ipsissimus*."[14] By contrast, the Satanic frenzy that gripped fin-de-siècle France was fueled by perceived threats to identity, a fear of aliens and outsiders. While the world of the Decadent Magus had been one of narcissistic solitude – unpopulated except for the chilly company of the illuminati – the paranoid realm of the fin-de-siècle Satanist teemed with toxic bacilli, pullulated with malevolent larvae like those Bois describes attacking Saint Francesca of Rome: biting, licking, shrieking, breaking furniture, emitting the stench of the corpse she was fated to become. Rare are those who are high enough or exceptional enough to resemble us. Many are those who, by embodying our disavowed vices, are projected as the accursed other.

Whereas turn-of-the-century white magic moved toward coalescence with one's neighbor, devil worship was often motivated by a horror of the stranger. In an era witnessing widespread institutional destabilization – secularism's attack on the church, democracy's undermining of social hierarchy, subversion of long-standing belief systems – change once considered as cultural happenstance became disquietingly transmogrified, endowed with malevolent intention, attributed to infernal enemies. Freud's identification of the *Unheimlich* described it as what was both unrecognizable and familiar, alien in the same way as one's reflection in a mirror. As Hawthorne had written more than a century earlier: "The fiend in his own shape is less hideous than when he rages in the breast of man."[15]

In Huysmans's *Là-bas*, the devil's journey had described his unsettling approach: from the Middle Ages, out of the subterranean slaughter-dungeon of Gilles de Rais, into the present day, to sanctuaries in the nearby neighborhoods of Paris. Defamiliarized, distorted, Satan was the one who inevitably came back. He is "nothing else than the personification of the repressed unconscious instinctual life."[16]

Xenophobia and anti-Semitism had become more pronounced in the fin de siècle, as France had become polarized in the aftermath of Dreyfus. Edouard Drumont, in *La Libre Parole*, propagated the most virulent forms of bigotry, opposing a romanticized vision of France's pastoral history to its rootless, capitalistic present. Portable wealth controlled by Jews had caused a disintegration of national identity, yet evil was manifested by the very multiplicity of one's adversaries: bankers, Protestants, Freemasons, Republicans, all conspiring with the Jews in their schemes of world conquest.

Fin-de-siècle supernaturalism had hinged on this dialectical exchange: between an exalted self and a hated other, between familiarity and estrangement. The most terrifying Satan was the one most closely resembling the subject, the reflection he disavowed, the brother he disinherited. Thus, at the turn of the century, the infiltration of the Fallen One into contemporary life had blurred the clarity of established taxonomies, inverting moral antipodes, confusing metaphysical adversaries. From the narcissism of the occult master and his delirium of imaginary emulation, one moved to the paranoia of the demonophobe drowning in an ocean of alien malevolence. Unlike magic, predicated on the grandeur of a self that enveloped admiring others, the fear of Lucifer had been fueled by fears of sameness. How can we recognize our antagonist and be prepared to fight against him if Satanists, Jews, and Freemasons are identical to us? The saturation of space with imps and larvae corresponded to this projection of the multiplication of others. The Magus had stood alone and filled the astral light with his uniqueness, while the Satan-fighter was embattled by evil Doppelgänger.

Retreating into the fortress of his ethnicity, faith, and caste, the enemy of Satan had been as isolated as the thaumaturge. Protected by prayers and counter-spells, he was similarly defended by precautionary xenophobia. Unlike the devout who worshipped God, the Satanist enlisted the devil to come and serve him. Listen to his promises, as Jules Bois writes in his *Evocation du Diable* [Evocation of the Devil]: "Ask me, and I will make a naked girl dance for you. Beat urine, and I will make it thunder and hail. With magnetic powder strewn on braziers, I unleash earthquakes and lightening. I cure hemorrhoids and scabies. I bestow treasure and prevent suffering."[17] In a universe where God is sovereign, there is infinite transcendence. In a microcosm where the devil serves, space is shrunk to the dimensions of one's desires.

In the Decadent mirror-box of ipseity, where only the ego had been beautiful, the Devil relinquished his grandeur at the same time that the self became idealized. In Durtal's view of the medieval world, where mystery was uncompromised by science, Satan was unseen and his power appeared immeasurable. But when worshippers knelt at vanity's altar, the devil had been domesticated, becoming another cynical roué, like Félicien Rops's monocle-wearing clubman. In the fin de siècle, Satanism was just another vice like showgirls or roulette.

The virtue of Léo Taxil's magnificent fin-de-siècle hoax – his creation of the imaginary worldwide Luciferian cult of Palladism – had been to operate on dual registers. To the worldly intellectual, for whom the devil offered entertainment, Taxil's global narrative of far-flung Masonic lodges housing Satanic orgies afforded a diversion whose anti-hero was as amusingly wicked as themselves. To the Catholic reactionary, for whom science was a force of metaphysical evil, a Satanic confederation of Freemasons and Jews resurrected a worthy adversary whose stature was as great as the church crusader who fought them. Taxil's mystification proposed the devil as joke and bugbear, inciting the Vatican to join in a cosmic clash of good against evil, pleasing jaded readers with serialized stories of adventures with Asmodeus. In Taxil, Satan was the Prince of Darkness and a ridiculous anachronism, a nightmare from which one awakened feeling foolish for believing it.

The Decadents who mourned a devil greater than the banality of their perversions longed for some cause to serve, some entity to adore. Taxil's imposture had spread the theater of metaphysical warfare across the globe. Anglophones and Semites, nymphomaniacs and Asians formed an alliance of aliens threatening Judeo-Christian westernism. But then, like the prestidigitator who explains how his sleight of hand worked, Taxil had confessed to his deception, and the theater had gone dark. There was nothing more to fear than the embarrassment of having been duped.

While those fearful of the devil had retreated into a fortress filled with those resembling them and believing as they did – while the Magus had withdrawn to the mountaintop castle of his disdainful superiority – the mystic had also undergone indescribable experiences alone. Like the Magus, whose arcane knowledge precluded its being shared with the uninitiated, the mystic was plunged into an ineffably solitary dissolution in the divine. The autism of the mystic's raptures surpassed the lexicon of the common people, just as the wisdom of the hermeticist was communicable only in numbers and symbols.

Yet what distinguished fin-de-siècle literature of the transcendental was its radical inversion of superiority and abjection. Péladan's Magus had still been affiliated with an aristocracy of intelligence; Papus had still denigrated the poverty of the seminarian's education. But the anti-intellectualism triggered by the idolatry of science was accompanied by an overthrow of traditional virtues and ideals. Prosperity, intelligence, and happiness were stigmatized while a cultivated poverty, an embrace of suffering on behalf of others became the appanage of a new elite of the disinherited and despised.

Emptied of egotism, the mystic had made room for the divine, as annihilation of personal will allowed for a consummation of self in God. Of course, the ecstasy of the visionary was still inescapably narcissistic. Indescribable in speech, the mystic's fusion with the Lord afforded a community of seekers no opportunity to participate. Yet unlike the Magus, sequestered in the stronghold of his secrecy, the mystic had aimed at reconnection with another, acquiescing to humility as the price paid for love.

In the tidal sweep of Eugène Vintras's homiletic rhetoric, there had been Biblical execrations of the pomp and pageantry of Roman Masses, jeremiads against the Pope and his assertions of infallibility, denunciations of a church drunk with opulence and power. However, the popularity of Vintras's teachings had come from their glorification of the downtrodden, their elevation of visionary women, their championing of the poor as members of Christ's crucified body.

Vintras's *Glaive sur Rome* had begun by deploring the mercantilism of the church. As Jesus told the prophet: "I was sold for money; I was hated, tormented, and persecuted because of gold."[18] When Jesus had been hungry, the clergy had strewn diadems on altars; when he was naked, priests had dressed themselves in "all the sumptuous things of the world."[19] Vintras's elevation of the poor foreshadowed the apotheosizing of the peasant girls to whom the Virgin had appeared – Bernadette Soubirous in Lourdes and Mélanie Calvat in La Salette – reinforcing the fin-de-siècle ideal of naïveté and simplicity. In the generation following Vintras, culture and erudition became spiritual impediments, filtering out what, for the unlettered, was a direct apprehension of the divine. This glorification of poverty, analphabetism, and guilelessness had joined in a dialectic in which self-forgetfulness brought remembrance of God.

Among the reactionary Catholics examined here, the celebration of the forsaken, the rejection of reason and the invocation of ignorance as a virtue had been accompanied by an honoring of women seen as intuitive and visionary, as humble conduits of the divine. Thus, the fin-de-siècle rehabilitation of Eve as a precursor of Mary had been part of a redefinition of women, first as sinners, then as saviors.

In Vintras's church, women had been raised to positions of authority; spreading the Marian gospel, they were voices of fin-de-siècle mysticism. Yet countering the image of the Virgin as nurturer and intercessor was the reactionary view of her as the Mater Dolorosa. Richard Burton notes the preference among certain fin-de-siècle Catholics for the Virgin of La Salette, whose message was threatening and ominous, to the Virgin who appeared in Lourdes, promising forgiveness, cures, and comfort. According to Huysmans, the inaccessibility of La Salette had tested pilgrims' resoluteness. "But physical remoteness was not the sole reason for setting La Salette above Lourdes. To the extent that the Virgin's message at Lourdes was in essence one of healing and love, it could [...] be reconciled not just with existing society with its visceral 'hatred of Pain' but also with the will to existence itself, the sheer animal instinct to live and to be, whence the site's huge popularity with the mass of 'ordinary' life-loving, pain- and death-fearing Catholics. But when the Virgin spoke to Mélanie and Maximin on the mountain, she seemed to be opposed to *everything*: to society as it is, to the contemporary Church, to reason, to the body, and, ultimately, to existence itself."[20]

For Léon Bloy, reverence for Mary as the One Who Weeps – "Celle qui pleure" – had expressed a recognition of women's value as the source of pain's secretions: the sacred blood and holy tears that washed away the stain of sin, drowning the world in a new Flood of angry lamentation, undoing a flawed creation before the forthcoming apocalypse and the world's resurrection in the reign of the Holy Spirit. For Bloy, Eve's transgression had caused man's expulsion from the Garden, and so Mary's good offices had been necessary for him to re-enter paradise. In Bloy's writings, Eve and Mary wept eternally – from remorse for the first sin, out of compassion for the sinner. The disobedience of man's mother had necessitated intervention by Christ's mother, so that Eve and Mary functionally became complementary halves of a single whole.

However, in the economy of Dolorism, the trespasser's sin entailed the victim's punishment, as the debt of human guilt was liquidated by the Crucifixion of the one offended. All man's efforts, all the world's suffering intended a return to the beginning, restoration of a state of innocence, a welcoming back to Eden, whence the idealization among fin-de-siècle Catholic mystics of the innocence of childhood.

Analysis of the theology of fin-de-siècle Catholic reactionaries shows their revalorizing women's roles in a revolutionary fashion. By yielding to the temptation to eat the forbidden fruit of knowledge, Adam and Eve had been banished to a world in which knowledge itself had caused unhappiness. It was not concupiscence but *libido sciendi* that had brought about the Fall, exile to a barren place like the realm of scientific reason.

God's punishment of the first man had been a requirement that he work: "cursed is the ground because of you; in toil shall you eat of it all the days of your life" (Genesis 3. 17). To Eve God had announced that her labor would be similarly painful: "I will greatly multiply your pain in childbearing; in pain shall you bring forth children" (Genesis 3. 16). The spiritual aesthetic of authors like Bloy and Hello had been to practice art as its undoing. Writers toiled, and women suffered so that their guilt might be expunged, cleansing them so that no new books and no new children would be engendered. The Great Work of human history had been an act of cancellation: the Passion endured on Calvary so that original sin was washed away. In order to participate in the ongoing task of man's redemption, the pain assumed by Christ had to be undergone by women whose child was sorrow conceived and born of love.

Women were no longer seen as anatomically disadvantaged. Rather, these authors exhibited a kind of suffering-envy, a desire to experience torments culminating in the delivery, not of an artwork, but a Messiah. Eve's guilt was the precondition for the fecundity of Mary, who was proleptically absolved of sin, accorded an Immaculate Conception, as she bore the child who saved man from his wretched exile on the earth. The Mother of humanity, Mary cried for man's iniquity, and her sadness extended the childbirth pain that had been visited on Eve. The Virgin's tears were like Christ's blood in washing away the stain of history: "The Holy Virgin's Compassion was the Passion in its most terrible form."[21]

Yet the end of the world had not come, and the human race had kept on living, committing new atrocities, raising the rate of increase on sin as debt. New martyrs had been required to balance the ledger with their bleeding wounds and weeping eyes, so that the sum of what was owed could return again to zero. In the apocalyptic mentality of the fin-de-siècle mystics – in the Third Age of the Paraclete whose advent Vintras promised – the bride of Christ who joined with him in the consummation of self-sacrifice would give birth to the innocence which they represented as nothing.

Inevitably, fin-de-siècle mysticism had begotten a literature of silence, as unsustainable, peak states had fallen outside the realm of fiction, condemned, like life, to continue in a world of bodies, loss, and compromise.

Essentially, mystical literature belonged to an aristocracy of art, in which even authors and their audiences could not take part in the transports of the character. As the Magus was alone with the insignia of his genius, possessing wisdom encrypted in an idiolect of the enlightened, Christ's betrothed also betrayed a form of "selfishness between two people," enjoying an unsurpassable experience unamenable to the language of the tribe. In Huysmans's reconstruction of the life of Lydwine, and in

Bloy's novel of a modern saint, the agonies of the heroine exceeded the benefits of those they suffered for.

Yet, if only gradually, fin-de-siècle literature of the mystical and occult moved from the private experience of the subject to the shared ventures of a community, migrating from the chamber of the Magus to the Rosicrucian enclave – from the library of the lonely aesthete to the teeming pilgrimage site of Lourdes. In the final volume of Péladan's *Ethopée*, *La Vertu suprême*, Mérodack's brothers at Montségur had been urged to adopt the principles of the Albigensians: denial of the Incarnation, a renunciation of the flesh, a desire to rejoin God in the Uncreated Light. The end point of the Dolorist's mission, after securing the deliverance of souls from Purgatory, had been to reward the sufferer with the death that repatriated her in heaven. Huysmans's Lydwine had quit a shell that was already crucified and broken, and had risen to meet the Bridegroom in a scene of indescribable bliss. Bloy's heroine, Clotilde Chapuis, awaited a similar liberation, an end to separation in the Gehenna of her loneliness on earth. The rapture these women anticipated came from what Denis de Rougemont calls Eros or Endless Death, disappearance into the night that preceded Creation.

But when Guaïta had described descending the ladder from the firmament to the world – when Péladan's Magus had chosen to impart his occult knowledge to a novice – there was a reintegration into the world, an affirmation of solidarity with the other. From the Thanatotic literature of mystical asceticism came a pastoral art recommending service to our brothers here below. As Rougemont writes: "to love is no longer to flee and persistently to reject the act of love. Love now still begins beyond death, but from that beyond it returns to life. And in being thus converted, love brings forth our *neighbor*."[22]

In its final stages, fin-de-siècle supernaturalism rejected an art of hypersubjectivity, abandoning the Decadent *culte du moi* in favor of cooperative effort and self-sacrifice. The literature of the transcendental became a vehicle for "morality," which Jean Pierrot identifies with the final years of the nineteenth century. "Everything changed after 1898. Intellectuals recognized their solidarity with a society on which they acted; they felt responsible for its future and integrated into its destiny."[23]

In Huysmans's *Les Foules de Lourdes*, suffering had motivated service, and the privileged subject had made way for the unfortunate he hoped to solace. Poverty was no longer cultivated as self-eradicating mysticism – as the disposal of material goods and a detachment from the ego – and miracle-workers became those committed to comforting their brothers. By dedicating themselves to life and work, they exchanged Eros for Agape or Christian Love.

The final fin-de-siècle staging ground for manifestations of the supernatural ceased to be the Christ-flooded consciousness of martyrs whose pain had turned to joy and instead became the fallen world described as a prison house or hospital. There, refugees and patients awaited succor or release, and they were helped, not by saints who writhed in silence on their beds, but by volunteers whose calling was to comfort and assuage. "Suffering with," they expressed compassion as an interactive practice rather than as solitary prayer.

For Huysmans, in a world normally governed by pleasure-seeking and self-interest, the presence of wealthy women working as attendants to the crippled and bath attendants to the stricken was the surest proof of the miraculous. The Virgin's presence was felt less strongly in the broken who were made whole than in the actions of an army of caregivers cured of their customary apathy. In Lourdes, Huysmans – once a member of an aristocracy of aesthetes – observed the operation of a will to well-being that was democratically expressed. No longer crucified with Jesus, the faithful did the work of Christ by dedicating themselves to pain's abatement. Miracles, no longer witnessed in the flamboyance of theophanies, were evident in the ordinariness of selfless deeds done with humility.

How far fin-de-siècle thinking had come by the time of Huysmans's writing – from the chamber of the Magus, with its directive to become like God, to Lourdes's helpers who worked in sickrooms where the privileged mingled with the forsaken. The new century saw a rejection of the inwardness of mystic thinking. It marked an end of the occult tendency toward exclusivity and secrecy: assignment of numerological values to the Arcana of the Tarot, enclosure of spagyrical science in impenetrable symbols. The etiolated recluse who had poured over grimoires in his sanctuary had been dragged out, as Camille Mauclair writes, "into the violent, sacred sun, into the magnificence of life, away from nostalgia and self-reflection."[24] Even before the outbreak of the Great War, France had been re-politicized, the anarchist movement had been infused with new energy, religious introversion had been abandoned. Adolphe Retté had inveighed against the "final avatar" of Christianity with its "mystical corruption" – responsible, he claims, for France's "morbid state of mind."[25]

But even before the century ended with the obsolescence of Decadent aesthetics – not with the glorious apocalypse that many had anticipated – the supernatural had relocated from the occultist's brain to the world of action. Péladan's thaumaturge no longer guarded esotericism's secrets for himself but imparted them to others, sharing their meaning in works of art. In Huysmans, Satan had been exposed as the prideful self that one adored. In Taxil, devil religion had been revealed as ethnocentric paranoia. The Catholic mystics who once proclaimed the sanctity of women suffering for souls in Purgatory not only honored the poor as the crucified members of Christ's body, but also sought to implement Christ's teaching by comforting the afflicted. No longer was the burning of souls in hell or the conflagration of saints in God an indescribable drama playing out in the theater of the afterlife. Instead, the blessed assisted people condemned to hell on earth: victims of elephantiasis, chorea, and lupus, the hydrocephalics who stormed Lourdes' flaming grotto with their prayers. God's servants no longer aspired to a solitary marriage with their Redeemer but joined in a commitment to the service of humanity. I act in memory of Christ when I perform the occult act of self-transcendence. Not martyrdom for me: God's work on earth for you.

Notes

Introduction

1. Lézinier, p. 193.
2. Qtd. in Huysmans, *A rebours*, p. 69.
3. Huysmans, "Emile Zola et *L'Assommoir*," p. 162.
4. Huysmans, *Là-bas*, p. 4.
5. Huysmans, *A rebours*, p. 68.
6. Burton, *Blood in the City*, p. 161.
7. Qtd. in Baldick, p. 161.
8. Baldick, p. 210.
9. Baldick, p. 166.
10. Baldick, p. 214.
11. Pierrot, p. 158.
12. Huysmans, *Là-haut* , p. 43.
13. Huysmans, *Là-haut*, p. 45.
14. Huysmans, *Là-haut*, p. 49.
15. Bois, p. 29.
16. Huysmans, *Là-bas*, p. 244.
17. Huysmans, *Sainte Lydwine de Schiedam*, Vol. II, pp. 126–7.
18. Qtd. in Seillan, pp. 216, 218.

1 The Satanist

1. "The 'Black Art' in France," *The Manchester Guardian*, December 1897.
2. Waite, *Devil Worship in France*, p. 100.
3. Waite, *Devil Worship in France*, p. 119.
4. Waite, *Devil Worship in France*, pp. 233–4.
5. Waite, *Devil Worship in France*, p. 233.
6. Pierrot, p. 117.
7. Guaïta, *Le Temple de Satan*, p. 155.
8. Pierrot, p. 131.
9. Papus, *Le Diable et l'occultisme*, p. 9.
10. Papus, *Le Diable et l'occultisme*, p. 13.
11. Papus, *Le Diable et l'occultisme*, p. 34.
12. Péladan, *Comment on devient mage*, p. 228.
13. Péladan, *Comment on devient mage*, p. 229.
14. Péladan, *Comment on devient mage*, p. 81.
15. Bois, p. 181.
16. Bois, p. 157.
17. Bois, p. 159.
18. Bois, p. 164.

19. Bois, p. 167.
20. Chasseguet-Smirgel, p. 395.
21. Bois, p. 164.
22. Bois, p. 170.
23. Bois, p. 169.
24. Bois, p. 169.
25. Bois, p. 170.
26. Bois, p. 171.
27. Huysmans, *Certains*, p.78.
28. Baldick, p. 148.
29. Huysmans, *Certains*, p. 76.
30. Huysmans, *Certains*, p. 72.
31. Huysmans, *Certains*, p. 90.
32. Hall, p. 96.
33. Huysmans, *Certains*, p. 106.
34. Waite, *Devil Worship in France*, p.12.
35. Guaïta, *Le Temple de Satan*, p. 106.
36. Guaïta, *Le Temple de Satan*, p. 111.
37. Guaïta, *Le Temple de Satan*, p. 52.
38. Guaïta, *Le Serpent de la Genèse*, p. 91.
39. Guaïta, *Le Serpent de la Genèse*, p. 100.
40. Guaïta, *Le Serpent de la Genèse*, p. 502.
41. Guaïta, *Le Serpent de la Genèse*, p. 501.
42. Guaïta, *Le Serpent de la Genèse*, p. 504.
43. Guaïta, *Le Serpent de la Genèse*, p.517.
44. Guaïta, *Le Serpent de la Genèse*, p. 524.
45. Schwob, *Le Livre de Monelle*, pp. 69–70.
46. Schwob, *Le Livre de Monelle*, p. 20.
47. Guaïta, *Le Serpent de La Genèse*, p. 525.
48. Guaïta, *Le Serpent de la Genèse*, p. 524.
49. Guaïta, *Le Serpent de la Genèse*, p. 519.
50. Lévi, *Dogme et Rituel de la Haute Magie*, p. 30.
51. Guaïta, *Le Serpent de la Genèse*, p. 52.
52. Rougemont, *The Devil's Share*, p. 132.
53. Wallis, p. 155.
54. Jean-Martin Charcot and Paul Marie Louis Pierre Richer, *Les démoniaques dans l'art*, 1887.
55. Huysmans, Preface to Bois's *Le Satanisme et la magie*, p. vii.
56. Huysmans, Preface to Bois's *Le Satanisme et la magie*, p. xii.
57. Waite, *Devil Worship in France*, p. 10.
58. Qtd. in Baldick, p. 157.
59. Huysmans, *Là-bas*, Vol. I, p. 24.
60. Huysmans, *Là-bas*, Vol I, p. 24.
61. Huysmans, *Là-bas*, Vol. I, p. 25.
62. Papus, *Le Diable et l'Occultisme*, p. 31.
63. Huysmans, *Là-bas*, Vol. I, p. 6.
64. Huysmans, *Là-bas*, Vol II, p. 164.
65. Huysmans, *Là-bas*, Vol. II, p. 164.
66. Huysmans, *Là-bas*, Vol. I, p. 216.

67. Huysmans, Preface to Bois's *Le Satanisme et la magie*, p. xx.
68. Bois, p. 41.
69. Bois, p. 41.
70. Borie, p. 19.
71. Huysmans, *Là-bas*, Vol. I, p. 185.
72. Bois, pp. 278–9.
73. Huysmans, *Là-bas*, Vol. I, p. 172.
74. Huysmans, *Là-bas*, Vol. II, p. 45.
75. Bois, p. 279.
76. Baldick, p.156.
77. Huysmans, Preface to Bois's *Le Satanisme et la magie*, p. xxi.
78. Huysmans, Preface to Bois's *Le Satanisme et la magie*, p. xxii.
79. Huysmans, Preface to Bois's *Le Satanisme et la magie*, p. xiv.
80. Huysmans, Preface to Bois's *Le Satanisme et la magie*, p. xx.
81. Huysmans, *Là-bas*, Vol. II, p. 109.
82. Miller, p. 225.
83. Huysmans, *Là-bas*, Vol. II, p. 182.
84. Huysmans, *Certains*, p. 72.
85. Péladan, *Le Vice Suprême*, p. 210.
86. Qtd. in Huysmans, Preface to Bois's *Le Satanisme et la magie*, p. xvi.
87. Chasseguet-Smirgel, p. 4.
88. Chasseguet-Smirgel, p. 11.
89. Huysmans, *Là-bas*, Vol. I, pp. 216–17.
90. Bricaud, p. 21.
91. Bois, p. 244.
92. Bois, p. 246.
93. Huysmans, *Là-bas*, Vol. I, p. 82.
94. Hall, p. 154.
95. Bois, p. 36.
96. Bois, p. 87.
97. Huysmans, *Là*-bas, Vol. II, p. 34.
98. Huysmans, *Là-bas*, Vol. II, p. 35.
99. Huysmans, *Là-bas*, Vol. II, p. 35.
100. Huysmans, *Là-bas*, Vol. II, p. 36.
101. Huysmans, *Là-bas*, Vol. II, p. 36.
102. Bois, p. 247.
103. Huysmans, *Là-bas*, Vol. II, pp. 195–6.

2   The Hoaxer

1. Huysmans, Preface to Bois's *Le Satanisme et la magie*, p. xv.
2. Weber, "Religion and Superstition," p. 399.
3. Weber, "Religion and Superstition," p. 400.
4. Weber, "Religion and Superstition," p. 404.
5. Huysmans, Preface to Bois's *Le Satanisme et la magie*, p. xv.
6. Weber, "Religion and Superstition," p. 404.
7. Weber, *Satan Franc-Maçon*, p. 201.
8. Berchmans, p. 11.

9. Waite, *Devil Worship in France*, p. 71.
10. Weber, *Satan Franc-Maçon*, p. 190.
11. Qtd. in Weber, *Satan-Franc-Maçon*, p. 168.
12. Weber, *Satan Franc-Maçon*, p. 158.
13. Papus, *Le Diable et l'Occultisme*, p. 11.
14. Waite, *Devil Worship in France*, p. 28.
15. Closson, p. 318.
16. Qtd. in Closson, p. 316.
17. Huysmans, *Là-bas*, Vol. II, p. 165.
18. Huysmans, *Là-bas*, Vol. II, p. 162.
19. Waite, *Devil Worship in France*, p. 26.
20. Berchmans, p. 58.
21. Closson, p. 319.
22. Qtd. in Weber, *Satan Franc-Maçon*, p. 170.
23. Closson, p. 331.
24. Waite, *Devil Worship in France*, p. 116.
25. Durand, p. 364.
26. Chasseguet-Smirgel, p. 10.
27. Eliade, *Mephistopheles and the Androgyne*, p. 141.
28. Closson, p. 328.
29. Waite, *Devil Worship in France*, p. 117.
30. Hall, p. 89.
31. Closson, p. 324.
32. Closson, p. 323.
33. Frankfurter, p. 76.
34. Qtd. in Weber, *Satan Franc-Maçon*, p. 62.
35. Eliade, *The Forge and the Crucible*, p. 52.
36. Weber, *Satan Franc-Maçon*, p. 69.
37. Qtd. in Weber, *Satan Franc-Maçon*, p. 75.
38. Waite, *Devil Worship in France*, p. 143.
39. Eliade, *The Forge and the Crucible*, p. 157.
40. Qtd. in Weber, *Satan Franc-Maçon*, p. 84.
41. Qtd. in Weber, *Satan Franc Maçon*, p. 176.
42. Qtd. in Weber, *Satan Franc-Maçon*, p. 30.
43. Qtd. in Weber, *Satan Franc-Maçon*, p. 32.
44. Qtd. in Weber, *Satan Franc-Maçon*, p. 142.
45. Qtd. in Weber, *Satan Franc-Maçon*, p. 173.
46. Margiotta, pp. 53–4.
47. Margiotta, p. 241.
48. Qtd. in Weber, *Satan Franc-Maçon*, p. 37.
49. Qtd. in Weber, *Satan Franc-Maçon*, p. 156.
50. *Taxil, Les Soeurs Maçonnes*, p. 179.
51. Closson, p. 332.
52. Carpenter, p. 174.

3   The Magus

1. Pierrot, p. 103.
2. Griffiths, p. 129.

3. Péladan, *Comment on devient mage*, p. 30.
4. Qtd. in Hayes, p. 101.
5. Huysmans, *Là-bas*, Vol. II, p. 235.
6. Péladan, *La Vertu suprême*, p. 390.
7. Péladan, *Comment on devient mage*, p. 143.
8. Péladan *Comment on devient mage*, p. 76.
9. Bois, pp. 75–6.
10. Péladan, *Comment on devient mage*, p. 23.
11. Hall, p. 156.
12. Péladan, *Comment on devient mage*, p. 25.
13. Qtd. in Pierrot, p. 144.
14. Pierrot, p. 145.
15. Waite, Biographical and Critical Essay, *Mysteries of Magic*, p. 39.
16. Mercier, p. 43.
17. Qtd. in Waite, Biographical and Critical Essay, *Mysteries of Magic*, p. 47.
18. Waite, Biographical and Critical Essay, *Mysteries of Magic*, p 73
19. Qtd. in Waite, Biographical and Critical Essay, *Mysteries of Magic*, p. 73.
20. Guaïta, *Au Seuil du mystère*, pp. 16–17.
21. Guaïta, *Au Seuil du mystère*, p. 18.
22. Péladan, *Le Vice suprême*, p. 159.
23. The *Sepher Yetzirah*, qtd. in Hall, p. 114.
24. Guaïta, *Au Seuil du mystère*, pp. 35–6.
25. Papus, *Le Tarot des Bohémiens*, p. 25.
26. Durand, pp. 364–5.
27. Lévi, *Dogme et Rituel de la Haute Magie*, p. 345.
28. Hall, p. 130.
29. Qtd. in Hall, p. 130.
30. Jung, p. 329.
31. Waite, Biographical and Critical Essay, *Mysteries of Magic*, p. 39.
32. Péladan, *Comment on devient mage*, p. 91.
33. Huysmans, *Sainte Lydwine de Schiedam*, pp. 126–7.
34. Bois, p. 76.
35. Jankélévitch, p. 52.
36. Péladan, *Comment on devient mage*, p. 148.
37. Péladan, *Comment on devient mage*, p. 150.
38. Péladan, *Comment on devient mage*, pp. 155–6.
39. Péladan, *La Vertu suprême*, p. 390.
40. Péladan, *Le Vice suprême*, p. vi.
41. Papus, *Le Diable et l'Occultisme*, p. 30.
42. Péladan, *Comment on devient mage*, p. 268.
43. Papus, *Le Diable et l'Occultisme*, p. 50.
44. Péladan, *Comment on devient mage*, p. 276.
45. Péladan, *Comment on devient mage*, p. 281.
46. Péladan, *Le Vice suprême*, p. 293.
47. Berg, p. 96.
48. Péladan, *Comment on devient mage*, p. 287.
49. Péladan, *Comment on devient mage*, p. 288.
50. Péladan *Comment on devient mage*, p. 292.
51. Lévi, *Dogme et Rituel de la Haute Magie*, p. 58.

52. Pierrot, p. 147.
53. Bois, *Le Satanisme et la magie*, p. 107.
54. Schuré, p. 456–7.
55. Lévi, *Dogme et Rituel de la Haute Magie*, p. 12.
56. Jung, p. 331.
57. Jung, p. 97.
58. Guaïta, *Le Serpent de la Genèse*, p. 451.
59. Guaïta, *Le Serpent de la Genèse*, pp. 452–3.
60. Guaïta, *Au Seuil du mystère*, p. 66.
61. Guaïta, *Au Seuil du mystère*, p. 97.
62. Guaïta, *Au Seuil du mystère*, p. 97.
63. Qtd. in Waite, *The Mysteries of Magic*, p. 295.
64. Péladan, *Comment on devient mage*, p. 292.
65. *Hebrews* 7:3.
66. Pierrot, p. 107.
67. Pierrot, p. 109.
68. Villiers de l'Isle-Adam, *Axël*, p. 549.
69. Villiers de l'Isle-Adam, *Axël*, p. 549.
70. Villiers de l'Isle-Adam, *Axël*, p. 665.
71. Hall, p. 139.
72. Villiers de l'Isle-Adam, *Axël*, , p. 547.
73. Villiers de l'Isle-Adam, *Axël*, p. 635.
74. Villiers de L'Isle-Adam, *Axël*, pp. 637–8.
75. Péladan, *Comment on devient mage*, p. 293.
76. Pierrot, p. 87.
77. Pierrot, p. 86.
78. Pierrot, p. 90.
79. Kohn, p. 245.
80. Péladan, *Comment on devient mage*, p. 288.
81. Beaufils, p. 12.
82. Péladan, *Comment on devient mage*, p. xix.
83. Péladan, *Comment on devient mage*, p. 36.
84. Péladan, *Comment on devient mage*, p. 19.
85. Bois, p. 256.
86. Bois, p. 258.
87. Péladan, *L'Occulte catholique*, p. 13.
88. Péladan, *L'Occulte catholique*, p. 13.
89. Lévi, *Dogme et Rituel de la Haute Magie*, p. 121.
90. Péladan, *Le Vice suprême*, p. 387.
91. Péladan, *Le Vice suprême*, p. 140.
92. Kohn, p. 242.
93. Beaufils, p. 77.
94. Beaufils, p. 77.
95. Péladan, *Comment on devient mage*, p.189.
96. Péladan, *Comment on devient mage*, p. 271.
97. Péladan, *Comment on devient mage*, p. 293.
98. Péladan, *Comment on devient mage*, p. 293.
99. Péladan, *Finis Latinorum*, p. 195.
100. Papus, *Le Diable et l'Occultisme*, p. 52.

101. Péladan, *Finis Latinorum*, p.146.
102. Péladan, *L'Occulte catholique*, p. 166.
103. Péladan, *L'Occulte catholique*, p. 168.
104. Péladan, *Finis Latinorum*, p. 50.
105. Péladan, *L'Occulte catholique*, p. 70.
106. Péladan, *Finis Latinorum*, p. 50.
107. Péladan, *La Vertu suprême*, p. 390.
108. Péladan, *La Vertu suprême*, p. 390.
109. Péladan, *La Vertu suprême*, p. 396.
110. Péladan, *Comment on devient mage*, p. 113.
111. Péladan, *Le Vice suprême*, pp. 258–9.
112. Péladan, *La Vertu suprême*, p. 35.
113. Péladan, *La Vertu suprême*, p. 35.
114. Péladan, *La Vertu suprême*, p. 295.
115. Rougemont, *Love in the Western World*, p. 68.
116. Rougemont, *Love in the Western World*, p. 80.
117. Péladan, *La Vertu suprême*, p. 376.
118. Péladan, *La Vertu suprême*, p. 378.
119. Péladan, *La Vertu suprême*, p. 384.
120. Péladan, *la Vertu suprême*, p. 394.
121. Péladan, *La Vertu suprême*, p. 200.
122. Péladan, *Comment on devient mage*, pp. 138–9.
123. Péladan, *La Vertu suprême*, p. 391.
124. Péladan, *La Vertu suprême*, p. 391.
125. Kohn, p. 239.
126. Kohn, p. 240.
127. Kohn, p. 251.
128. Péladan, *La Vertu suprême*, p. 394.
129. Péladan, Préface, *Le Vice suprême*, p. vi.
130. Péladan, *La Vertu suprême*, p. 400.

4 The Mystic

1. Hayes, pp. 90–1.
2. Hayes, p. 241.
3. Qtd. in Hayes, p. 246.
4. Vintras, *Le Glaive sur Rome* (*The Sword Over Rome*), pp. 147, 148.
5. Griffiths, p. 124.
6. Garçon, pp. 15–16.
7. Garçon, p. 72.
8. Griffiths, p. 125.
9. Vintras, *Opuscule sur des communications annonçant l'Oeuvre de la Miséricorde*, qtd. in Garçon, pp. 33–4.
10. Qtd. in Garçon, p. 43.
11. *L'Eternel Evangile*, p. 476.
12. Vintras, *L'Eternel Evangile*, p. 461.
13. Vintras, *L'Eternel Evangile*, p. 459.
14. Huysmans, *Là-bas*, Vol. II, pp. 196–7.

15. Huysmans, *Là-bas*, Vol. II, p. 197.
16. Burton, *Holy Blood, Holy Tears*, p. xiii.
17. Griffiths, p. 128.
18. Qtd. in Griffiths, p.128.
19. Vintras, *Le Glaive sur Rome*, p. 33.
20. Vintras, *L'Eternel Evangile*, p. 590.
21. Vintras, *L'Eternel Evangile*, p. 690.
22. Huysmans, *Sainte Lydwine de Schiedam*, Vol. I, p. 99.
23. Huysmans, *Sainte Lydwine de Schiedam*, Vol. II, p. 100.
24. Baldick, p. 214.
25. Baldick, p. 214.
26. Qtd. in Baldick, pp. 344–5.
27. Huysmans, *Sainte Lydwine de Schiedam*, Vol. II, p. 37.
28. Qtd. in Garçon, p. 60.
29. Hopkins, p. 258.
30. Hopkins, p. 257.
31. Griffiths, p. 127.
32. Lévi, *Histoire de la Magie*, p. 484.
33. Lévi, *Histoire de la Magie*, p. 484.
34. Guaïta, *Le Serpent de la Genèse*, p. 448.
35. Lévi, *Histoire de la Magie*, p. 485.
36. Guaïta, *Le Serpent de la Genèse*, p. 451.
37. Guaïta, *Le Serpent de la Genèse*, p. 451.
38. Guaïta, *Le Serent de la Genèse*, p. 448.
39. Guaïta, *Le Serpent de la Genèse*, p. 453.
40. Guaïta, *Le Serpent de la Genèse*, p. 454.
41. Vintras, *Le Glaive sur Rome*, p. 377.
42. Vintras, *Le Glaive sur Rome*, p. 385.
43. Vintras, *Le Glaive sur Rome*, p. 385.
44. Vintras, *Le Glaive sur Rome*, p. 379.
45. Vintras, *Le Glaive sur Rome*, p. 390.
46. Vintras, *Le Glaive sur Rome*, p. 390.
47. Papus, *Le Diable et l'Occultisme*, p. 34.
48. Papus, *Le Diable et l'Occultisme*, p. 31.
49. Vintras, *Le Glaive sur Rome*, p. 395.
50. Vintras, *L'Eternel Evangile*, p. 623.
51. Vintras, *L'Eternel Evangile*, p. 623.
52. Griffiths, p. 128.
53. Vintras, *Le Glaive sur Rome*, p. 455.
54. Vintras, *Le Glaive sur Rome*, p. 454.
55. Vintras, *Le Glaive sur Rome*, pp. 380–1.
56. Bloy, *Le Sang du Pauvre*, p. 24.
57. John Ruskin, *Unto this last*, qtd. in Brown, *Life Against Death*, p. 257.
58. Vintras, *Le Glaive sur Rome*, p. 431.
59. Vintras, *L'Eternel Evangile*, p. 690.
60. Citti, p. 69.
61. Vintras, *Le Glaive sur Rome*, p. 474.
62. Vintras, *Le Glaive sur Rome*, p. 474.
63. Vintras, *Le Glaive sur Rome*, p. 476.

64. Qtd. in Garçon, p. 131.
65. Qtd. in Garçon, p. 146.
66. Garçon, p. 151.
67. Burton, *Holy Blood, Holy Tears*, p. 229.
68. Vintras, *Le Glaive sur Rome*, p. v.
69. Qtd. in Bloy, *Ici on assassine les grands hommes*, p. 25.
70. Barrès, p. 80.
71. Barrès, p. 89.
72. Fumet, p. 182.
73. Barrès, p. 115.
74. Koos, p. 13.
75. Griffiths, p. 138.
76. Bloy, *Ici on assassine les grands hommes*, p. 20.
77. Kéchician, p. 70.
78. Bloy, *Ici on assassine les grands hommes*, p. 20.
79 Kéchichian, p. 70.
80. Polet, "Ernest Hello, un inspirateur de Léon Bloy," p. 124.
81. Polet, "Ernest Hello, un inspirateur de Léon Bloy," p. 125.
82. Fumet, p. 192.
83. Smeets, p. 86.
84. Qtd. in Smeets, p. 86.
85. Fumet, p. 192.
86. Qtd. in Bloy, *Ici on assassine les grands hommes*, p. 28.
87. Hello, *Prières et méditations*, p. 14.
88. Hello, "Ludovic," p. 37.
89. Hello, "Ludovic," pp. 41–2.
90. Brown, p. 245.
91. Hello, "Ludovic," p. 42.
92. Hello, "Ludovic," p. 49.
93. Hello, "Ludovic," p. 49.
94. Hello, "Ludovic,"p. 51.
95. Hello, "Ludovic," p. 58.
96. Fumet, p. 208.
97. Hello, *Philosophie et athéisme*, qtd. in Fumet, p. 213.
98. Hello, "Prière à sainte Cathérine, *Prières et méditations*, p. 37.
99. Polet, "Ernest Hello, un inspirateur de Léon Bloy," p. 129.
100. Hello, "L'Infini," *Prières et méditations*, p. 8.
101. Hello, "Prière à sainte Catherine," *Prières et méditations* 37.
102. Polet, "Ernest Hello, un inspirateur de Léon Bloy," p. 128.
103. Polet, "Ernest Hello, un inspirateur de Léon Bloy," p. 128.
104. Hello, "Prière à sainte Catherine," *Prières et méditations*, p. 37.
105. Hello, "Prière à sainte Catherine" *Prières et méditations*, p. 37.
106. Hello, "Prière à sainte Catherine," *Prières et méditations*, p. 38.
107. Hello, "Prière à l'Esprit-Saint," *Prières et méditations*, p. 28.
108. Baldick, p. 156.
109. Seillan, p. 395.
110. Huysmans, *Là-bas*, Vol. II, p. 199.
111. Huysmans, *Là-bas*, Vol. II, p. 264.

112. Seillan, p. 401.
113. Huysmans, *Là-bas*, Vol. II, p. 235.
114. Seillan, p. 400.
115. Dec. 25, 1900, qtd. in Emery, p. 208.
116. Emery, p. 203.
117. Emery, p. 212.
118. Seillan, p. 394.
119. Seillan, p. 396.
120. Brown, p. 278.
121. Vircondelet, p. 159.
122. Huysmans, *A Vau-l'eau* [*Downstream*], p. 85.
123. Seillan, p. 284.
124. Huysmans, *L'Oblat*, Vol. II, p. 156.
125. Huysmans, *L'Oblat*, Vol. II, p. 159.
126. Huysmans, *L'Oblat*, Vol. II, p. 159.
127. Huysmans, *Sainte Lydwine de Schiedam*, Vol. I, p. 104.
128. Huysmans, *Sainte Lydwine de Schiedam*,Vol. I, pp. 36–7.
129. Huysmans, *Sainte Lydwine de Schiedam*,Vol. I, p. 41.
130. Seillan, p. 385.
131. Huysmans, *Sainte Lydwine de Schiedam*, Vol. I, p. 88.
132. Huysmans, *Sainte Lydwine de Schiedam*, Vol. I, p. 192.
133. Huysmans, *Sainte Lydwine de Schiedam*, Vol. I, p. 192.
134. Huysmans, *Sainte Lydwine de Schiedam*, Vol. II, p.126.
135. Brown, p. 276.
136. Huysmans, *Sainte Lydwine de Schiedam*, Vol. II, p. 13.
137. Huysmans, *Sainte Lydwine de Schiedam*, Vol. II, p. 120.
138. Huysmans, *Sainte Lydwine de Schiedam*, Vol. I, p. 103.
139. Huysmans, *Sainte Lydwine de Schiedam*, Vol. I, p. 102.
140. *A Mirror for Novices*, qtd. in Merkur, p. 60.
141. Huysmans, *Sainte Lydwine de Schiedam*, Vol. I, p. 106.
142. Huysmans, *Sainte Lydwine de Schiedam*, Vol. I, p. 106.
143. Qtd. in Merkur, p. 65.
144. Huysmans, *Sainte Lydwine de Schiedam*, Vol. I, p. 91.
145. The Song of Solomon I. 13; Saint Bonaventure, *Lignum vitae*, qtd. in Merkur, p. 64.
146. Huysmans, *Sainte Lydwine de Schiedam*, Vol. I, p. 106.
147. Huysmans, *Sainte Lydwine de Schiedam*, Vol. I, p. 109.
148. Huysmans, *Sainte Lydwine de Schiedam*, Vol I, p. 174.
149. Camus, p. 6.
150. Huysmans, *Sainte Lydwine de* Schiedam, Vol. I, p. 174.
151. Smeets, p. 192.
152. Huysmans, *Sainte Lydwine de Schiedam*, Vol. I, p. 194.
153. Huysmans, *Sainte Lydwine de Schiedam*, Vol. II, p. 68.
154. Huysmans, *Sainte Lydwine de Schiedam*, Vol. II, p. 86.
155. Merkur, p. 86.
156. Huysmans, *Sainte Lydwine de Schiedam*, Vol. II, p. 55.
157. Huysmans, *Sainte Lydwine de Schiedam*, Vol. II, p. 57.
158. Huysmans, *Sainte Lydwine de Schiedam*, Vol. II, p. 58.

159. Solal, p. 135.
160. Vintras, *Entretiens de Saint Joseph*, Les Fonds Lambert, Bibliothèque de l'Arsenal.
161. Coombes, p. 16.
162. Burton, *Holy Tears, Holy Blood*, p. 15.
163. Bloy, *Le Symbolisme de l'Apparition*, p. 22.
164. Bloy, *Le Symbolisme de l'Apparition*, pp.103, 113.
165. Béguin, p.16.
166. Bloy, *Le Sang du Pauvre*, p. 90.
167. Griffiths, p. 50.
168. Griffiths, p. 51.
169. Bloy, *Le Désespéré*, p. 175.
170. Bloy, *La Femme pauvre*, p. 107.
171. Bloy, *La Femme pauvre*, p. 107.
172. Bloy, *La Femme pauvre*, p. 111.
173. Griffiths, p. 128.
174. Bloy, *La Femme pauvre*, p. 111.
175. Bloy, Introduction, *Vie de Mélanie*, p. xxv.
176. Bois, pp. 28–9.
177. Huysmans, *Là-bas*, Vol. II, pp. 64–5.
178. Bloy, *Le Sang du Pauvre*, p. 23.
179. Bloy, *La Femme pauvre*, p.137.
180. Bloy, *Le Désespéré*, p.106.
181. Bloy, *Au Seuil de l'Apocalypse (On the Threshold of the Apocalypse)*, p. 2007.
182. Bloy, *Le Désespéré*, p. 39.
183. Bloy, *Le Désespéré*, p. 360.
184. Bloy, *Le Désespéré*, p. 354.
185. Bloy, *Le Désespéré*, p. 11.
186. Bloy, *Le Désespéré*, p. 143.
187. Polet, "Ernest Hello, un inspirateur de Léon Bloy," p. 127.
188. Bloy, *Le Symbolisme de l'Apparition*, p. 15.
189. Bloy, *Le Symbolisme de l'Apparition*, p. 15.
190. Bloy, *Le Désespéré*, p. 126.
191. Coombes, p. 18.
192. Polet, "Le Purgatoire de Léon Bloy," p. 137.
193. Bloy, *La Femme pauvre*, p. 21.
194. Rodwell, p. 149.
195. Bloy, *La Femme pauvre*, p. 114.
196. Bloy, *La Femme pauvre*, p. 115.
197. Bloy, *La Femme pauvre*, p. 314.
198. Bloy, *La Femme pauvre*, p. 179.
199. Bloy, *Le Symbolisme de l'Appraition*, p. 173.
200. Polet, "Le Purgatoire de Léon Bloy," p. 138.
201. Polet, "Le Purgatoire de Léon Bloy," p. 140.
202. Bloy, *La Femme pauvre*, p. 186.
203. Bloy, *La Femme pauvre*, p. 55.
204. Bloy, *La Femme pauvre*, p. 255.
205. Bloy, *La Femme pauvre*, p. 321.
206. Bloy, Introduction, *Vie de Mélanie*, p. xlix.

207. Bloy, *La Femme pauvre*, p. 326.
208. Bloy, *La Femme pauvre*, p. 66.
209. Bloy, *La Femme pauvre*, p. 326.
210. Bloy, *La Femme pauvre*, p. 411.
211. Bloy, *La Femme pauvre*, p. 416.
212. Bloy, *La Femme pauvre*, p. 418.
213. Bloy, *la Femme pauvre*, p. 418.
214. Roswell, p. 144.
215. Coombes, p. 17.
216. Bloy, *La Femme pauvre*, p. 423.
217. Bloy, *La Femme pauvre*, p. 423.
218. Bloy, *La Femme pauvre*, p. 428.
219. Bloy, *La Femme pauvre*, p. 425.
220. Bloy, *La Femme pauvre*, p. 423.
221. Bachelard, p. 25.
222. Bloy, *La Femme pauvre*, p. 426.
223. Bloy, *La Femme pauvre*, p.426.
224. Polet, "Le Purgatoire de Léon Bloy," p.144.
225. Bachelard, p. 16.
226. Bloy, *La Femme pauvre*, p. 430.
227. Bloy, *La Femme pauvre*, p. 431.
228. Bloy, *La Femme pauvre*, p. 431.
229. Bloy, *La Femme pauvre*, pp. 431–2.
230. Bloy, *La Femme pauvre*, p. 430.
231. Bloy, *La Femme pauvre*, p. 432.

5   The Miracle-worker

1. Seillan, p. 216.
2. Seillan, p. 302.
3. Seillan, p. 305.
4. Huysmans, *Les Foules de Lourdes*, p. 315.
5. Baldick, p. 319.
6. Huysmans, *Les Foules de Lourdes*, p. 93.
7. Huysmans, *Les Foules de Lourdes*, p. 28.
8. Borie, p. 78.
9. Huysmans, *Les Foules de Lourdes*, p. 76.
10. Huysmans, *En Route*, p.32.
11. Huysmans, *Là-bas*, Vol. II, p. 209.
12. Huysmans, *Préface*, *En Route*, p. x.
13. Huysmans, *Les Foules de Lourdes*, p. 290.
14. Citti, p. 31.
15. Huysmans, *Les Foules de Lourdes*, p.184.
16. Huysmans, *Les Foules de Lourdes*, p. 184.
17. Huysmans, *Les Foules de Lourdes*, p. 185.
18. Huysmans, *Les Foules de Lourdes*, p.185.
19. Huysmans, *Les Foules de Lourdes*, p.109.
20. Huysmans, *Les Foules de Lourdes*, p. 154.

21. Huysmans, *Les Foules de Lourdes*, p. 320.
22. Huysmans, *Les Foules de Lourdes*, p.73.
23. Huysmans, *Les Foules de Lourdes*, p. 143.
24. Huysmans, *Les Foules de Lourdes*, p. 198.
25. Jourde, p. 248.
26. Huysmans, *Les Foules de Lourdes*, p. 197.
27. Huysmans, *Là-bas*, Vol. I, p. 11.
28. Huysmans, *Là-bas*, Vol. II, p. 19.
29. Huysmans, *Sainte Lydwine de Schiedam*, Vol. II, p. 126.
30. Peylet, p. 139.
31. Huysmans, *Les Foules de Lourdes*, p.42.
32. Duran, p. 238.
33. Jankélévitch, p. 37.
34. Jankélévitch, pp. 37–8.
35. Pierrot, p. 313.
36. Jourde, p. 249.

Conclusion

1. Lorrain, p. 50.
2. Pierrot, p. 107.
3. Pierrot, p. 105.
4. Qtd. in Pierrot, p. 112.
5. Guaïta, *Au Seuil du Mystère*, p. 9.
6. Guaïta, *Au Seuil du Mystère*, p. 23.
7. Brottman, p. 475.
8. Brottman, p. 474.
9. Papus, *Le Tarot des Bohémiens*, p. 26.
10. Papus, *Le Tarot des Bohémiens* , p. 20.
11. Bois, p. 75.
12. Péladan, *La Vertu suprême*, p. 336.
13. Péladan, *La Vertu suprême*, p. 389.
14. Péladan, *Comment on devient mage*, p. 148.
15. Hawthorne, "Young Goodman Brown," p. 8.
16. Freud, p. 296.
17. Bois, p. 115.
18. Vintras, *Le Glaive sur Rome*, p. 226.
19. Vintras, *Le Glaive sur Rome*, p. 43.
20. Burton, *Holy Tears, Holy Blood*, p. 15.
21. Bloy, *Le Symbolisme de l'Apparition*, p. 192.
22. Rougemont, p.68.
23. Pierrot, p. 234.
24. Qtd. in Pierrot, p. 302.
25. Qtd. in Pierrot, p. 300.

References

Bachelard, Gaston. *The Psychoanalysis of Fire*. Trans. Alan C. M. Ross. Boston: Beacon Press, 1964.

Baldick, Robert. *The Life of J.-K. Huysmans*. Oxford: Oxford at Clarendon Press, 1955.

Barrès, Maurice. *La Colline inspirée*. Paris: Plon, 1961.

Beaufils, Christophe. *Le Sâr Péladan 1858–1918: Bibliographie critique*. Paris: Aux Amateurs de Livres.

Béguin, Albert. *Léon Bloy: Mystique de la douleur*. Paris: Labergerie, 1948.

Berchmans, Michel. *Le Diable au XIXe siècle: La mystification du Dr. Bataille*. Verviers: Bibliothèque Marabout, 1973.

Berg, Christian. "Théodicées victimales au dix-neuvième siècle en France (de Joseph de Maistre à J.-K. Huysmans)." *Victims and Victimization in French and Francophone Literature*. French Literature Series. Vol. XXXII. Rodopi: Amsterdam, 2005, 87–100.

Bloy, Léon. *Le Désespéré*. Paris: Union Générale d'Editions, 1983.

Bloy, Léon. *La Femme pauvre*. Paris: Union Générale d'Editions, 1983.

Bloy, Léon. *Ici on assassine les grands hommes*. Paris: Edition du Mercure de France, 1895.

Bloy, Léon. Introduction. *Vie de Mélanie*. Paris: Mercure de France, 1919.

Bloy, Léon. *Le Pélerin de l'Absolu*, suivi de *Au Seuil de l'Apocalypse*. *L'Oeuvre Complète de Leon Bloy (1846–1917)*. Paris: François Bernouard, 1948.

Bloy, Léon. *Le Sang du Pauvre*. Paris: Stock, 1909.

Bloy, Léon. *Le Symbolisme de l'Apparition*. Paris: Edition Payot et Rivages, 2008.

Bois, Jules. *Le Satanisme et la Magie*. Paris: Chailley, 1895.

Borie, Jean. *Huysmans: Le Diable, le célibataire et Dieu*. Paris: Grasset, 1991.

Bricaud, Joanny. *Huysmans Occultiste et Magicien*. Paris: Bibliothèque Chacornac, 1913.

Brottman, Mikita. "Psychoanalysis of Magic: Then and Now." *American Imago* 66(4) (2009): 471–89.

Brown, Norman O. *Life Against Death: The Psychoanalytical Meaning of History*. Middletown, CT: Wesleyan UP, 1955.

Burton, Richard. D. E. *Blood in the City: Violence and Revelation in Paris 1789–1945*. Ithaca: Cornell UP, 2001.

Burton, Richard D. E. *Holy Tears, Holy Blood: Women, Catholicism, and the Culture of Suffering in France, 1840–1970*. Ithaca: Cornell UP, 2005.

Camus, Albert. *The Myth of Sisyphus*. Trans. Justin O'Brien. New York: Random House, 1955.

Carpenter, Scott. *Aesthetics of Fraudulence in Nineteenth-Century France: Frauds, Hoaxes, and Counterfeits*. Surrey: Ashgate, 2009.

Chasseguet-Smirgel, Janine. *Creativity and Perversion*. New York: Norton, 1984.

Citti, Pierre. *Contre la décadence: Histoire de l'imagination française dans le roman 1890–1914*. Paris: Presses universitaires de France, 1987.

Closson, Marianne. *"Le Diable au xixe siècle* de Léo Taxil: ou les 'mille et une nuits' de la démonologie." *Fictions du diable: démonologie et littérature de Saint-Augustin à Léo Taxil.* Eds. Françoise Lavocat, Pierre Kapitaniak, and Mary Closson. Geneva: Droz, 2007, 313–32.

Coombs, John E. "Léon Bloy." *Dictionary of Literary Biography: Nineteenth-Century French Fiction Writers.* Vol. 123. Ed. Catharine Savage Brosman. Detroit: Gale, 1992, 15–25.

Duran, Sylvie. "Les bocaux de la tératologie" I." *Voix de l'écrivain: Mélanges offertes à Guy Sanges.* Ed. Jean-Louis Cabanès. Toulouse: Presses universitaires du Mirail, 1996, 231–45.

Durand, Gilbert. *Les Structures anthropologiques de l'imaginaire.* Paris: Bordas, 1969.

Eliade, Mircea. *The Forge and the Crucible: The Origins and Structures of Alchemy.* Trans. Stephen Corrin. Chicago: University of Chicago Press, 1962.

Eliade, Mircea. *Méphistophélès et l'Androgyne.* Paris: Gallimard, 1962.

Emery, Elizabeth. "Ecrire la fin: *Sainte Lydwine de Schiedam* de J.-K. Huysmans." *Cahiers naturalistes* 75 (Scpt. 2001): 203–14.

Frankfurter, David. *Evil Incarnate: Rumors of Demonic Conspiracy and Satanic Abuse in History.* Princeton: Princeton University Press, 2006.

Freud, Sigmund. "Character and Anal Eroticism" (1908). *The Freud Reader.* Ed. Peter Gay. New York: Norton, 1989.

Fumet, Stanislas. *Ernest Hello ou La Drame de la Lumière.* Paris: Editions Saint-Michel, 1928.

Garçon, Maurice. *Vintras Hérésiarque et Prophète.* Paris: Librairie Critique, Emile Nourry, 1928.

Griffiths, Richard. *The Reactionary Revolution: The Catholic Revival in French Literature, 1870–1914.* New York: Frederick Ungar, 1965.

Guaïta, Stanislas de. *Au Seuil du Mystère: Essais de sciences maudites.* Paris: Chamuel, 1895.

Guaïta, Stanislas de. *Le Temple de Satan. Le Serpent de la Genèse.* Paris: Librairie du Merveilleux, 1891.

Hall, Manly. *The Secret Teachings of All Ages.* Los Angeles: The Philosophical Research Society, 1977.

Hawthorne, Nathanael. "Young Goodman Brown." *40 Short Stories.* Ed. Beverly Lawn. Boston: Bedford/Saint-Martin's, 2001, 1–13.

Hayes, Carlton J. H. *Contemporary Europe Since 1870.* New York: Macmillan, 1958.

Hello, Ernest. *Contes extraordinaires.* Brussels: Durendal, 1934.

Hello, Ernest. *Prières et méditations.* Paris: Arfuyen, 1994.

Hopkins, Brooke. "Jesus and Object Use: A Winnicottian Account of the Resurrection Myth." *Transitional Objects and Potential Spaces.* Ed. Peter Rudnytsky. New York: Columbia UP, 1993.

Huysmans, J.-K. *A rebours.* Paris: Gallimard, 1977.

Huysmans, J.-K. *A Vau-l'eau. Oeuvres complètes V.* Geneva: Slatkine, 1972.

Huysmans, J.-K. "Emile Zola et *L'Assommoir. Oeuvres complètes II.* Geneva: Slatkine, 1972.

Huysmans, J.-K. *En Route. Oeuvres complètes XIII.* Geneva: Slatkine, 1972.

Huysmans, J.-K. "Félicien Rops." *Certains. Oeuvres complètes X.* Geneva: Slatkine, 1972.

Huysmans, J.-K. *Les Foules de Lourdes. Oeuvres complètes XVIII.* Geneva: Slatkine, 1972.

Huysmans, J.-K. *Là-bas. Oeuvres complètes XII.* Geneva: Slatkine, 1972.

Huysmans, J.-K. *Là-haut ou Notre-Dame de La Salette.* Nancy: Presses universitaires de Nancy, 1988.

Huysmans, J.-K. *L'Oblat. Oeuvres complètes XVII.* Geneva: Slatkine, 1972.

Huysmans, J.-K. "Préface écrite vingt ans après le roman." *A rebours.* Paris: Gallimard, 1977.

Huysmans J.-K "Préface." *Le Satanisme et la magie.* By Jules Bois. Paris: Chailley, 1895.

Huysmans J.-K. *Sainte Lydwine de Schiedam. Oeuvres complètes XV.* Geneva: Slatkine, 1972.

Jankélévitch, Vladimir. "La Décadence." *Dieu, la chair et les livres.* Ed. Sylvie Thorel-Cailleteau. Paris: Honoré Champion, 2000, 33–63.

Jung, C. G. *Alchemical Studies. The Collected Works of C. G. Jung.* Vol. 13. Princeton: Princeton University Press, 1967.

Kéchichian, Patrick. Postface. *Prières et méditations.* By Ernest Hello. Paris: Arfuyen, 1993.

Kohn, Ingeborg. "The Mystic Impresario: Joséphin Péladan, Founder of *Le Salon de la Rose+Croix.*" *Secret Texts: The Literature of Secret Societies.* Eds. Marie-Mulvey Roberts and Hugh Ormsby-Lennon. New York: AMS Press, 1995, 228–57.

Koos, Leonard. "Maurice Barrès." *Dictionary of Literary Biography: Nineteenth-Century French Fiction Writers.* Vol. 123. Ed. Catharine Brosman. Detroit: Gale, 1992, 3–15.

Lévi, Eliphas. *Dogme et Rituel de la Haute Magie.* Paris: Editions Niclaus, 1972.

Lévi, Eliphas. *Histoire de la Magie.* Paris: Guy Trédaniel, 2008.

Lévi, Eliphas. *Mysteries of Magic: A Digest of the Writings of Eliphas Lévi.* Ed. Alfred Waite. 1896. Whitefish, MT: Kessinger Publishing, 2005.

Lézinier, Michel de. *Avec Huysmans: Promenades et souvenirs.* Paris: Delpeuch, 1928.

Lorrain, Jean. *Histoires de masques.* Paris: Ollendorff, 1900.

Margiotta, Domenico. *Le Palladisme: Culte de Satan-Lucifer dans les triangles maçonniques.* Grenoble: Biblioteca Esotérica Herrou Aragón, 1895.

Mercier, Alain. *Les Sources Esotériques et Occultes de la Poésie Symboliste.* Paris: Nizet, 1969.

Merkur, Dan. *Crucified with Christ: Meditation on the Passion, Mystical Death, and the Medieval Invention of Psychotherapy.* Albany: SUNY Press, 2007.

Miller, J. Hillis. "The Critic as Host." *Deconstruction and Criticism.* Eds. Harold Bloom et al. New York: Seabury Press, 1987.

Papus (Gérard Encausse). *Le Diable et l'Occultisme.* Nimes: Lacour, 1996.

Papus. *Le Tarot des Bohémiens.* St. Jean de Braye: Editions Dangles, 1977.

Péladan, Joséphin. *Comment on devient mage* (Paris: Chamuel, 1892). Reprinted by Elibron Classics, 2005.

Péladan, Joséphin. *Finis Latinorum.* Paris: Flammarion, 1890.

Péladan Joséphin. *L'Occulte catholique.* Paris: Charcornac, 1902.

Péladan Joséphin. *La Vertu suprême.* Paris: Flammarion, 1900.

Péladan Joséphin. *Le Vice suprême.* Geneva: Slatkine, 1979.

Pierrot, Jean. *L'Imaginaire decadent (1880–1900).* Paris: Presses universitaires de France, 1977.

Polet, Jean-Claude. "Ernest Hello, un inspirateur de Léon Bloy." *La Revue des lettres modernes* (1989): 932–7.

Polet, Jean-Claude. "Le Purgatoire de Léon Bloy: Une Lecture de *La Femme pauvre*." *Léon Bloy au tournant du siècle*. Ed. Pierrre Glaudes. Toulouse. Presses universitaires du Mirail, 1992, 137–52.

Rodwell, Rosemary. "Léon Bloy and the Earthly Paradise." *Journal of European Studies* 27(2) (June 1997): 143–59.

Rougemont, Denis de. *The Devil's Share*. Trans. Haaken Chevalier. Washington, D C: Pantheon Books (Bollingen Series), 1944.

Rougemont, Denis de. *Love in the Western World*. Trans. Montgomery Belgion. New York: Pantheon, 1956.

Schuré. Edouard. *The Great Initiates: A Study of the Secret History of Religions*. Trans. Gloria Raspberry. San Francisco: Harper and Row, 1961.

Schwob, Marcel. *Le Livre de Monelle*. Paris: François Bernouard, 1928.

Seillan, Jean-Marie. *Huysmans: politique et religion*. Paris: Editions Classiques Garnier, 2009.

Smeets, Marc. *Huysmans l'inchangé: Histoire d'une conversion*. Amsterdam: Rodopi, 2003.

Solal, Jérôme. "Le divin lait de Lydwine: érotique du chez-soi et théorie du dehors." *J.-K. Huysmans chez lui*. Ed. Marc Smeets. *CRIN* 52 (2009): 121–36.

Taxil, Léo. *Les Soeurs Maçonnes*. Paris: Letouzy et Ané, 1895.

Villiers de l'Isle-Adam. *Axël. Oeuvres complètes*. Vol. 2. Paris: Gallimard, 1986.

Vintras, Eugène. *L'Eternel Evangile*. London: Trübnel, 1857.

Vintras, Eugène. *Le Glaive sur Rome et ses complices! Venue et Enseignement d'Elie sur l'Avènement Glorieux de Jésus-Christ*. London: Dulau, 1855.

Vircondelet, Alain. "Huysmans et l'expérience de la douleur." *J.-K. Huysmans: Littérature et religion*. Ed. Samuel Lair. Rennes: Presses universitaires de Rennes, 155–63.

Waite, Alfred. Biographical and Critical Essay. *Mysteries of Magic: A Digest of the Writings of Eliphas Lévi*. 1896. Whitefish, MT: Kessinger Publications, 2005, 1–41.

Waite, Alfred. *Devil Worship in France*. London: G. Redway, 1896.

Wallis, C. G. Review. *La Part du Diable*. By Denis de Rougemont. *Kenyon Review* 6(1) (Winter 1944): 150–6.

Weber, Eugen. "Religion and Superstition in Nineteenth-Century France." *The Historical Journal* 31(2) (June 1988): 399–423.

Weber, Eugen. *Satan Franc-Maçon: La Mystification de Léo Taxil*. Paris: Collection Archives, 1964.

Index

CPSIA information can be obtained at www.ICGtesting.com
Printed in the USA
BVOW012107140513

320714BV00004B/16/P

9 780230 293083